An Introduction to
PROGRAMMING USING

JAVA™

JONES & BARTLETT
LEARNING

World Headquarters
Jones & Bartlett Learning
40 Tall Pine Drive
Sudbury, MA 01776
978-443-5000
info@jblearning.com
www.jblearning.com

Jones & Bartlett Learning
Canada
6339 Ormindale Way
Mississauga, Ontario L5V 1J2
Canada

Jones & Bartlett Learning
International
Barb House, Barb Mews
London W6 7PA
United Kingdom

Jones & Bartlett Learning books and products are available through most bookstores and online booksellers. To contact Jones & Bartlett Learning directly, call 800-832-0034, fax 978-443-8000, or visit our website, www.jblearning.com.

Substantial discounts on bulk quantities of Jones & Bartlett Learning publications are available to corporations, professional associations, and other qualified organizations. For details and specific discount information, contact the special sales department at Jones & Bartlett Learning via the above contact information or send an email to specialsales@jblearning.com.

Production Credits
Publisher: Cathleen Sether
Senior Acquisitions Editor: Timothy Anderson
Associate Editor: Melissa Potter
Production Director: Amy Rose
Senior Marketing Manager: Andrea DeFronzo
V. P., Manufacturing and Inventory Control: Therese Connell
Composition: Northeast Compositors
Cover Design: Kristin E. Parker
Cover Image: © Péter Gudella/Dreamstime.com
Printing and Binding: Malloy, Inc.
Cover Printing: Malloy, Inc.

Library of Congress Cataloging-in-Publication Data
Dos Reis, Anthony J.
   An introduction to programming using Java / Anthony J. Dos Reis.
       p. cm.
   Includes bibliographical references and index.
   ISBN-13: 978-0-7637-9060-8 (pbk.)
   ISBN-10: 0-7637-9060-5 (pbk.)
   1. Java (Computer program language) I. Title.
   QA76.73.J38D665 2011
   005.13'3--dc22
                                    2010030853

6048
Printed in the United States of America
14 13 12 11 10   10 9 8 7 6 5 4 3 2 1

To my wife, with love

Contents

Preface

One of Woody Allen's jokes goes like this:

> I took a speed reading class. I read *War and Peace* in ten minutes. I think it's about Russia.

War and Peace has always been the undisputed exemplar of a book too long to read. However, today it has competition for that honor from all the standard Java™ textbooks. These textbooks have enormous page counts—right up there with *War and Peace*. And they are harder to read. Most students have neither the time nor the diligence to plow through the typical 1,000 page textbook.

Our textbook, *An Introduction to Programming Using Java*, is the solution to the problem. It's not an outline or a reference, but a comprehensive, easy-to-read tutorial. Its most important feature, however, is its size. Its 448 pages cover just about everything the 1,000 page textbooks cover and, *mirabile dictu*, include a lab manual as well.

Of course, a textbook with 448 pages cannot possibly have everything a 1,000 page textbook has. But with Java textbooks, more is less. Back in the days of my youth, when I was in the Army, the master sergeant would occasionally assemble the troops to inform us of the latest news, such as the times at which he would be bringing us bagels and lox. But instead of simply saying "I'll be there at 10 a.m. so you can sleep in until then," he would ramble on endlessly about something or other. I could never pay attention for more than a minute or so. When our assemblies ended, I always had two reactions: "Boy, I'm glad that's over," and "What did he say?" The fact is, the more he said, the less I absorbed. The same is true with Java textbooks. The longer they are, the less a student learns from them.

We achieved the compression of 1,000 pages of material into 448 pages by trimming four areas in which excessive verbiage is typically found:

- **Overviews**
  Overviews are important but they should be brief and, most important, intelligible to the student. Some Java textbooks start with an extensive discussion of object-oriented programming—encapsulation, information hiding, inheritance, and polymorphism—much of which is incomprehensible to a beginning student. We do discuss object-oriented programming in Chapter 1, but we limit our discussion to a level that a beginner can comprehend.
- **Programming examples**
  Students learn the most by writing programs—not by reading programs. Programming examples should be as simple as possible. Simple concepts should not be illustrated with complex programs.
- **Warnings of potential errors**
  Some textbooks warn students of the errors they are likely to make. A better approach is to have students intentionally make errors in the lab through guided exercises. Students learn and retain more by making mistakes than by reading about making mistakes.
- **Sidebars**
  Sidebars are distracting. Reading a text with many sidebars is like attending a class in which two professors are lecturing simultaneously. Sidebars presumably contain optional material. But, perhaps, some sidebars are not really optional. Thus, for every sidebar, the reader has the distraction of deciding whether to read it.

One unusual feature of our book is the inclusion of sample exams at various checkpoints in the text. The idea of sample exams came from a professor, now retired, who many years ago made the following observation about his classes: If he covers topics A, B, C, and D, and tells students before an exam that they are responsible for topics A, B, C, and D, they study A, B, C, D, and do well on the exam. However, if he simply says that they are responsible for the topics covered, students inexplicably won't study one or more of the required topics. In this case, students do poorly on the exam. "Oh," a student would say. "I didn't know we were responsible for topic C." And the professor would reply, "But we covered topic C two weeks ago. How could you not know you were responsible for it?"

Students respond to specificity. So before every exam, I give a sample exam as a homework assignment. If I want my students to know A, B, C, and D, I give a sample exam on

A, B, C, and D. And as sure as the sun rises in the east, my students learn A, B, C, and D before the real exam. The sample exam is an *unbelievably* effective motivator. Try it!

Other noteworthy features of the book:

- Introduces objects early (in Chapter 1).
- Provides plenty of material for a one-semester course.
- Uses the computer in the lab exercises to teach students some of the fine points of Java. This approach is more efficient, effective, and stimulating than a tedious enumeration in the text proper.
- Each lab includes a set of prep questions. Requiring students to hand in the answers to these questions at the *beginning* of a lab will ensure that they are adequately prepared to do the lab.
- Each lab provides enough exercises to keep even the speediest student working productively during a two or three hour lab session.
- Introduces linked structures. I have found that introducing linked structures in the first programming course makes for a more successful second course (on data structures).
- Explains abstract classes and interfaces in the context of generic programming. With this approach, students quickly grasp the conceptual and technical aspects of these constructs.
- Liked by students. It gives them precisely what they need from a textbook.
- Available supplements include source code for all the programs in the textbook, PowerPoint® and PDF slides, and an Instructor's Manual.

The introductory computer course is an important component in any math, science, or engineering curriculum. Don't use a textbook that will make students say, "I think it's about Java." We believe we have a better alternative.

Laura and I would like the thank Professor Andy Pletch for his helpful critique, Tim Anderson at Jones & Bartlett Learning for his assistance with this project, and Mom for everything else.

Anthony J. Dos Reis
Laura L. Dos Reis

CHAPTER 1

Two Simple Java Programs

OBJECTIVES

- Understand the nature of programming
- Understand basic computer organization
- Edit, compile, and run a simple Java program
- Edit, compile, and run a Java program that creates objects
- Understand encapsulation and information hiding

1.1 Fundamental Problem with Computers

Once upon a time, an engineer was assigned the task of designing a bridge. Rather than design the bridge himself, he programmed a computer to do it. Unfortunately, he programmed the computer incorrectly. As a result, the computer produced a design that was grossly (and obviously) incorrect: It called for beams that were only 1 inch in diameter. When he showed the design to his boss, the boss immediately recognized the error and said, "This couldn't be right." The engineer responded by saying, "But this design was produced by the computer." "Oh," the boss replied, "in that case, it must be right."

Our engineer and his boss thought the design *had* to be correct because a computer produced it. However, computers are not infallible super-brains. To the contrary, computers are quite dumb. They are electronic machines that simply follow the instructions they are provided. When you program a computer, you provide it with these instructions. If you give a computer incorrect instructions, it will blindly follow them.

Obviously, if we program a computer, we should be sure to give it the correct instructions. But this goal is not easy to accomplish. The fundamental problem with computers is that they require programming, and programming is so difficult to do correctly. However, there is a plus side to programming: It gives computers their incredible flexibility. A toaster can only toast, but with the proper programming, a computer can do almost anything. For example, it can design bridges, play chess, and even diagnose rare diseases (who needs Dr. House?).

Computers often make mistakes because the programmers fail to program them to handle all the possibilities that can occur in real life. For example, many years ago the IRS sent a letter to a taxpayer asking for an explanation for an unauthorized name change. The letter—computer generated, no doubt—wanted to know why Mr. Dos Reis had changed his name to "DosReis" without going through the proper legal procedures. Mr. Dos Reis had not changed his name. Apparently, on the return in question, his name was entered into the computer *without* a space, but the IRS had his name from previous returns *with* a space. The resulting mismatch of names caused a computer to generate the letter of inquiry. The computer's program failed to check if the mismatch was simply due to a missing space rather than a genuine name change.

1.2 Computer Organization

All the information within a computer is stored in the form of binary numbers. **Binary numbers** consist of 0's and 1's. We call symbols that make up binary numbers—the 0's and 1's—**bits**.

Binary numbers work very much like decimal numbers. Consider the decimal number 235. Each digit has a weight, depending on its position (see Fig. 1.1a). Weights from right to left are the successive powers of 10, starting with $10^0 = 1$. Thus, the digits from right to left in 235 have the weights $10^0 = 1$, $10^1 = 10$, and $10^2 = 100$. Each digit contributes its own value times its weight to the value of the number. For example, the weight of the 3 digit in 235 is 10. Thus, this 3 digit contributes $3 \times 10 = 30$ to the value of the number.

Now consider the binary number 111. The weights from right to left are the successive powers of 2 starting from $2^0 = 1$. The weights of the three bits in 111 from right to left are $2^0 = 1$, $2^1 = 2$, and $2^2 = 4$. Thus, the bits from right to left contribute 1×1, 1×2, and 1×4 to the value of the number (see Fig. 1.1b). Thus, 111 in binary numbers equals $1 + 2 + 4 = 7$ in decimal numbers.

The value of a binary number is simply the sum of the weights corresponding to the 1 bits. For example, the value in decimal of the binary number 101 is 5, which is the sum of 1 (the weight of the right 1) and 4 (the weight of the left 1).

Computers use binary representation because devices that store binary numbers are inexpensive and reliable. Each bit in a binary number requires only a simple off/on switch. The off position can represent 0; the on position can represent 1. In contrast, each position in a decimal number has 10 possibilities: 0, 1, . . . , 9. Thus, each position in a decimal number requires a 10-position switch, which, of course, would be more complicated and expensive than the simple 2-position switch required by binary. Moreover, binary numbers are not restrictive in any way. They, of course, can represent numbers just as well as decimal. But, with the proper encoding, they can also represent letters, punctuation, pictures, sound, movies, and so on. For example, if we assign a distinct binary code to each letter of the alphabet, we can then use these codes within a computer to represent their corresponding letters.

A computer system consists of **software** (the programs and data) and **hardware** (the circuits, wires, cabinets—anything you can touch). The software consists of two types: **system software** (software that manages the computer system itself) and **application**

a) Decimal

2	3	5	digits
10^2	10^1	10^0	weights

Value = $2 \times 10^2 + 3 \times 10^1 + 5 \times 10^0 = 235$ decimal

b) Binary

1	1	1	bits
2^2	2^1	2^0	weights

Value = $1 \times 2^2 + 1 \times 2^1 + 1 \times 2^0 = 7$ decimal

Figure 1.1

software (software that satisfies a user's end need). An example of system software is the **operating system**—the large, complex program that manages all the resources of the computer, and provides an interface that allows a user to interact with the computer. Examples of application software are word processors and spreadsheet programs.

The principal hardware components of a computer system are the central processing unit, main memory (sometimes called primary memory), secondary memory, input devices, and output devices. The **central processing unit** (CPU) is the computational unit of a computer system. It can add, subtract, multiply, divide, and compare numbers. The CPU also controls the operation of the other units in the computer. The CPU, however, cannot do anything unless it is provided with instructions. The only kind of instructions the CPU can use are called **machine language instructions**. Machine language instructions are binary numbers that specify the operations the CPU is to perform. When we say that the CPU is **executing** an instruction, we mean that the CPU is simply performing the operations specified by that instruction.

The CPU gets the machine language instructions that tell it what to do from **main memory**. A program can be executed *only if it is in main memory*. Thus, to execute a program that resides on a hard disk, the program must first be copied from the hard disk into main memory. This requirement is the reason why a program does not start immediately when you click on its screen icon. Before it can start (i.e., before the CPU can execute its instructions), it has to be copied into main memory.

Main memory typically consists of billions of individual memory cells. The CPU can access these cells in any order. For example, it can directly access the third cell without first accessing the first and second cells. For this reason, main memory is sometimes referred to as **random access memory** (RAM). Main memory is **volatile**. That is, the data and instructions it holds are lost whenever power is turned off.

Secondary memory is nonvolatile memory. That is, its contents are not lost when power is turned off. A hard disk is a typical secondary memory device. Secondary memory is the depository of all the programs and data available on a computer system. Because main memory is volatile and of limited size, you obviously cannot use it for this purpose.

When you create a document with a word processing program, the document (as well as the word processing program and the operating system) sits in main memory. If your computer loses power, even for an instant, you will lose your document because main memory is volatile. For this reason, it is always a good idea to frequently save your document. Saving your document copies it from main memory to a secondary memory device. If your computer then loses power, the copy in main memory is lost but not the copy on the secondary memory device.

An **input device** provides information to the computer from the outside world. Examples of input devices are the keyboard and mouse. An **output device** provides information in the computer to the outside world. Examples of output devices are the LCD display and the printer.

The CPU and main memory are all electronic. They have no moving parts to slow them down. Thus, once main memory has the instructions and data required for a computation, the CPU can perform that computation at an incredible speed. Secondary memory devices, such as a hard disk, typically have moving parts. Thus, their operation is considerably slower than the CPU and main memory. *A computer is fast because its core components—the CPU and main memory—are all electronic.*

It is generally advantageous to have a large amount of main memory. Recall that a program must be in main memory to be executed. With a large amount of main memory, the operating system can simultaneously keep itself and all the active programs in main memory. Then, because all the active programs are already in main memory, the CPU can then switch from executing one program to another virtually instantaneously.

1.3   Let's Start Programming—Some Initial Considerations

When writing Java™ programs, you must pay attention to small details. For example, wherever a Java program requires a left brace ({), you must use a left brace—not a left parenthesis (() or a left square bracket ([). You must also pay attention to the case of the letters you use. For example, the words `class`, `public`, `static`, and `void` must in lowercase. The words `String` and `System` must start with a capital letter followed by lowercase letters. Java is **case sensitive**. That is, it treats words spelled the same but differing in case as distinct words.

The Java language allows a program to be **formatted** (i.e., laid out on the page) in a variety of ways. For example, you can insert any number of spaces, tabs, or blank lines between any two **tokens** (i.e., meaningful units) of a program but not within a token. For example, you may write the following Java statement

```
System.out.println(20+3);
```

in this format (with spaces surrounding the plus sign):

```
System.out.println(20 + 3);
```

or in this format (with each token on a separate line):

```
System
.
Out
.
println
(
20
+
3
)
;
```

All three of these formats are equivalent from the computer's point of view. You may not, however, write

```
S ystem.ou t.pri ntln(2 0 + 3);
```

because `System`, `out`, `println`, and `20` are all single tokens, and, therefore, cannot have any embedded spaces.

Although the Java language does not require a specific format, you should, nevertheless, format your programs in the same way the sample programs in this textbook are format-ted. Using this format, you will be less likely to make errors when you write programs. It will also make your programs easier to read and understand.

It is easy to make mistakes when writing a computer program. Even the best program-mers make mistakes *all the time*. We call these mistakes **bugs**. **Debugging** is the process of eliminating the bugs in a program. Debugging is fun to do (no kidding). An incorrect program that you have written is a puzzle of your own making that you have to solve. When you figure out what's wrong, you'll get a wonderful sense of satisfaction.

1.4 Structure of a Java Program

A Java program consists of one or more classes. A class is the basic unit of a Java program. It has the following structure:

```
class class name
{
    .
    .
    .
}
```

A class can contain methods as well as other items that we will discuss later. A **method** is a named sequence of Java statements. A method has the following structure:

```
method header
{
        statements  } method body
}
```

The **header** of a method contains the name of the method as well as several other items. It is followed by the **body** of the method. The body consists of a sequence of statements enclosed by braces. When a computer **executes** a method, it performs the operations specified by the statements in its body.

A simple Java program—one consisting of a single method inside a single class—has the following structure:

```
class class name
{
    method header
    {
        statements
    }
}
```

Although not required by the Java language, it is a good idea to start the word `class` and its associated braces in the leftmost column. Then indent the left margin of the method from the left margin of the class. This indentation serves an important purpose: It shows us that the method is a subpart of the class. Also indent the statements in the method body from the enclosing braces.

Figure 1.2 shows a simple Java program. This program contains a single method named `main` inside a class named `Program1`. Although just about as simple as can be, this program

```
        Class name        Method name         Parameter
              ↓                |                   |
                              |                   |
    class Program1            |                   |
    {                         ↓                   ↓
        public static void main(String[] args)   } Method header
        {
            System.out.println(20 + 3);            } Method
            System.out.println("20 + 3");          } body
        }
    }
```

Figure 1.2

necessarily uses some features of Java that you will not be able to fully understand until you learn more about Java. So for now, just try to understand the program as much as you can.

Let's examine the components of the program in Fig. 1.2 in order of appearance.

class   Indicates the beginning of a class. Words like `class` that have a pre-defined meaning are called **reserved words** or **keywords.**

Program1   This is the class name. You choose the class name, but it cannot be a reserved word. For example, you can use `Butterfly` or `Rocket` instead of `Program1`. By convention, class names should start with an uppercase letter, although the Java language does not require this.

{   The left brace marks the beginning of the body of the class. Braces look very much like parentheses on a computer screen. *Be sure you use a brace here—not a parenthesis.*

public   This is the start of the header for the `main` method. `public` indicates that access to this method is unrestricted. That is, it is "available to the public." `public` is a reserved word.

static   Indicates that we can execute the method without first creating an object. We will discuss objects later in this chapter. `static` is a reserved word.

void   This is the **return type** of the method. `void` indicates that the method does not return (i.e., give back) a value. `void` is a reserved word. We will discuss return types in Chapter 5.

main   This is the method name. Every Java program must have a method named `main`. `main` is always executed first. By convention, method names should start with a lowercase letter.

(The left parenthesis marks the beginning of the **parameter list**. It consists of a list of zero or more parameters, each preceded by its type and separated from the next by a comma. In this particular parameter list, only one parameter, args, is specified, preceded by its type, `String[]`.

String[]   This is a data type. The square brackets in `String[]` stand for "array." Thus, `String[]` stands for "`String` array." Its use here indicates that the next item in the program (the parameter args) has the type `String[]`. We will discuss `String` arrays in Chapter 9.

args   This is the name of the **parameter**. You choose the name. It does not have to be args. We will discuss parameters in Chapter 5.

)   The right parenthesis marks the end of both the parameter list and the method header.

{   This left brace marks the beginning of the body of the method.

```
System.out.println(20 + 3);
```
When executed, this statement causes the computer to evaluate 20 + 3 and display the result on the display screen. Thus, this statement displays 23 at the current location of the display cursor. It then positions the display cursor at the beginning of the next line. Notice the semicolon at the end of the statement. Semicolons mark the ends of statements.

```
System.out.println("20 + 3");
```
This statement displays the sequence of characters inside the quotes and then positions the display cursor at the beginning of the next line. A string of characters enclosed in double quotes is called a **literal String constant**. Arithmetic expressions inside a literal String constant are not evaluated. Thus, this statement displays 20 + 3 rather than 23.

}　　　　　This right brace marks the end of the body of the method.

}　　　　　This right brace marks the end of the body of the class.

main requires the specific header shown in Fig. 1.2, except for the name of the parameter (for example, you can substitute parms for args). Whenever you write a main method, use this header.

1.5　Compiling and Running a Java Program

To work with Java programs, you need to install the **Java Development Kit** (JDK) on your computer unless you have a Macintosh (the Macintosh comes with the JDK pre-installed). If you have a Windows or Linux system, see the Appendix for installation instructions.

To run (i.e., execute) the program in Fig. 1.2, you first have to create a file that contains the program. The name of this file should be the class name used in the program followed by a period and the extension java. The class name of the program in Fig. 1.2 is Program1. Thus, you should create a file whose name is Program1.java.

To create the file Program1.java, use a program called a **text editor**. A text editor allows you to enter text into a computer, edit (i.e., modify) the text if necessary, and then save the text to a computer file. Most computer systems come with a simple text editor. Windows, for example, has notepad and edit. To use notepad, simply click on its icon (which is under Accessories in the All Programs menu). To use edit, first switch to **command-line mode** by clicking on the Command Prompt icon (which is under Accessories in the All Programs menu). Then enter edit followed by the name of the file you wish to edit. Linux and Macintosh systems usually have one or more of the following simple text editors: pico, nano, or joe. To use any of these programs, activate the Terminal program (which switches you to command-line mode). Then enter pico, nano, or joe followed by the name of the file you wish to edit.

After you create the file Program1.java that contains the program, you have to **compile** (i.e., translate) the program in this file. The CPU of a computer cannot directly execute Java instructions. Recall that the only type of instructions the CPU can directly execute are machine language instructions. Thus, before you can run a Java program, you must translate it to machine language. The Java compiler, javac, in the JDK performs this translation for you. To compile the program in Program1.java, put your computer in command-line mode if you have not already done so (see instructions above). Then enter

```
javac Program1.java
```

javac (the Java compiler) will then translate the Java program in the file Program1.java to machine language and output it to a file named Program1.class. The name of the output file created by the compiler consists of the name of the class in the program followed by a period and the extension class.

Different types of computers have different machine languages. The javac compiler translates Java programs to a particular machine language called bytecode. **Bytecode** is the name of the machine language for the **Java Virtual Machine** (JVM). To run the bytecode in Program1.class, you must run the java interpreter. The java **interpreter** makes your computer act like the JVM. The name of the Java interpreter is java. To run the java interpreter on Program1.class (which causes the execution of the program in Program1.class), enter

```
java Program1
```

Note that you specify the class name (Program1), not the file name (Program1.class) of the translated program when you invoke the interpreter. After you enter this command, the java interpreter will execute the program in Program1.class. You will then see the following output (produced by the program in Program1.class):

```
23
20 + 3
```

Be sure to use the correct case when entering these commands. If, for example, you enter

```
java program1
```

with a lowercase letter p at the beginning of the class name, the program will not run.

The two files—`Program1.java` and `Program1.class`—contain the same program but in different forms. `Program1.java` contains the Java **source program** (i.e., the original Java program). `Program1.class` contains the corresponding bytecode.

When we interact with the computer when it is in command-line mode, we say that we are using the **command-line interface**. To edit, compile, and run a Java program when we are using the command-line interface, we enter commands on the keyboard to invoke the programs that perform those functions. Another approach to editing, compiling, and running Java programs is to use an **integrated development environment** (IDE). An IDE combines everything we need for program development into a single, convenient package. It also typically includes a **debugger**—a tool that facilitates the debugging of programs. If you use an IDE, you will be able to write and debug programs more easily than if you use the command-line interface. The disadvantage of IDEs is that you have to learn how to use them. For this reason, it is probably best to start out with the command-line interface so initially you can focus all your efforts on learning Java. Once you have learned the basics of Java, you can switch over to an IDE. Two excellent (and free) IDEs that are well-suited for students learning Java are DrJava (available at `http://www.drjava.org`) and BlueJ (available at `http://www.bluej.org`). Both are easy to learn and easy to use. Tutorials on how to use DrJava and BlueJ are available at their respective websites.

Java programs are **portable**—that is, Java programs can be executed without modification on any computer that has a `java` interpreter. The Java interpreter for a computer makes that computer act like the JVM. Thus, any machine language program for the JVM can run without modification on every computer with a Java interpreter. For example, the program in `Program1.class` can run on any computer system with a Java interpreter, regardless of the type of system on which it was created. For example, we can create `Program1.class` on a Windows system (by compiling `Program1.java`) and then run `Program1.class` on a Macintosh system (by running the `java` interpreter on the Macintosh). The portability of Java is one of its most attractive features, and distinguishes it from most other computer languages.

Instead of programming in Java and then using the Java compiler to translate our programs to machine language, why don't we program directly in machine language? We could do this, but it would be far more difficult and time-consuming than programming in Java. It would be like using a toothbrush to clean your basement floor.

One brief note on terminology: The term **code** refers to some portion of a program. For example, when we say "the *code* on Lines 4 through 7," we mean that portion of the program on Lines 4 through 7.

1.6 Syntax, Logic, Compile-Time, and Run-Time Errors

A `syntax error` is a violation of the rules of a programming language. For example, if you use a left parenthesis in a Java program where a left brace is required, you have made a syntax error—you have violated the rules of the Java language. If, on the other hand, you tell the computer to do the wrong thing using correct syntax, you have made a **logic error**. For example, suppose you want to compute and display the sum of 20 and 3. To do this, you write a program that contains the following statement:

```
System.out.println(200 + 3);
```

Unfortunately, this statement contains a mistake: It computes the sum of 200 and 3 rather than 20 and 3. It, however, is a perfectly legal instruction. When you run the program, it will display 203, an incorrect answer to the problem you wanted the computer to solve.

Errors that the compiler can detect are called **compile-time errors**. The `javac` compiler knows all the rules of the Java language. Thus, it can detect all syntax errors. It, however, cannot detect most logic errors. How, for example, could the compiler know in the preceding example that you want to compute the sum of 20 and 3 rather than 200 and 3? It cannot. Thus, this logic error would go undetected by the compiler.

A **run-time error** is an error that is detected at run time (i.e., during program execution). For example, dividing by zero (which is an illegal operation) is a run-time error. What happens when a run-time error occurs depends on the program. One alternative is to terminate execution immediately. Another alternative is to **recover from the error** (i.e., handle the error in such a way that the program can continue executing). When a run-time error causes a program to terminate, we often say (over-dramatically) that the program has "crashed" or has "blown up."

Logic errors are far more insidious than syntax errors. You can easily determine if your program has syntax errors: simply compile your program. If it has any syntax errors, the compiler will generate error messages. However, logic errors generally do not produce error messages at compile time. And they may not produce any error messages at run time. So you may have logic errors in your program but not know it. Your program may be providing an answer that is completely wrong. *Just because a computer provides an answer for some problem does not mean the answer is correct.*

1.7 A Program with Objects

Java is an **object-oriented** (OO) programming language. That is, Java programs, when executed, can create and use objects. An **object** is a structure that contains both data and the methods that operate on that data.

```
 1 class Program2
 2 {
 3    public static void main(String[] args)
 4    {
 5        String p, q;                     // create references p and q
 6        p = new String("hello");         // create object
 7        q = p.toUpperCase();             // create second object
 8        System.out.println(p);           // display p-string
 9        System.out.println(q);           // display q-string
10        String r = new String("bye");    // create ref r and object
11        String s = "all done";           // create ref s and object
12        System.out.println(r);           // display r-string
13        System.out.println(s);           // display s-string
14    }
15 }
```

Comments

Figure 1.3

Object-oriented programming languages have significant advantages over other types of programming languages. We will begin investigating the OO features of Java in Chapter 6. So that we don't have to wait until then to get a taste of object-oriented programming, let's now look at a simple program that creates objects.

Objects are constructed from classes. A class is a blueprint for an object. The Java programming language comes with many predefined classes. Thus, we do not have to create classes before we can create objects; we can simply use the predefined classes as long as they satisfy our requirements. The program in Fig. 1.3 constructs objects from the predefined class named String. An object constructed from the String class contains data (a string) and a collection of methods that operate on that string.

Let's now examine Fig. 1.3 in detail. The line numbers on the left are not part of the program—we have added them so that we can easily refer to specific lines. If you create a file for this program, it should *not* contain these line numbers. However, the **comments**, the items on the right that start with two slashes, are part of the program. We are using comments here to inform the human reader what each statement does. We have added color to our comments to make them stand out from the rest of the program. However, when you enter comments in a program, you should enter them in the same way you enter everything else in the program. Comments have no effect on how the program is compiled—they are only for the benefit of the human reader. Comments can make a program easier to read and understand (even for the programmer who wrote the program!). You should always comment your programs. But do not over-comment. Specifically, do not comment on what should be obvious to the intended reader. Such comments waste the reader's time.

Line 5 in Fig. 1.3 creates two String reference variables, one named p and one named q (see Fig. 1.4a). A **variable** is a named location in memory in which a value can be stored. Line 6 is an **assignment statement**, which works this way: The right side of the assignment statement produces a value. This value is then stored in the variable on the left side. The new operator on the right side triggers the construction of an object from the class whose name appears right after new. Thus, here the new operator triggers the construction of an object from the String class. This object contains a string (the string within the quotes on Line 6) and methods that operate on that string. One of these methods is named toUpperCase (see Fig. 1.4b). The new operator not only triggers the construction of the object, it also returns the **reference value** that "points to" the object. This returned value becomes the value of the right side of the assignment statement. It is assigned to p, the variable on the left side of the assignment statement. A reference value is a binary number that designates the location in memory at which an object resides. Thus, it, in effect, points to that object, so we represent it in our diagrams with an arrow. The net effect of Line 6 is to create a String object and assign to p the reference value that points to the new object. Thus, p points to the new object.

An object has no name. However, we can access an object via the reference that points to it. For example, to **invoke** or **call** (i.e., to cause to be executed) the toUpperCase method in the object created by Line 6, we use

```
7        q = p.toUpperCase();              // create new object
```

toUpperCase() on the right side of this assignment statement indicates that the toUpperCase method is to be invoked. But which toUpperCase method? The initial p on the right side indicates that it is the toUpperCase method *in the object to which p points*. When invoked, toUpperCase creates a second object identical to the object in which the invoked toUpperCase method resides, except that in the new object all the letters in the string are in uppercase. Thus, Line 7 creates a new String object that contains the string HELLO (see Fig. 1.4c). It also returns a reference value to the new object. This reference is then assigned to q by the action of the assignment statement in Line 7. Note that Line 7 contains parentheses to the right of the method name. Parentheses are required when we invoke a method.

Lines 8 and 9 do *not* display the reference values in p and q. Instead, they display the string data in the objects to which they point. Thus, these lines display hello and HELLO, respectively.

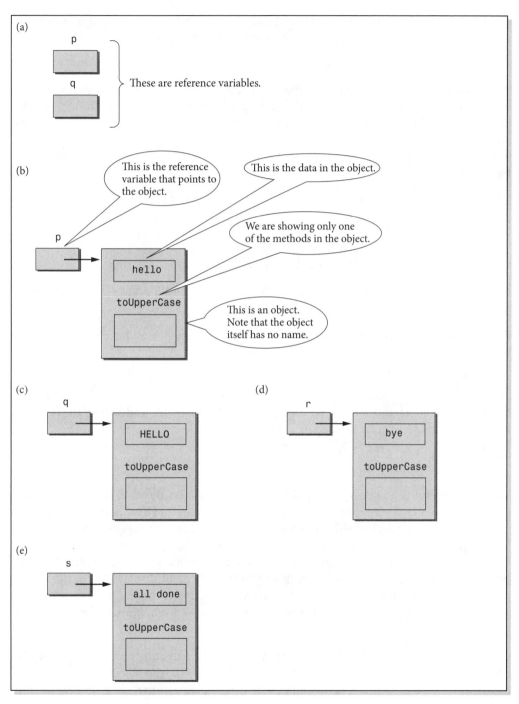

Figure 1.4

On line 10 we create a reference variable r, construct an object containing bye, and assign r the reference to the object, all in one statement (see Fig. 1.4d):

```
10        String r = new String("bye");// create reference r and object
```

Strings are used so often in programs that a shorthand technique for constructing String objects is allowed: If we simply specify a string within quotes, a String object is automatically constructed that contains that string. We do not have to use the new operator and specify the String class. For example, line 11 creates the reference variable s and a String object containing all done. It then assigns to s the reference to the object (see Fig. 1.4e):

```
11        String s = "all done";        // create reference s and object
```

Lines 12 and 13 then display the r and s strings:

```
12        System.out.println(r);        // display r-string
13        System.out.println(s);        // display s-string
```

That is, they display the strings in the objects to which r and s point—namely, bye and all done.

Because objects do not have names, when talking about objects, we have to refer to them by using the reference variables that point to them. For example, to refer to the object to which p points, we say "the p object." This phrase is shorthand for the phrase "the object to which p points."

Now that we understand something about objects, we can better understand the program in Fig. 1.2. Let's reexamine the two println statements in this program:

```
System.out.println(20 + 3);
System.out.println("20 + 3");
```

These statements are actually method invocations. System.out is a reference variable that points to an object that contains the println method. Thus, each of these statements invoke the println method in this object. The value of the **argument** (i.e., what is inside the parentheses in a method invocation) is passed to the println method when it is invoked. In the first println statement, 20 and 3 are first added. The result, 23, is then passed to the println method. Thus, this println statement displays 23. In the second println statement, the string "20 + 3" is passed. The println method simply displays the string it is passed—it does not look inside the string for arithmetic expressions to evaluate. Thus, this println statement displays 20 + 3.

Generally, to invoke a method in an object, we first have to construct the object. However, some objects are automatically constructed for us—like the object that contains the println method to which System.out points. Thus, we can use these objects without first having to construct them.

In the invocation of toUpperCase on Line 7 in Fig. 1.3, we are not passing any arguments (the arguments, if there were any, would be specified inside the parentheses). toUpper-Case does not need any arguments passed to it because it operates on the data—the string hello—in the object.

The program in Fig. 1.3 illustrates two important features of objects. Each object combines data and methods into a *single* functional unit. We access the data in an object via the methods in the object. We call this feature **encapsulation**. We have no direct access to the data in an object (we access the data only via the methods in an object). Moreover, we can use the object without knowing how the data it holds is represented within the object. We call this feature **information hiding**. For example, consider the string "do". It is represented in computer memory by the binary code for 'd' followed by the binary code for 'o'. But suppose in the next memory slot there just happens to be the binary code for some other character, say 't'. In that case, do we have the string "do" or the string "dot"? To avoid this sort of ambiguity, a string is represented either by recording its length (i.e., the number of characters) in addition to its binary codes, or by terminating its sequence of binary codes with a special code that means "end of string." With the first approach, we store the string "do" by storing the binary codes for the letters 'd' and 'o', and the length 2 (see Fig. 1.5a). With the second approach, we store the binary codes for 'd' and 'o', followed by the end-of-string code (see Fig. 1.5b). With either approach, the string is well defined—that is, we know for sure where it ends.

But we don't need to know any of these details to use a String object that holds the string "do". If, for example, we want an uppercase version, we simply invoke its toUpperCase method.

Because of encapsulation and information hiding, you can easily use classes someone else has written—*you do not have to know the internal details of a class to use it.* By using classes

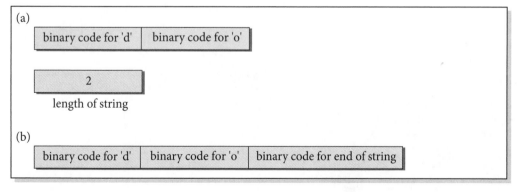

Figure 1.5

someone else has written, you can dramatically cut down the time to implement complex programs. Suppose, for example, a professional programmer wants to write a simple word processing program that uses a **graphical user interface** (i.e., an interface that uses graphical components such as drop-down menus and buttons). If the programmer writes the entire program from scratch, it will take, perhaps, 1 year. If, however, the programmer takes advantage of Java's predefined classes, it will take, perhaps, 1 day. *Making code easy to share is one of the principal advantages of object-oriented programming.*

1.7.1 Note on Prep, Laboratory, and Homework Exercises

Any Java code that appears in the prep, laboratory, and homework exercises is available in the collection of source code that accompanies this textbook. *Don't waste your time typing in this code—use the source code provided.* The names of the files in the source code collection include the chapter number, the category letter ("p" for prep, "e" for lab exercise, and "h" for homework) and the exercise number. For example, C1p4.java is the code for Chapter 1, Lab Prep 4; C1e5.java is the code for Chapter 1, Lab Exercise 5; C6h1.java is the code for Chapter 6, Homework 1. Use the same file naming system when you create files for which a source code file does not already exist. For example, use C1e11.java for the program you create for Chapter 1, Lab Exercise 11.

Include a comment containing your name at the beginning of your programs. Include additional comments to explain any nonobvious features of your code. Properly format your programs (use the sample programs in this textbook as models).

Laboratory 1 Prep

1. Invent a mnemonic (i.e., something that aids memory) so that you can easily remember the header required for the `main` method (see Fig. 1.2).

2. Which of the following identifiers are the names of Java classes: `main`, `Random`, `public`, `String`, `int`, and `Integer`.

3. What are the binary equivalents for the decimal numbers 0 through 15?

4. What is wrong with the following command,

   ```
   javac Program1
   ```

   and the following Java statement:

   ```
   System.out.println[2 + 2]
   ```

5. Write a single statement that creates a `String` reference variable `s`, creates a `String` object that contains the string `"dog"`, and assigns `s` the reference to the object created.

Laboratory 1

1. Compile and run the program in Fig. 1.2 by entering

   ```
   javac Program1.java
   java Program1
   ```

   Now try running the program again by entering (with a lowercase p)

   ```
   java program1
   ```

   What happens?

2. Compile and run the program in `C1e2.java`. Verify that the program compiles and runs correctly. Change `args` to `goofy`. Verify that the program still compiles and runs correctly. Java does not require the name `args` for the name of the parameter in the `main` method.

3. Compile and run the program in `C1e3.java` in the source code package. Verify that the program compiles and runs correctly. Remove the semicolon at the end of the first `println` statement. Compile the program and inspect the compile-time error that results. Does the error message correctly indicate the location of the error in the source program?

LABORATORY

4. What's wrong with the following program:

```
Class C1e4
{
    public static void Main(String args)
    {
        system.out.println("C1e4");
    }
}
```

Compile and run it to check your answer. Fix the program so that it runs correctly.

5. Compile the following program to verify it has four syntax errors. For each error, what is the error message produced by the compiler?

```
clas s C1e5
{
    public static void main(String[] args)
    {
        System.out.println("Good
        bye");
        System.out.println("Go od by e");
        System.out.println("all done);"
    )
}
```

Fix the program so it runs correctly.

6. Verify that the following program runs correctly:

```
class
  C1e6
  { public static
    void main(String[] args) {System.out.println("hello");
  }}
```

Reformat the program so that it is easier to read. You should never write a program with sloppy formatting because it makes the program difficult to read. Always format your programs the way the programs in this textbook (except for this one) are formatted. When you indent, always indent the same number of columns (three columns is a good choice) from the start of the previous line. Don't indent fewer than three columns (it will make it difficult for your eye to pick up the indentation). *Indentation is essential! Always indent properly.*

7. Does the following program work? Note that public follows static in the method header.

```
class C1e7
{
    static public void main(String[] args)
    {
        System.out.println("hello");
    }
}
```

Now switch the positions of void and public. Does the program still work? The return type of method must immediately precede the method name. Thus, void (which is the return type of main) must immediately precede main and follow public and static. public can either precede or follow static, although it is customary to put public first.

8. Insert the following statement in an otherwise correct program. What happens when you run the program?

```
System.out.println(5/0);
```

9. Write a program that displays your name. Use a file named C1e9.java. Use the class name C1e9. Compile and run.

10. Compile and run the following program:

```
1 // escape sequences example
2 class C1e10
3 {
4   public static void main(String[] args)
5   {
6       System.out.println("hel\"lo"); // escape sequence
7   }
8 }
```

The initial quote on Line 6 is a *special* quote. It is special in the sense that it starts the string constant. The third quote on Line 6 is also a *special* quote. It is special in the sense that it ends the string constant. The middle quote is an *ordinary* quote in the sense it does not act in a special way (it does not end the string constant). This quote is made ordinary by the preceding backslash character. (*Rule:* A backslash that precedes a character that is normally special makes that character ordinary.) We call sequences that start with a backslash **escape sequences**. When the preceding program runs, it displays:

```
hel"lo
```

The backslash-quote sequence is displayed as a single quote. Now delete the backslash character in the println statement on Line 6 to get

```
System.out.println("hel"lo"); // escape sequence
```

Because the middle quote is now not backslashed, it is a special quote. That is, it ends the string constant, making the characters to its right look like garbage. Verify that the program no longer compiles correctly.

Like the quote, a backslash can be either a special character (if it is not preceded by a special backslash) or an ordinary character (if it is preceded by a special backslash). Change Line 6 to

```
System.out.println("hel\\\"lo"); // escape sequence
```

Compile and run. We now have two consecutive escape sequences: \\ followed by \". The first backslash makes the second backslash an ordinary character. The third backslash makes the middle quote an ordinary character. Note that in sequence

```
\\\"
```

the third backslash is not an ordinary backslash even though it is preceded by a backslash because the middle backslash is an ordinary backslash by virtue of the first backslash. Thus, this sequence represents an ordinary backslash followed by an ordinary quote. This println statement displays the following seven characters:

```
hel\"lo
```

11. Write a program that displays the following sequence of eight characters:

    ```
    /\/\"/\"
    ```

12. Can a blank line be inserted anywhere in a Java program? Run a test program to determine the effect of blank lines.

13. Determine the effect of

    ```
    System.out.print("hello");
    System.out.print("hello");
    ```

    How does it differ from

    ```
    System.out.println("hello");
    System.out.println("hello");
    ```

    and from

    ```
    System.out.println("hello"); System.out.println("hello");
    ```

    (*Hint:* The "ln" in println means "go to the beginning of the next line.")

14. Run a test program to determine the effect, if any, of

    ```
    System.out.println();
    ```

15. Is the following a legal statement:

```
System.    out  .    println("hello");
```

Compile a program that contains it to check your answer.

16. Write a program that computes and displays the sum of 1, 2, 3, 4, and 5.

17. What does the following program display?

```
class C1e17
{
    public static void main(String[] args)
    {
        String s = "hellobirdbye";
        System.out.println(s);
        System.out.println(s.length());
        String t = s.substring(0,5);
        System.out.println(t);
        System.out.println(s.equals(t));
        System.out.println(t.equals("hello"));
    }
}
```

length, substring, and equals are methods in String objects. length returns the number of characters in the string. substring creates a new object that contains the specified substring of the given string. Its first argument specifies the position at which the substring starts (0 corresponds to the first character). Its second argument specifies the position in the given string that is just beyond the end of the substring. equals compares two strings for equality.

Homework 1

1. Write a program that displays your name in a box, like so:

```
+--------------------------+
|                          |
|        your name         |
|                          |
+--------------------------+
```

2. Write a program that displays a plus sign formed with asterisks. The vertical and horizontal strokes of the plus sign should each be formed with 11 asterisks.

3. Write a program that displays the following sequence of characters:

```
\""\\"""\\\""""\\\\
```

LABORATORY

4. Write a program that *computes* and *displays* the sum of 5 and −20. Your program should produce a display that looks like this:

```
5 + -20 = -15
```

(*Hint:* Use a print statement to display "5 + -20 = " [see Lab Exercise 13]. Then use a println statement to compute the sum of 5 and −20 and display the result.)

5. Is there a toLowerCase method in string objects? Run a test program to find out.

6. Write a program that creates three String reference variables. Each variable should point to the *same* object. This object should contain the string "MeMeMe". Display the string pointed to by each reference variable. (*Hint:* Use the assignment statement to assign one reference variable to another.)

7. Write a program that creates three String reference variables. Each variable should point to a different object. One object should contain the string "UPPER", one object should contain the string "lower", and one object should contain the string "MiXeD". Display the string in each object. For each object, invoke the toUpperCase method and display the string in the new object created.

Constants, Variables, and Operators

2.1 Naming Rules and Conventions

Identifiers are the words we use in a Java program. The categories of identifiers are

- Reserved words, which are identifiers reserved for a specific purpose. Examples of reserved words are `class`, `public`, `static`, and `void`. For a complete list of the reserved words in Java, see Fig. 2.1.
- Identifiers that are not reserved words but are already in use. Examples of this category are `System`, `String`, and `main`.
- Identifiers we make up when writing a program. Examples of this category are the class name `Program1` and the parameter `args` shown in Fig. 1.2.

When you make up an identifier to use in your program, you must obey the following rules:

- Use any combination of letters, digits, the underscore (_), and/or the dollar sign ($), but do not start an identifier with a digit.
- Do not embed any **whitespace** in the identifier. Whitespace is an invisible character such as the space, tab, or the **newline** character (the newline character corresponds to the Enter key).
- Do not match any reserved word.

In addition, an identifier you make up should not conflict with an identifier already in use. For example, you should not use `String` for the class name of your program because `String` is already in use. Using `String` for the class name is *not* illegal, but it will make your program unrunnable (see Lab Exercise 14).

You should also follow some conventions when naming identifiers. These conventions are not required by the Java language, but they make reading Java programs easier.

abstract	assert	boolean	break	byte	case
catch	char	class	const	continue	default
do	double	else	enum	extends	false
final	finally	float	for	goto	if
implements	import	instanceof	int	interface	long
native	new	null	package	private	protected
public	return	short	static	strictfp	super
switch	synchronized	this	throw	throws	transient
true	try	void	volatile	while	

Figure 2.1   Reserved Words

- Class names should start with an uppercase letter. Method and parameter names should start with a lowercase letter.
- Use an uppercase letter at the beginning of any noninitial word in a multiple-word identifier. For example, in the method name `getMaximumScore` and in the class name `ScoreExamProgram`, we capitalize the first letter of every noninitial word (in the latter, we also capitalize the first letter of the initial word because the identifier is a class name). This type of capitalization is called **camelcase**.
- Use meaningful identifiers, such as `Program1` and `getMaximumScore`.

2.2   Literal Constants

A **literal constant** is a value used in a program. For example, 3, `"3"`, and 3.0 are literal constants. All literal constants in Java have a **type**. The type of a constant determines how it can be used and how it is stored in the computer. For example, the type of 3 is int (int means "integer"). The type of `"3"` is String (because it is enclosed in quotes). What is the type of 3.0? A good guess is int. However, int is wrong. The type of 3.0 is double. Although 3 and 3.0 are mathematically equivalent, they have different types in Java. They are represented quite differently inside the computer. 3 is represented as a regular binary number. Only whole numbers can be represented in this format. 3.0, on the other hand, is represented in a special binary format called **floating point format**. Floating point format allows a number to have a fractional part. In Java, any number with a decimal point is represented in floating point format.

Here are the rules in Java on literal constants:

- Commas are not allowed in arithmetic constants. For example, you may *not* write one thousand and five as 1,005.
- double constants are arithmetic constants that contain a decimal point or use **E notation**. In E notation, the letter E (upper or lowercase) followed by an integer represents a power of 10. For example, the double constant 1200.0 can be represented in E notation as 1.2E3. E3 here represents the third power of 10. Thus, 1.2E3 equals 1.2×10^3. E notation is convenient when the whole part of a double number has many trailing zeros, or the fractional part has many leading zeros. For example, it is easier to write 1.2E14 and 1.2E–14 than their equivalents 120000000000000 and 0.000000000000012. If the number that precedes E does not have a decimal point, it is treated as if the decimal point were right before the E. For example, 12E3 is equal to 12.E3. The number that follows E must be an integer.

- Whenever we use double quotes, we always get a `String` constant. Thus, 3 (without quotes) is an `int` constant, but "3" (with quotes) is a `String` constant. `int` and `String` constants are stored differently inside the computer. Moreover, the operations that can be performed on `int` constants are different than the operations that can be performed on `String` constants. For example, we can tell the computer to subtract 2 from 3 and display the result with the statement

```
System.out.println(3 - 2);      // displays 1
```

But we cannot tell the computer to subtract the string "2" from the string "3". Thus, the following statement is illegal:

```
System.out.println("3" - "2");  // illegal statement
```

2.3 Operators and Operands

Symbols like "+" and "−" that represent operations are called **operators**. The items on which they operate are called **operands**. For example, in 11 − 7, the minus sign is the operator, and 11 and 7 are the operands. Spaces surrounding an operator are not required. For example, we can write either 11 − 7 or 11−7.

One of the operations we can perform on strings is **concatenation**. This operation combines two strings into one longer string. For example, if we concatenate the strings "down" and "town", we get "downtown". Java uses the plus sign for the concatenation operator. Thus, in the statement,

```
System.out.println("down" + "town");   // concatenation, not addition
```

we are concatenating—not adding—two strings. This statement concatenates these two strings and then displays the result, `downtown`.

The plus sign is an example of an operator that can have different meanings, depending on the operands that surround it. If a plus sign is surrounded by arithmetic operands, the plus sign is the addition operator. But if the plus sign is surrounded by string operands, then the plus sign is the concatenation operator. We say an operator that has multiple meanings is **overloaded**.

Now consider the following statement :

```
System.out.println("11" + "7");  // displays 117
```

The operands surrounding the plus sign are both strings (because they are enclosed in quotes). Thus, the plus sign here functions as the concatenation operator, concatenating the string `"11"` and the string `"7"` to get the string `"117"`. 117 is then displayed on the screen.

What happens if one operand is arithmetic and the other is a string, as in the following statement:

```
System.out.println(11 + "7");    // displays 117
```

Here, we have operands with different types: the left operand has type `int`; the right operand has type `String`. In this situation, the operand that is not a string is converted to a string. The two strings are then concatenated. Thus, the integer 11 is converted to the string `"11"` and then concatenated with `"7"` to give the string `"117"`. 117 is then displayed on the screen.

Here are the common arithmetic operators in Java:

+   addition
−   subtraction
*   multiplication
/   division
%   remainder

Let's use these operators in `println` statements and examine the results.

Our first statement displays 5:

```
System.out.println(2 + 3);    // addition
```

Because both operands of the plus sign are arithmetic, they are added.

The next statement multiplies 2 and 3:

```
System.out.println(2*3);        // multiplication
```

To multiply, we must always explicitly specify the multiplication operator "`*`". Thus, the following statements are *illegal*:

```
System.out.println((2)(3));    // illegal because missing *
System.out.println(2×3);       // illegal because cannot use ×
```

The division operator "`/`" represents two types of divisions. If both operands have an integer type, then "`/`" yields their quotient with the remainder discarded. For example, the statement

```
System.out.println(5/2);    // displays 2
```

displays the quotient of 5 divided by 2, which is 2. The remainder, which is 1, is discarded. However, if the operands have `double` values, "/" yields a result that includes a fractional part. For example,

```
System.out.println(5.0/2.0);
```

displays 2.5. If only one operand is a `double`, the other operand—if it is arithmetic—is automatically converted to a `double`. The division then yields a fractional result. For example, in the statement

```
System.out.println(5.0/2);   // 2 converted to 2.0
```

the `int` constant 2 is converted to 2.0. 5.0 is then divided by 2.0, yielding 2.5.

"%" is the remainder operator. It yields the remainder in a division with integers. For example,

```
System.out.println(5%2);
```

displays 1, the remainder when 5 is divided by 2.

Symbols for operators within a string are treated as ordinary characters. That is, they do not trigger an operation. For example, the statement

```
System.out.println("5/2");
```

simply displays the characters that make up the string (excluding the quotes):

```
5/2
```

2.4 Precedence

The rules of precedence for arithmetic operations in Java are the same as in conventional mathematics. For example, multiplication and division have higher precedence than addition and subtraction. Thus, in the statement

```
System.out.println(6 + 27/3);      // displays 15
```

the division of 27 by 3 occurs before the addition of 6. 6 + 27/3 equals 6 + 9, which equals 15. Note that if the addition were performed first (which it is not), you would get a different answer: 6 + 27 equals 33. 33 divided by 3 equals 11.

As in mathematical notation, we can force the addition to be performed before a higher-precedence operation by using parentheses. For example, in the following statement, the parentheses force the addition of 6 and 27 to occur before the division by 3:

```
System.out.println((6 + 27)/3);      // displays 11
```

All the operators we have discussed so far are **left associative**. That is, operations of equal precedence are evaluated left to right, unless overruled by parentheses. For example, in

```
System.out.println(10 − 5 − 3);    // displays 2
```

the subtraction of 5 from 10 is performed first because it appears leftmost. To force the right operation first, we can use parentheses:

```
System.out.println(10 − (5 − 3));   // displays 8
```

2.5   Variables and the Assignment Statement

A **variable** is a named location in computer memory in which a value can be stored, and from which a value can be retrieved. If we put 5 into a variable named x, then the **contents** of x becomes 5. We can then represent the current state of x with the following picture:

```
       x
    ┌───────┐
    │   5   │
    └───────┘
```

Actually, this representation is not quite correct. The x variable would contain a binary number whose value is equal to decimal 5. All numbers are stored in a computer in binary form. Rather than complicate our diagrams by using the actual binary numbers, we will show the values of arithmetic variables using decimal numbers. But keep in mind that everything stored in the computer is stored in some binary form.

If we now put 7 into x, then the 7 replaces the 5. We get

```
       x
    ┌───────┐
    │   7   │
    └───────┘
```

All variables have a type and store values only of that type. For example, a variable x of type int can store the int constant 7 but not the double constant 7.0.

To use a variable in a Java program, we must declare it. A **variable declaration** specifies the type and name of a variable, and optionally an initial value. For example, the declaration

```
int x, y, z = 1;
```

declares x, y, and z to be type int variables. It also initializes z (and only z) to 1. In a declaration, the type comes first, followed by a list of variables (with optional initial values) separated by commas. A semicolon at the end terminates the declaration.

The following code is illegal:

```
int x, y, z;
int x;          // illegal!!!
```

Here we are declaring two variables with the name x. This duplicate declaration of x would make any statement that refers to x ambiguous. Thus, it is illegal.

We can put a value into a variable with an **assignment statement**. For example, the following is an assignment statement that puts 5 into the variable x:

```
x = 5;
```

You should read this statement as "x is assigned 5." The equals sign is the **assignment operator**. If we then want to assign 7 to x, we can use

```
x = 7;
```

When executed, this statement replaces the 5 in x with 7.

Suppose we use a variable in a program in place of a literal constant. Then the current value in the variable is used in the evaluation process. Consider, for example, the program in Fig. 2.2 (we have added line numbers so we can easily refer to individual lines).

Once we declare x on Line 5, we can use it. After assigning 7 to x on Line 6, we use x in the next three statements. In each instance, the computer uses the current value in x (which is 7). Thus, Lines 7, 8, and 9 display on the screen

```
7
11
7
```

Notice that Line 7 *displays the value in* x, not the character x itself:

```
7       System.out.println(x);            // displays 7
```

However, Line 10 displays the character x—not the value in x—because x is in quotes:

```
10      System.out.println("x");          // displays x
```

On Line 8 the value in x is not changed. The computer makes a copy of the value in x to which it adds 4 and then displays the result 11. Thus, the value in x is unaffected. We can, of course, change the value in x with additional assignment statements, which we do with

```
11      x = 20;                           // x now 20
```

```
 1 class Variables
 2 {
 3    public static void main(String[] args)
 4    {
 5       int x;                              // declare x
 6       x = 7;                              // x is now 7
 7       System.out.println(x);              // displays 7
 8       System.out.println(x + 4);          // displays 11
 9       System.out.println(x);              // x is still 7
10       System.out.println("x");            // displays x
11       x = 20;                             // x now 20
12       System.out.println(x);              // displays 20
13       x = x + 1;                          // adds 1 to x
14       System.out.println(x);              // displays 21
15       x++;                                // adds 1 to x
16       System.out.println("x = " + x);     // displays x = 22
17       x--;                                // subtracts 1 from x
18       System.out.println("x = " + x);     // displays x = 21
19
20       double y, z;                        // declares y and z
21       y = 5.0;                            // y is now 5.0
22       y = y/2.0;                          // divides y by 2.0
23       System.out.println(y);              // displays 2.5
24       z = y/2.0;                          // y still 2.5, z is 1.25
25       System.out.println(z);              // displays 1.25
26    }
27 }
```

Figure 2.2

which changes the value of x to 20. Then the statement

```
13        x = x + 1;                        // adds 1 to x
```

adds 1 to x. With this statement, we are *not* asserting that x is equal to x + 1 (a mathematical impossibility). The equals sign does *not* mean equality. *It is the assignment operator.* It means that the value of its right side, x + 1 (which is 21 because x is 20 at this point), should be assigned to the variable on the left side, which happens to be x. Thus, the effect of this statement is to assign 21 (1 more than the current value of x) to x, thereby increasing the value of x by 1. Line 15 illustrates another way to increase x by 1. It uses the **increment operator**, "++," whose effect is to add 1 to the variable to which it applies (it works only on variables with integer types):

```
15        x++;                              // adds 1 to x
```

x is now 22. Thus, Line 16 displays x = 22:

```
16        System.out.println("x = " + x);   // displays x = 22
```

Here the plus sign is the concatenation operator because one of its operands is a string. The int value in x (22) is converted to the string "22", and concatenated to the string "x = ". The left x in this statement is within quotes. Thus, the character x itself appears in the message displayed. However the right x is not within quotes. Thus, its value appears—not the character x—in the message displayed. The **decrement operator**, "- -", subtracts 1 from x:

```
17          x--;                              // subtracts 1 from x
```

Starting on Line 20, we declare double variables y and z, assign 5.0 to y, divide it by 2.0, and then display the final value in y.

```
20          double y, z;                      // declares y and z
21          y = 5.0;                          // y is now 5.0
22          y = y/2.0;                        // divides y by 2.0
23          System.out.println(y);            // displays 2.5
```

The statement on Line 22 is similar to the statement on Line 13. In both cases, the value of the expression on the right of the assignment statement is computed and assigned to the variable on the left. Thus, the effect of Line 22 is to divide a copy of the value in y (which is currently 5.0) by 2.0, producing the result 2.5. 2.5 is then assigned to y. Thus, the value in y is halved. In contrast, in the assignment statement

```
24          z = y/2.0;                        // y still 2.5, z is 1.25
```

we divide a copy of the value in y by 2.0 but assign the result to z. Thus, Line 24 does not change the value in y. *Assignment statements change the value in the variable on the left of the assignment operator.*

Variables declared inside a method are **local** to that method—that is, they can be used only inside that method. For this reason, we call variables declared within a method **local variables**. The **scope** (i.e., where an item can be used in a program) of a local variable is the method in which it is declared from its point of declaration forward to the end of the method. Thus, you cannot use a local variable before its declaration. For example, the following code is illegal:

```
m = 2;      // illegal
int m;
```

You also cannot access the value in a local variable before it has been given one. For example the following code is illegal:

```
int n, m;   // local variables n and m have no values initially
m = n + 1;  // illegal because n has no value
```

n and m here have no initial values. Thus, a value cannot be computed for the right side of the assignment statement.

Laboratory 2 Prep

1. Determine by hand the value of each of these Java expressions:

```
1 – 2 – 3 – 4 – 5 – 6 – 7 – 8 – 9 – 10
2 * 4 / 2 * 2
100 % 5 / 4
2 / 2 / 2
2 % 2 % 2
22 / 7.0
22 / 7 / 1.0
22 / (7 / 1.0)
2.1E3 + 2.4E2 + 1E1 + 1.5
```

2. What do the following statements display (assume they are embedded in a valid Java program):

```
System.out.println("2" + 3);
System.out.println(7E3);
System.out.println(7E–3);
```

3. What does the following statement display:

```
System.out.println(1 + 2 + 3 + "4" + 5 + 6);
```

4. Give a statement that declares int variables i, j, k and initializes j to 50. Give an assignment statement that decreases the value in j by 10, regardless of its current value.

5. Which of the following are legal Java identifiers: hEllo, 12x, _, $1234, bongo

Laboratory 2

Your programs should appropriately label any output it generates. For example, if your program computes and displays the average of a set of test scores, it should not simply display the average. It should display the average with a descriptive label, such as

```
Test Score Average = ___
```

1. Determine by hand the value of each of these Java expressions. Then check your answers by writing a Java program that displays their values.

```
10%2
11%2
12%2
13%2
14%2
```

if x%2 equals 0, what can you conclude about x? If x%2 equals 1?

2. What happens when you compile a program that contains the following statement:

```
System.out.println(5.0%2.0);
```

Why is this statement illegal?

3. Compile and run the following program to determine the effect of the "++" operator.

```
 1 class C2e3
 2 {
 3    public static void main(String[] args)
 4    {
 5       int x, y;
 6       x = 1;
 7       x++;
 8       System.out.println("x++; changes x from 1 to " + x);
 9       x = 1;
10       ++x;
11       System.out.println("++x; changes x from 1 to " + x);
12       x = 1;
13       y = x++;      // increment after assignment
14       System.out.println("y = x++; changes x from 1 to " + x);
15       System.out.println("y = x++; assigns y " + y);
16       x = 1;
17       y = ++x;      // increment before assignment
18       System.out.println("y = ++x; changes x from 1 to " + x);
19       System.out.println("y = ++x; assigns y " + y);
20    }
21 }
```

"++" is called the increment operator. The timing of the incrementation depends on whether "++" follows or precedes a variable. In Line 13, the value in x is incremented *after* the assignment to y. In Line 17, the value in x is incremented *before* the assignment to y.

Replace every occurrence of "++" in the preceding code with the decrement operator "--". Run the program to determine the effect of this change.

In the statement on Line 13, the expression ++x has a **side effect**. That is, in addition to providing a value that is then assigned to y, it does something else. In the case of x++, it increments x.

4. Incorporate the following code in a program and run. Do the first two println statements display different values for x? Do the last two println statements display different values for y? Explain the results.

```
int x, y;
x = 1;
y = ++x;
System.out.println("x = " + x + " y = " + y);
x = 1;
y = x + 1;
System.out.println("x = " + x + " y = " + y);

y = 1;
y = x + x++;        // avoid writing confusing statements like this
System.out.println(y);
x = 1;
y = x++ + x;        // avoid writing confusing statements like this
System.out.println(y);
```

5. Write a Java program in which you declare the int variables x, y, and sum. Assign 2 to x and 3 to y. Add x and y and assign the result to sum. Display the value of sum. When you run your program, you should see the following displayed on the screen:

```
sum = 5
```

6. Explain what happens when you compile the following program:

```
class C2e6
{
    public static void main(String[] args)
    {
        int x, y;
        x = y + 1;
    }
}
```

7. The following statement contains a minus sign.

```
y = -x + 10;
```

This minus sign is not the subtraction operator. It is the **negation operator**. It negates (i.e., changes the sign) of the operand that follows it. Because it operates on only one operand, it is called a **unary operator** ("unary" means "one"). The plus sign here is the addition operator. Because it operates on two operands, it is called a **binary operator** ("binary" means "two").

Unary operators have higher precedence than binary operands. Thus, in the preceding statement, a copy of the value in x is negated and then the result of the negation and 10 are added. Assume the value of x is 5. What value is assigned to y? Run a test

LABORATORY

program to check your answer. What value would be assigned to y if the addition operator had higher precedence than the negation operator?

8. Compile the following program by entering on the command line

```
javac C2e8.java
```

Then run the program by entering on the command line

```
java C2e8 bird deer
```

The additional items on the preceding command—bird and deer—are **command-line arguments**. They are passed to the args parameter in the main method. main can then access these command-line arguments using the args parameter as demonstrated in the program. We will learn more about argument passing in Chapter 5.

```
class C2e8
{
   public static void main(String[] args)
   {
      System.out.println(args[0]);   // displays bird
      System.out.println(args[1]);   // displays deer
   }
}
```

Run the program a second time by entering

```
java C2e8 cat dog
```

What is displayed this time? Now try

```
java C2e8 up
```

What's wrong with this command?

9. Run a program that contains the following two statements:

```
System.out.println("2" + 3 + 4);
System.out.println("2" + (3 + 4));
```

Why do these statements display different strings?

10. Include the following code in a Java program. What is the effect of each statement?

```
x = 1;
x += 2;
System.out.println(x);
x *= 10;
System.out.println(x);
x /= 15;
System.out.println(x);
```

"+=" means to add and then assign. "*=" means to multiply and then assign. "/="
means to divide and then assign. For example, the second statement in the preceding
code adds x and 2 and then assigns the result to x.

11. Run the following program. What is displayed?

```java
class C2e11
{
    public static void main(String[] args)
    {
        System.out.println("1"); /*
        System.out.println("2");
        System.out.println("3"); */
        System.out.println("4");
    }
}
```

Whatever is between "/*" and "*/" is treated as a comment by the compiler. This
type of comment can span multiple lines.

12. What happens when you compile the following program:

```java
class C2e12
{
    public static void main(String[] args)
    {
        int switch;
        switch = 3;
    }
}
```

What is wrong with the variable switch?

13. What do the following statements display:

```java
System.out.println(20);
System.out.println(020);
```

(*Hint:* Integer constants that have a leading zero are treated as octal constants. In
octal, the weights are powers of 8.)

14. Compile and run the following program (use the class name String):

```java
class String              // use the name String for this class
{
    public static void main(String[] args)
    {
        System.out.println("hello");
    }
}
```

LABORATORY

LABORATORY

This program will not run correctly because it redefines String. Thus, the args parameter now does not have the required type (it must be String[], where String is the *original* definition of String). *Once you compile this program, all the programs you subsequently compile will not run* because of the redefinition of String. To fix this problem, delete the String.class file you created when you compiled the preceding program. To do this on a Linux or Macintosh system, enter

```
rm String.class
```

On a Windows system, enter

```
del String.class
```

15. Is the following code legal:

```
int m = 3;
int n = m;  // can the initial value in a declaration be a variable?
```

Homework 2

1. Write a program that displays five command-line arguments. For example, if you run your program with

```
java C2h1 u v w x y
```

your program will display

```
u
v
w
x
y
```

(*Hint:* See Lab Exercise 8.)

2. Write a program that assigns 1.5, 22.4, −44.8, 0.333, and 1.123 to the variables a, b, c, d, and e, respectively. Next, compute their sum. Assign the result to a variable named sum. Next, compute the average of the values in these variables. Assign the result to a variable named average. Display the values in sum and average with appropriate labels.

3. 5 factorial is the product of 5, 4, 3, 2, and 1. 10 factorial is the product of the integers 10 down to 1. Write a program that computes and displays the value of 5 factorial. In the same program compute and display the value of 10 factorial making use of the result you computed for 5 factorial. Be sure to display your results with appropriate labels.

4. Write a program that computes and displays with an appropriate label the value of

$$\frac{(5)\,(6)\,(7)}{(2)\,(3)}$$

5. The number of characters in a String object is returned by the length method in the object. For example, if s is a reference to a String object, then the following statement displays the number of characters in its string:

```
System.out.println(s.length());
```

Write a program that creates three String objects. Your program should then determine and display the length of each string. Test your program with the following strings: "yes", "yes   ", and "". The string "" is the **null string**—the string with zero characters.

Primitive Types and Casts

- Learn how primitive types are represented
- Learn how to use casts
- Learn how mixed types are handled in arithmetic expressions
- Learn how to use relational and boolean operators
- Learn more precedence rules

3.1 Representation of Primitive Types in Memory

int and double are examples of **primitive types**. A variable with a primitive type corresponds to single box in memory that has a name. Thus, a variable that has a primitive type can hold only one value at a time. We can access this value via the name of the box that holds it. For example, suppose within a method we have the following code:

```
int x;
double y;
x = 3;
y = 5.5;
```

After the two assignment statements are executed, the variables x and y can be represented with

```
     x                           y
  ┌────────────┐    ┌──────────────────────────┐
  │     3      │    │           5.5            │
  └────────────┘    └──────────────────────────┘
```

We show the y box bigger than the x box because it is, indeed, a bigger box in memory. A double value requires more memory space than an int value. However, both x and y correspond to single, named boxes—each of which can contain a single value. Nonprimitive types, like String, have more complicated structures associated with them.

At this point we need to digress a little to discuss how memory is organized in a computer. Everything—numbers, strings, instructions—in main memory is represented with **binary numbers**—numbers that contain only 0's and 1's. Each 0 or 1 in a binary number is called a **bit**. A sequence of 8 bits is called a **byte**.

Main memory is an array of individual cells, each of which can hold 1 byte. One cell of main memory—that is, 1 byte—is too small to hold the range of values that a variable of type int can have. So Java uses 4 consecutive cells—that is, it uses 4 consecutive bytes for a variable of type int. For a double variable, it uses 8 consecutive bytes.

What if we want to store an integer in a variable but it is too big to fit into an int variable? Recall that the box for an int variable is 4 bytes long. With 4 bytes, the values can range roughly from −2 billion to +2 billion. However, Java has another primitive type, long, that holds integers. A long variable uses 8 bytes. Because it uses more bytes than an int variable, a long variable can hold a much larger range of integers. long values range from roughly -10^{19} to 10^{19}. If you need to hold really large integers, use type long instead of type int.

Java also has two more types that are for integers: byte and short. byte variables use only 1 byte so its range is the least. short variables use 2 bytes so its range lies between

	Type	Size	Range
	byte	1 byte	−128 to 127
	short	2 bytes	−32768 to 32767
	int	4 bytes	approximately −2 billion to 2 billion
	long	8 bytes	approximately -10^{19} to 10^{19}
	float	4 bytes	approximately -10^{38} to 10^{38}, 8 significant digits
	double	8 bytes	approximately -10^{308} to 10^{308}, 16 significant digits
	char	2 bytes	can hold any single character
	boolean	1 byte	holds either true or false

Arithmetic types { byte, short, int, long, float, double }

Figure 3.1   Primitive Types

that of byte and int. Fig. 3.1 shows each primitive type in Java, along with its associated size and range.

Java has two types for numbers with a fractional part: double, which we have already seen, and float. These types differ in the number of bytes used by the corresponding variables. A double variable uses 8 bytes of memory; a float variable uses only 4 bytes. Because a variable of type double uses more bytes than a variable of type float, a double variable has greater range and can hold values with more precision (i.e., with more significant digits). double variables can hold double the significant digits that float variables can hold—hence the name double. If you perform computations with variables and constants of type double, you will, in general, get more accurate and more precise answers than if you use float. Thus, you should almost always use double rather than float to hold fractional numbers. The only circumstance that would make sense using float rather than double is if your program has to be as small as possible. Because float variables occupy less memory than double variables, a program with float variables would be smaller than the same program with double variables.

We distinguish literal constants of type double from literal constants of type float by appending the letter f to the end of float constants. For example, 3.33 is a double constant and will, therefore, be represented using 8 bytes. 3.33f, on the other hand, is a float constant and will, therefore, be represented using 4 bytes.

3.2 Casts

Suppose b, s, i, l, f, and d are variables of type byte, short, int, long, float, and double, respectively. Then the assignment statement

```
i = b;      // i is int, b is byte
```

is legal because the value in b will always fit into the variable i (recall type byte corresponds to 1 byte, and int corresponds to 4 bytes). For the same reason, the following statements are also legal:

```
s = b;      // s is short, b is byte
l = b;      // l is long, b is byte
f = b;      // f is float, b is byte
d = b;      // d is double, b is byte
```

For all these statements, a copy of the value in b is automatically converted to match the type of the variable on the left. The converted copy is then assigned to the variable on the left. We call this automatic type conversion **type coercion**. For example, if the value in b is 3, a copy of this value is converted to the double value 3.0 before it is assigned to d.

If we switch the left and right sides in each of the preceding assignment statements, they become illegal. For example, the following statement is illegal because the value in i (which occupies 4 bytes) may not fit into b (which occupies 1 byte):

```
b = i;      // illegal statement
```

This statement will cause a compile-time error. However, we can modify it to make it legal. We can insert a **cast** to force a type change. A cast consists of the name of a type surrounded by parentheses. For example, in the following statement, we are casting i to byte:

```
b = (byte)i;          // legal statement because of the cast
```

The cast here does not change the value in i or the type of i. Instead, it changes the type of a *copy* of the value in i to byte. The resulting value is then assigned to b. To change the value obtained from i to type byte, the value is **truncated** to 1 byte (i.e., its leftmost 3 bytes are chopped off). Obviously, if a value cannot fit in 1 byte, then its truncation to 1 byte will result in a different value. For example, if the value 257 is truncated to 1 byte, the resulting value is 1. Although the preceding assignment statement is legal, you probably would not want to use it unless you know in advance that i will have a value that fits in b. The range of values that fit in b is −128 to 127.

To assign d (which is type double) to b (which is type byte), we must cast d to byte:

```
b = (byte)d;
```

Here the *integer part* of a copy of the value in d is first truncated to 1 byte before it is assigned to b. Although the cast makes this statement legal, it does not ensure that the statement will work in a reasonable way when it is executed. If d contains 3.12, then the value of its integer part, 3, fits into b. Thus, the truncation of its integer part to 1 byte provides the integer part intact. b is assigned 3. The values of b and d, in this case, will differ by only the fractional part of d. But if d contains 3 billion, then the truncated value of its integer part will be some number between −128 and 127. In this case, the integer value assigned to b will be quite different from the integer part of the value in d.

The arithmetic types in Figure 3.1 form a hierarchy. As we go from byte to double in Fig. 3.1, the range of the corresponding variables gets progressively larger. A value of any arithmetic type in the table can be assigned without a cast to a variable of that type or any arithmetic type below it in the table. The simple operative rule is this: *You do not need a cast if the type of the variable to be assigned has a range equal to or greater than the range corresponding to the type of the value to be assigned.* For example, you can assign a byte value to an int variable without a cast because the range corresponding to int is greater than the range corresponding to byte.

Casts are not always legal. For example, the following cast is illegal:

```
x = (int)"hello";     // illegal cast
```

where x has type int. String and int are **incompatible types**. A string cannot be cast to an int, and vice versa.

3.3 Arithmetic Expressions with Mixed Types

A computer does not have circuitry to perform computations on mixed types. For example, it does not have circuitry to add an int value to a double value. Thus, to add an int value and a double value, one value must be converted to the type of the other value. Here is the rule for such conversions: *In a mixed-type operation, the value whose type corresponds to a smaller range of values is converted to match the type of the other value.* For example, in

```
System.out.println(2 + 3.5);     // displays 5.5
```

the 2 is automatically converted to 2.0 (i.e., it is converted to type double) so its type matches the type of 3.0. The 2 is converted to double rather than the 3.0 to int because the type of 2 (which is int) has a smaller range than the type of 3.0 (which is double).

Automatic type conversion occurs only when the two operands for an operator have different types. For example, in

```
System.out.println(1.0 + 7/2);                    // displays 4.0
```

the first operation performed is the division (because division has higher precedence than addition). Because both operands in this division (7 and 2) have type int, automatic type conversion does *not* occur. Because both operands have type int, the division is performed by the integer division circuitry in the computer. The result of the division is 3. Next, the double 1.0 and the int 3 are added. Because of the mixed type, the 3 is converted to the double 3.0. The addition then yields the result 4.0. If we want the entire expression to be evaluated using double values, we have to change at least one of the operands of the division to type double. That will, in turn, force the other operand to type double. For example, we can rewrite 7 as a double constant:

```
System.out.println(1.0 + 7.0/2);                  // displays 4.5
```

or we can cast 7 to double:

```
System.out.println(1.0 + (double)7/2);            // displays 4.5
```

Casts have higher precedence than all the arithmetic operators. Thus, in the preceding statement, the cast is applied to 7 *before* the division. The cast causes 7 to be converted to double, which, in turn, causes 2 to be converted to double. The division of these two double values results in 3.5. If the cast had lower precedence than division, then the division would be performed *before* the cast, in which case both operands in the division would be type int. If this were the case, the division would result in 3 rather than 3.5.

3.4 Type char

Another primitive type in Java is char. A char variable can hold a single character. A literal char constant consists of a single character enclosed by *single* quotes. For example, 'a', 'A', '5', and '&' are all char constants. Note that 'a' and "a" are not the same. 'a' (with single quotes) is a char constant. "a" (with double quotes) is a String constant.

Suppose we execute

```
c = 'A';
```

where c is declared with

```
char c;
```

We can then represent the variable c and its contents with

But what is actually inside the c box? Recall that all data in computer memory is in binary. Thus, the c box actually contains a binary number—the binary number that represents the uppercase letter A. Every character has a corresponding number that represents it. For example, the number that represents the character 'A' is 65 decimal. Thus, the c box shown actually contains the binary equivalent of the decimal number 65. The specific encoding of characters that Java uses is called Unicode.

To get the literal char constant for the symbol $, we simply surround $ with single quotes to get '$'. The left quote starts the char constant; the right quote ends the char constant. But how do we represent the char constant that is the single quote? If we write ''', the middle single quote ends the constant. The right quote then appears as garbage and will trigger a compile-time error. To remedy this problem, we simply backslash the middle quote to get '\''. The backslash makes the middle quote into an ordinary character—ordinary in the sense that it does not end the char constant. Sequences that start with the backslash are called **escape sequences**.

We can also use escape sequences to represent some special char constants. For example, '\n' represents the newline character (this is the character at the end of every line of a text file). Fig. 3.2 shows the common escape sequences that we can use in Java programs.

'\n' (the newline character), '\r' (the carriage return character), '\t' (the tab character), and the space character are called **whitespace** characters. These characters do not produce any marking on the display or on a paper when printed—hence, the name "whitespace."

\'	ordinary single quote (i.e., a quote that does not end a char constant)
\"	ordinary double quote (i.e., a quote that does not end a String constant)
\\	ordinary backslash
\n	newline character
\r	carriage return character
\t	tab character

Figure 3.2

We can use escape sequences individually in char constants or together with other characters in string constants. For example, in

```
char c;
c = '\'';
```

we are using the escape sequence \' in a char constant. In

```
System.out.println("I read \"War and Peace\" in 10 minutes.");
```

we are using the escape sequence \" twice within a string constant. This statement displays

```
I read "War and Peace" in 10 minutes.
```

3.5 Type boolean

There are many values of type int. They range from about −2 billion to 2 billion. However, there are only two values of type boolean: true and false. A variable whose type is boolean can be assigned only the values true or false. For example, the following code assigns true to boo1 and then assigns the value in boo1 to boo2:

```
boolean boo1, boo2;
boo1 = true;      // boo1 contains true
boo2 = boo1;      // contents of boo1 (true) assigned to boo2
```

Be sure *not* to use quotes around true and false because then you would get string constants. For example, if boo1 is a boolean variable, the following statement is illegal:

```
boo1 = "true";    // illegal because "true" is type String not boolean
```

3.6 Relational Operators

The relational operators are "<" (less than), "<=" (less than or equal), ">" (greater than), ">=" (greater than or equal), "==" (equal), and "!=" (not equal). The relational operators perform comparisons. They yield a boolean (i.e., true or false) result. For example, when we execute the following statement, true is displayed because 2 is less than 3:

```
System.out.println(2 < 3);              // displays true
```

The operands in the expression 2 < 3 are type int, but the result is boolean. Thus, if we want to assign the value of this expression to a variable, that variable should have the type `boolean`. For example, the following sequence assigns the value of `2 < 3` (which is `true`) to `boo` and then displays the value in `boo`:

```
boolean boo;
boo = 2 < 3;                        // true is assigned to boo
System.out.println(boo);            // displays true
```

As in arithmetic expressions, we can use variables in relational expressions. For example, if x and y are `int` variables, then `x < y` is a valid relational expression whose true/false value depends on the values of x and y. For example, in the following code, `x < y` is `true`:

```
int x, y;
x = 2;
y = 3;
System.out.println(x < y);          // displays true
```

Now consider the following code:

```
int x;
x = 2;
System.out.println(1 < x < 3);      // illegal!!!
```

x is equal to 2, which lies between 1 and 3. So you would expect the `println` statement here to display `true`. However, the expression `1 < x < 3` is, in fact, illegal in Java. You will get a compile-time error. Let's see why this happens. This expression has two operators. They are both "<" so they, of course, have the same precedence. Because "<" is left associative, the computer will perform the two "<" operations in left-to-right order. That is, it first evaluates `1 < x`, which yields the value `true` because 1 is less than x. The value `true` then becomes the left operand for the second "<" operator. That is, the second operation is, in effect, `true < 3`, which makes no sense. You cannot compare `true` with 3. We want to compare x—not `true`—with 3. We will learn how to correctly test if x is between 1 and 3 in Section 3.7.

Two warnings about the relational operators: First, the two-character operators, "<=" and ">=", must not have any embedded spaces. For example, you cannot write

```
System.out.println(2 < = 3);
```
                          ↑
               space here is illegal

Second, the equality operator uses two equal signs, not one. To test if x is equal to y use

```
x == y        // testing for equality
```

not

```
x = y         // assignment of y to x
```

For example, in the first assignment statement that follows, we test if x is equal to y and assign the result to boo. In the second assignment statement, we assign the value in y (which is 2) to x and then to z:

```
boolean boo;
int x = 1, y = 2, z;
```

This is the equality relational operator.

```
boo = x == y;      // boo is assigned false because x not equal to y
z = x = y;         // 2 is assigned to x and z
```

This is the assignment operator.

Multiple assignments in a single statement are performed right to left. Thus, in

```
z = x = y;
```

the value in y is first assigned to x and then to z. The assignment operator is **right associative**—that is, multiple assignments in a statement are performed right to left.

3.7 Boolean Operators

The boolean operators are "&&" (AND), "||" (OR), and "!" (NOT). Their operands must be boolean, and they yield boolean values. For example, suppose we declare p, q, and r with

```
boolean p = true, q = false, r;
```

and then execute

```
r = p && q;
```

The boolean operator "&&" yields true only if *both* p and q are true. In this example, q is false. Thus, the value of the right side is false. This value is assigned to r.

We can represent how the "&&" operator works with a truth table (see Fig. 3.3). A **truth table** shows the true/false value that an operator yields for every possible combination of values for its operands.

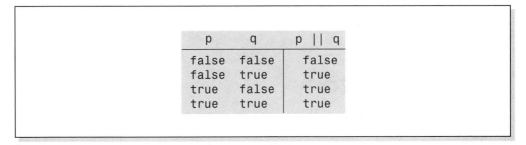

p	q	p && q
false	false	false
false	true	false
true	false	false
true	true	true

Figure 3.3

For example, the first line in Fig. 3.3 indicates that if p is `false` and q is `false`, then p `&&` q is also `false`. The only combination of operands for which the result is `true` is when both operands are `true`.

Fig. 3.4 shows the truth table for the `boolean` OR operator "`||`":

The "`||`" operator yields `true` if p or q or both are `true`.

The boolean NOT operator "`!`" takes only one operand so its truth table is simpler (see Fig. 3.5). This operator precedes the boolean value, variable, or expression on which it

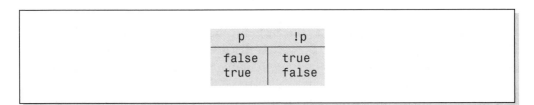

p	q	p || q
false	false	false
false	true	true
true	false	true
true	true	true

Figure 3.4

p	!p
false	true
true	false

Figure 3.5

operates. For example, to apply the NOT operator to the boolean variable p, we put "!" in front of p to get !p.

If p is false, then !p is true; if p is true, then !p is false. The "!" operator "flips" the truth value of its operand. "!" is an example of a unary operator. A **unary operator** takes only one operand. **Binary operators**, like "+" and "&&", take two operands.

The boolean operators are often used in conjunction with the relational operators. For example, consider the statement

```
boo = x > 1 && x < 3;
```

where boo has type boolean and x has type int. In this statement, x > 1 and x < 3 are evaluated first (because ">" and "<" have higher precedence than "&&"). The true/false values of these two relational expressions are then ANDed by the "&&" operator. Thus, the value of the entire right side is true only if both x is greater than 1 and x is less than 3. In mathematical notation, we would indicate that x is greater than 1 and less than 3 with

```
1 < x < 3
```

As we have already pointed out, this expression is illegal in Java. To capture this relationship in Java, we must use two relational expressions, x > 1 and x < 3, joined by the "&&" operator.

3.8 Sample Program

Let's now examine the program in Fig. 3.6. It uses a variety of primitive types.

The values of the right sides of the assignment statements on Lines 8 and 9 are boolean— that is, they are true or false. Thus, the type of the variables to which these values are assigned should also be boolean. The println statements on Lines 10, 11, and 12 display the true/false values of the boolean expressions they contain. On Line 16, the value in s is truncated to 1 byte, resulting in a value of 1. 1 is then assigned to b. On Line 19, both constants have type float because they are suffixed with the letter f. On Line 20, both constants have type double. Thus, the computation on Line 20 is performed with greater precision (i.e., more significant digits). We can see this from the output produced by Lines 22 and 23. The value displayed for d has twice the significant digits as the value

```
1 class PrimitiveTypes
2 {
3    public static void main(String[] args)
4    {
5        int x = 1, y = 2;
6        System.out.println(x < y);         // displays true
7        boolean boo1, boo2;
8        boo1 = x < y;                      // boo1 assigned true
9        boo2 = false;                      // boo2 assigned false
10       System.out.println(boo1 && boo2); // displays false
11       System.out.println(boo1 || boo2); // displays true
12       System.out.println(!boo2);         // displays true
13
14       byte b;
15       short s = 257;
16       b = (byte)s;                // truncated value assigned
17       System.out.println(b);     // displays 1
18
19       float f = 1.0f/3.0f;   // f suffix means float constant
20       double d = 1.0/3.0;     // no suffix means double constant
21
22       System.out.println(f);    // displays 0.33333334
23       System.out.println(d);    // displays 0.3333333333333333
24
25       d = 3.99999999;
26       long lg;
27       lg = (long)d;              // fractional part truncated
28       System.out.println(lg);   // displays 3
29    }
```

Figure 3.6

displayed for f. When d is cast to long in Line 27, its fractional part is truncated, leaving the integer 3, which is assigned to lg.

3.9 More on Operator Precedence

In the statement,

b = x > 2 && x < 4;

we do not have to use any parentheses because the relational operators, "<" and ">", have a higher precedence than the boolean operator, "&&". Thus, the relational subexpressions, $x > 2$ and $x < 4$, are evaluated first (which is the order we want). Their truth values are then ANDed by the "&&" operator.

Fig. 3.7 lists all the operators we have seen so far, from highest to lowest precedence.

Operator	Description	Highest precedence
!, ++, --,+, -	not, increment, decrement, unary plus, unary minus	
new, (type)	new operator, cast	
*, /, %	multiplication, division, remainder	
+, -	addition, subtraction	
<, > <=, >=	relational operators except equality/ inequality	
==, !=	equality/inequality relational operators	
&&	and	
||	or	
=	assignment	
		Lowest precedence

Figure 3.7

Laboratory 3 Prep

1. What values are assigned to b1, b2, b3, and b4 by the following code? Run the code to check your answers.

```
byte b1, b2, b3, b4;
int i = 3, j = 258;
double x = 4.999, y = 4.0E2;
b1 = (byte)i;
b2 = (byte)j;
b3 = (byte)x;
b4 = (byte)y;
```

2. Incorporate the following code in a program and compile. Why is there a compile-time error?

```
int x;
x = 999999999999;
```

3. Incorporate the following code in a program and compile. Why is there a compile-time error?

```
float x;
x = 2.0;
```

4. Why do the first and third println statements that follow display different values? Why do the second and fourth println statements display different values?

```
int x = 1;
System.out.println(x == 2);
System.out.println(x);
System.out.println(x = 2);
System.out.println(x);
```

5. What is displayed by the following statement:

```
System.out.println(100.0 + 50/4);
```

Laboratory 3

1. Run a program with the following code to determine if it is legal to concatenate two char constants, or to concatenate a char constant to a string.

```
System.out.println('a' + 'b');          // is this legal?
System.out.println('a' + "bcd");        // is this legal?
```

LABORATORY

2. Write a program that initializes the int variables x, y, and z to 1, 2, and 3, respectively, and then executes

```
x = y = z;
```

From the values assigned to x, y, and z, determine the order in which the assignments occur. Left to right, or right to left? Is the assignment operator left or right associative?

3. Is it legal to assign a char value to an int variable with a cast? For example, is the following code legal?

```
int i;
i = (int)'A';       // is this legal?
```

What value is assigned to i? Is the cast required? Is it legal to assign an int value to a char variable with a cast? Is a cast required? Run a test program to check your answers.

4. What is the effect of the following code:

```
char c = 'N';
c = (char)((int)'a' – (int)'A' + (int)c);
System.out.println(c);
```

Run a test program to check your answer. The code for every lowercase letter is 32 more than the code for the corresponding uppercase letter. Thus, (int)'a' – (int)'A' is equal to 32. If you add 32 to the character 'N', what character do you get?

5. Is it legal to cast a boolean constant to int. For example, is the following statement legal:

```
int i;
i = (int)true;
```

Run a test program to check your answer. If the code is legal, display the value assigned to i, and then repeat using the boolean constant false in place of true.

6. Write a program that determines if the value of x is less than 1 or greater than 10. If it is, your program should display true; otherwise, it should display false. Test your program for x equal to -3, 1, 5, 10, and 20.

7. Write a program that assigns 1.2345 to x, and then extracts from x and separately displays its integer part and its fractional part. x should have type double.

Homework 3

1. Write a program that computes and displays (with an appropriate label) the exact average of 1, 2, 3, and 4 (the correct answer is 2.5).

2. Write a program that outputs the truth table for the "&&" operator. Use the "&&" operator in your program to determine the values of p && q that appear in your table. For example, to display the value of "&&" when both operands are false, use

```
System.out.println("false    false    " + false && false);
```

Do *not* use

```
System.out.println("false    false    false");
```

Your output should look like this:

p	q	p && q
false	false	false
false	true	false
true	false	false
true	true	true

3. Write a program that computes and displays the truth table for !(p && q). Use the technique described in Homework Exercise 2.

4. Write a program that computes and displays the truth table for !p || !q. Use the technique described in Homework Exercise 2. Compare your results with those from Homework Exercise 3. The equivalence of !(p && q) and !p || !q is one of **DeMorgan's Laws** (see Homework Exercise 6 for the other DeMorgan's Law).

5. Write a program that computes and displays the truth table for !(p || q). Use the technique described in Homework Exercise 2.

6. Write a program that computes and displays the truth table for !p && !q. Use the technique described in Homework Exercise 2. Compare your results with those from Homework Exercise 5. The equivalence of !(p || q) and !p && !q is the one of **DeMorgan's Laws**.

7. Same as Homework Exercise 2, but use the "^" (exclusive OR) operator.

8. charAt is a method in a String object that returns the character at the specified position. For example, if c is type char and s is a reference to a String object, then the

LABORATORY

following assignment statement assigns c the first character in the String object to which s points:

```
c = s.charAt(0);
```

Write a program in which you assign "AB3cd$" to s. Display each character in this string on a separate line. Display all the letters in uppercase. Thus, your program should display AB3CD$. Your program should work for any five-character string. Do not use the toUpperCase method. (*Hint:* See Lab Exercise 4.)

if, if-else, and while Statements

OBJECTIVES

- Learn how to make decisions with the `if` and `if-else` statements
- Learn how to set up count-controlled loops with the `while` statement
- Learn how to set up condition-controlled loops with the `while` statement
- Learn how to use the `break` statement to create a loop with an interior exit test
- Learn how to input from the keyboard using the `Scanner` class

4.1 Two Versions of the `if` Statement

All but the simplest programs have to make decisions. Programs in Java make decisions with `if` statements. The `if` statement has two versions: one version has no `else` part; the other version has an `else` part. We call the former a **simple `if` statement**, the latter, an `if-else` **statement**.

A simple `if` statement has the following structure:

```
if (true/false expression)
    statement
```
                            ↑
                    No semicolon here

It contains a true/false expression inside parentheses followed by an embedded statement (i.e., a statement within the `if` statement). If the true/false expression is `true`, the embedded statement is executed. Otherwise, it is skipped. Note that a semicolon does not follow the parentheses that enclose the true/false expression.

Let's look at the following example of a simple `if` statement:

```
if (count <= 10)
    System.out.println("Too few");
```

When this statement is executed, if `count <= 10` is `true`, the embedded `println` statement is executed. If `count <= 10` is `false`, the `println` statement is skipped, in which case execution proceeds with the statement that follows the `if` statement.

Now consider this two-instruction sequence:

```
if (count <= 10)                    // first instruction
    System.out.println("Too few");
System.out.println("bye");          // second instruction
```

The first instruction is a simple `if` statement with an embedded `println` statement that displays `Too few`. The second instruction is a `println` statement that displays `bye`. The second `println` statement is not embedded within the `if` statement. It is a separate statement that follows the `if` statement. Thus, it is executed regardless of the action taken by the `if` statement. If `count <= 10` is `true`, this sequence of instructions displays

```
Too few
bye
```

But if `count <= 10` is `false`, it displays only

```
bye
```

In both cases, bye is displayed.

We indented the first println statement in the preceding example to show that it is a subpart of the if statement. We did not indent the second println statement because it is not a subpart of the if statement. If we change the indentation to

```
if (count <= 10)
    System.out.println("Too few");
    System.out.println("bye");
```

the code would work in exactly the same way. Indentation does not affect how the Java compiler translates programs. However, this new indentation incorrectly suggests that both println statements are embedded in the if statement. This example illustrates the importance of proper indentation. Without proper indentation, it is easy for a human reader to misinterpret the structure of a program.

An if-else statement has the following structure:

```
if (true/false expression)
    statement 1
else
    statement 2          No semicolon here
```

The if-else statement has two embedded statements. If the true/false expression is true, the first embedded statement is executed. Otherwise, the second embedded statement is executed. For example, consider

```
if (count <= 10)
    System.out.println("Too few");
else
    System.out.println("Enough");
System.out.println("bye");
```

If count <= 10 is true when the preceding code is executed, this code will display

```
Too few
bye
```

If count <= 10 is false, it will display

```
Enough
bye
```

In this example, the statement that displays bye follows the if-else statement. Thus, it is always executed regardless of the action of the if-else statement. We did not indent this statement because it is not a subpart of the if-else statement. Note that both of the embedded statements are terminated the way they always are—with semicolons.

The subparts of the simple if and if-else statements do not have to be single statements as in the previous examples. They can also be **compound statements**—a sequence of statements enclosed by braces. A compound statement can be used anywhere a single statement can be used. For example, consider

```
if (x <= 10)
{                                  // start of first compound statement
    System.out.println("incrementing x");
    x++;
}                                  // end of first compound statement
else
{                                  // start of second compound statement
    System.out.println("decrementing x");
    x--;
}                                  // end of second compound statement
System.out.println("bye");
```

If x <= 10 is true, the first compound statement is executed. If x <= 10 is false, the second compound statement is executed. After one of these compound statements is executed, the statement that follows the if-else statement is executed (the println that displays bye). Compound statements can also include variable declarations, in which case we typically refer to them as a **blocks**.

Be sure to format your if statements as shown. Place corresponding left and right braces in the same column. Also start else and its matching if in the same column

You can use braces in simple if and if-else statements regardless of the number of statements they delimit. For example, in the following code we are using braces even though they are unnecessary because the if and else parts do not have multiple statements:

```
if (count <= 10)
{
    System.out.println("Too few");
}
else
{
    System.out.println("Enough");
}
```

The braces are unnecessary, but they do no harm. Some programmers, in fact, prefer to always use braces in if statements. That way, if at some future time they add a statement to the if part or the else part, they do not have to add the braces (which then would be necessary). Moreover, because braces work for all cases, some programmers like to always use them for the sake of consistency.

4.2 Nested `if` Statements

The statements within an `if` statement can themselves be `if` statements. We call an `if` statement that contains one or more `if` statements a **nested `if` statement**. For example, Fig. 4.1a shows a nested `if` statement in which an `if-else` statement is nested within

```
a)
if (x == 3)                             // outer if
   if (y == 5)                          // inner if-else
      System.out.println("apple");
   else
      System.out.println("pear");
b)
if (x == 3)                   // outer if-else
{
   if (y == 5)                  // this is a simple if statement
      System.out.println("apple");
}
else
   System.out.println("pear");
c)
if (x == 3)
   if (y == 5)
      System.out.println("apple");
   else  // this else associates with the nearest (i.e., 2nd if)
      ;  // null statement
else
   System.out.println("pear");
d)
```

	Figure 4.1a	Figure 4.1b	Figure 4.1c
x = 3, y = 5	apple	apple	apple
x = 3, y = 6	pear		
x = 4, y = 5		pear	pear
x = 4, y = 6		pear	pear

Figure 4.1

a simple `if` statement. The outer `if` statement is a simple `if` statement. The value of x determines whether or not the statement it contains (which happens to be an `if-else` statement) is executed. If x is not equal to 3, the inner `if-else` statement is skipped. If, however, x is equal to 3, then the inner `if-else` statement is executed. In this case, either `apple` or `pear` is displayed depending on the value of y. For example, if x is 4, nothing is displayed because the inner `if-else` statement is skipped. If x is 3, the inner `if-else` is executed. In this case, if y is 5, `apple` is displayed; if y is not 5, `pear` is displayed.

An `else` always associates with the nearest `if` that is not already associated with an `else`. Thus, the `else` in Fig. 4.1a associates with the second `if`. However, this rule does not apply to an `else` if it is outside a compound statement that contains the `if`. For example, in Fig. 4.1b, the braces force the `else` to associate with the first `if`. We can achieve the same effect without braces by adding another `else` followed by a null statement (see Fig. 4.1c). Here, the first `else` associates with the second `if` (by our nearest `if` rule). Thus, the second `else` is forced to associate with the first `if`. Fig. 4.1d shows what the `if` statements in Fig. 4.1a, Fig. 4.1b, and Fig. 4.1c display for several combinations of values for x and y.

4.3 Multiway Branches

An `if-else` statement is a two-way branch. We execute either its `if` part or its `else` part. We, however, can nest `if` statements in a way that creates a multiway branch. For example, the following statement is a four-way branch:

```
if (x == 5)
    statement 1        } Do this statement if x equals 5
else
    if (x == 6)
        statement 2
    else
        if (x == 7)
            statement 3          } Do this statement if x is not equal to 5
        else
            statement 4

                    Do this statement if x is neither 5 nor 6
```

If x is 5, Statement 1 is executed. Otherwise, the nested `if` statement following the first `else` is executed. Thus, if x is 6, Statement 2 is executed. If x is neither 5 nor 6, then the `if-else` statement following the second `else` is executed. Thus, if x is 7, Statement 3 is executed. If x is neither 5 nor 6 nor 7, the `else` part of the third `else` is executed—that is, Statement 4 is executed. Among Statements 1, 2, 3, and 4, only one is executed.

4.4 Count-Controlled Loops

Suppose we want to determine the product of 1.2345 and 3.1415. To do this, we could write, compile, and run a Java program that contains

```
System.out.println(1.2345*3.1415);
```

However, we could get our answer more quickly using a simple electronic calculator. We simply enter the sequence 1.2345, *, 3.1415, and =. The product then appears in the calculator's display window.

If a simple calculator is easier to use and quicker (and cheaper) than a computer, why would we ever want to use a computer? The answer is that we can make a computer—but not a simple calculator—execute loops that we provide. A **loop** is a sequence of instructions that is executed repeatedly.

Suppose we create, compile, and run a program that contains a five-instruction loop. Entering the instructions that make up the loop and the additional instructions to make a complete program would not take long. We then compile and run the program. Let's say the loop executes one million times when the program runs. Because computers are so fast, the program would probably complete in a few seconds. The whole process—entering, compiling, and running the program—would take only a few minutes. Now, consider what we would have to do if we used a simple calculator instead of a computer. Because a simple calculator has no loop capability, we would have to repeatedly enter the keystrokes corresponding to the five-instruction loop one million times. This process would take years! Moreover, we would likely make many keystroke errors. Clearly, in this scenario, a computer is a lot better than a calculator. *Loops give computers their computational power.*

Java has three types of loops: the while, for, and do-while loops. For now, we will use only the while loop. After you become comfortable with the while loop, we will introduce the for and do-while loops.

The while loop has the following structure:

```
while (true/false expression)
    statement
```
No semicolon here

The statement within a while loop can be a simple statement or a compound statement (a sequence of statements enclosed in braces). We call the statement or compound statement within a while loop the **loop body**. The flowchart in Fig. 4.2 describes the action of a while loop.

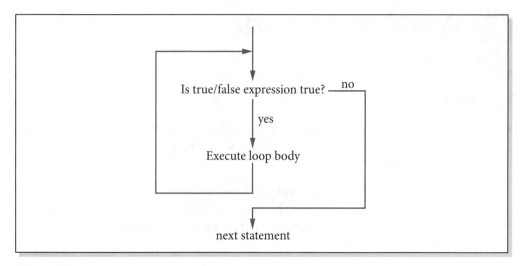

Figure 4.2

The action of the while loop consists of three steps:

1. Test the true/false expression. If it is true, then proceed to Step 2. Otherwise exit the loop (i.e., proceed to the statement that follows the loop). The testing of the true/false expression is called the **exit test** because it determines if the exit from the loop occurs.
2. Execute the loop body.
3. Go back to Step 1.

Because the first action of a while loop is the exit test, we say that the while loop has a **leading exit test**. Because a while loop has a leading exit test, the loop body is not executed at all if the true/false expression is initially false.

Consider the program in Fig. 4.3.

The true/false expression, count <= 3, on Line 7 is initially true because count initially equals 1. Thus, we enter the loop body (with count equal to 1). Each time the loop body is executed, line 11 increments count. On the first execution of the loop body, count is incremented from 1 to 2. On the second execution, count is incremented from 2 to 3. On the third execution, count is incremented from 3 to 4. In the exit test that follows the third execution, the true/false expression is false (count is 4 at this point), triggering

```
 1 class CountControlled1
 2 {
 3    public static void main(String[] args)
 4    {
 5
 6       int count = 1;
 7       while (count <= 3)
 8       {
 9          System.out.println("star");
10          System.out.println("moon");
11          count++;
12       }
13       System.out.println("good night");
14    }
15 }
```

Figure 4.3

an exit from the loop. Each time the loop body executes, it displays star and moon. It is executed three times. Thus, the total effect of the while loop is to display

```
star
moon
star
moon
star
moon
```

The statement that follows the while loop then displays

```
good night
```

We call the variable count in Fig. 4.3 a **counter** because it counts the number of times the loop executes. We say the loop is **count controlled** because its exit test depends on a count.

The true/false expression in a while loop should eventually go false. If it never goes false, then the loop is an **infinite loop** (i.e., a loop that never ends). For example, if we delete Line 11 in Fig. 4.3 (the line that increments count), the expression count <= 3 would remain true because count would retain its initial value of 1. We would then have an infinite loop.

Infinite loops do not really run forever. We can always force them to stop. One way, of course, is to turn off the computer. A better way, however, is to enter a keyboard sequence that forces the termination of the running program. The keyboard sequence that does this on most computer systems is ctrl-c: While holding down the ctrl key, hit the c key. If ctrl-c does not work, try ctrl-d, ctrl-z, or ctrl-break.

Always make sure that your `while` loops are not infinite loops. The body of the loop should do something *that will ultimately make the true/false expression go* `false`.

The `while` loop in Fig. 4.3 displays three `star/moon` pairs. If we want it to display some other number of `star/moon` pairs, we can simply change the true/false expression. For example, for 1000 `star/moon` pairs, we would simply replace

```
count <= 3
```

in the true/false expression with

```
count <= 1000
```

The counter variable in a count-controlled loop does not have to start at 1. It also does not have to count up—it can count down instead. For example, in the following count-controlled loop, `count` is initialized to 3, and it counts down:

```
count = 3;              // start at 3 and count down
while (count >= 1)
{
   ...                  // loop body executed three times

   count--;             // subtract 1 from count
}
```

Here we are decrementing `count` each time through the loop. Thus, the loop is counting down. The loop body in this example executes three times, for `count` equal to 3, 2, and 1.

In a count-controlled loop, the body of the loop can use the variable that is acting as the counter. For example, in the `while` loop in Fig. 4.4, `count` is acting as the counter, but it is also used within the loop body on Line 9.

How many times will Line 9 in Fig. 4.4 be executed? It is executed once for each value of `count`, starting with 1 up to and including 10. Thus, it is executed 10 times. In this example, `count` has two distinct uses:

1. It serves as the loop counter.
2. It contains the value added to `sum` each time the loop body executes.

```
 1 class CountControlled2
 2 {
 3    public static void main(String[] args)
 4    {
 5       int count = 1, sum = 0;
 6
 7       while  (count <= 10)
 8       {
 9          sum = sum + count;      // add n to sum
10          count++;                // add 1 to count
11       }
12       System.out.println("sum = " + sum);
13    }
14 }
```

Figure 4.4

The first time we execute Line 9, count is 1, so we add 1 to sum. The next time count is 2, so we add 2 to sum. As this loop continues, we add 3, 4, ... , 10 to sum. Because sum is initialized to 0, its value at the conclusion of the loop is the sum of the integers 1 to 10.

Notice that in Line 12 in Fig. 4.4, the statement that displays the sum follows the loop. It makes sense to display sum only *after* the loop has completed its computation. Thus, this statement should follow the loop rather than appear inside it or before it. The initialization of count and sum, of course, has to occur before the loop. Accordingly, Line 5, which declares and initializes count and sum, precedes the loop.

The structure of the preceding code is very common. It consists of three parts in this order:

1. Initialization
2. Loop
3. Use the result computed by the loop

Remember, initialize *before* the loop, and use the computed result *after* the loop.

When you are given a programming problem, you will need to determine if it needs any loops. If it does, you need to determine how many times each loop should execute. For example, to sum the integers 1 to 10, you have to perform an operation repeatedly— namely, adding an integer to a variable. Moreover, because the problem calls for adding 10 numbers, the operation should be repeated 10 times. Clearly, a loop that executes 10 times is indicated. Once you have completed this sort of analysis, it is generally quite easy to implement the required loop.

Let's apply this loop-analysis technique to a slightly different problem: Determine the sum of the squares of the integers from 1 to 10. That is, determine the sum of 1^2, 2^2, 3^2, ..., 10^2. Again we clearly need a loop. But how many times should this loop execute? 10 times? $10^2 = 100$ times? We still have to add up 10 items (the 10 squares), so we again need a loop that executes 10 times. Thus, the loop structure of this program should be the same as the loop structure for the program in Fig. 4.4. To sum the first 10 squares, we need to make only one small modification to the program in Fig. 4.4: Change Line 9 to

```
sum = sum + count*count;        // add count*count to sum
```

Each time through this loop, count*count is added to sum. count varies from 1 to 10. Thus, the loop sums the first 10 squares.

4.5 Condition-Controlled Loop

Suppose we want to write a program that displays all the squares of positive integers that are less than 5000. We clearly have to perform some action (display a square) repeatedly. This observation leads us to conclude that we need a loop. However, a count-controlled loop is not appropriate here. We do not know how many squares are less than 5000. So we do not know how many times the loop body should execute. To set up a count-controlled loop, we need to know the number of times its body is to execute *prior to the start of its execution.*

For this program, we want to continue executing the loop body as long as the computed square is less than 5000. Thus, the exit test should test for this condition. The code we need is shown in Fig. 4.5.

```
 1 class ConditionControlled1
 2 {
 3    public static void main(String[] args)
 4    {
 5       int x = 1;
 6
 7       while (x*x < 5000)
 8       {
 9          System.out.println(x + " squared = " + x*x);
10          x++;
11       }
12    }
13 }
```

Figure 4.5

The exit test for this loop tests if the square of x is less than 5000. Because the exit test depends on a condition other than a count reaching some value, we call this kind of loop a **condition-controlled loop**. When it is executed, we will see all the squares less than 5000:

```
1 squared = 1
2 squared = 4
      .
      .
      .
70 squared = 4900
```

4.6 break Statement

An inefficiency of the loop in Fig. 4.5 is that for each x it computes x*x twice—once on Line 7 and once on Line 9. A more natural and efficient loop structure for this problem is given in Fig. 4.6.

In this structure, we compute x*x only once for each value of x and save it in a variable named square. We then use the value in square in two places in the loop body: in the exit test and in the statement that displays the square. This structure, however, does not correspond to a while loop because its exit test is in the middle of the loop body, not at the beginning as in a while loop. However, by using an if statement in conjunction

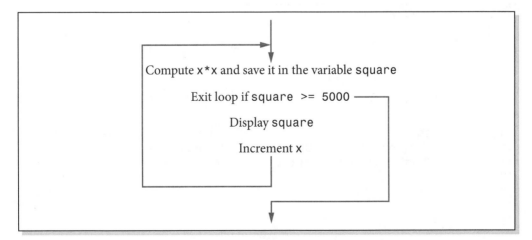

Figure 4.6

with a break statement, we can, in fact, place the exit test anywhere within the body of a while loop.

A break statement forces an immediate exit from a loop. For example, suppose we place the following statement within the body of a loop:

```
if (square >= 5000) break;
```

Then if square is greater than or equal to 5000, the break statement is executed, forcing a loop exit. This statement creates an exit test wherever it appears in a loop. Let's now rewrite the program in Fig. 4.5 using this approach. Fig. 4.7 shows the result.

The while loop in Fig. 4.7 appears to be an infinite loop because its true/false expression on Line 7 is the boolean constant true, which, of course, is always true. But the loop is not infinite because the if statement on Line 10 will trigger a loop exit when the square of x equals or exceeds 5000.

An alternative approach that also avoids the duplicated squaring of x appears in Fig. 4.8. This approach does not use a break statement.

Here we are using a normal while loop. We use an if-else statement within the loop body to perform the exit test. To exit, we set keepGoing to false, which, in turn, forces a loop exit when control returns to the top of the loop.

A third approach appears in Fig. 4.9. In this approach, the code to square x appears in two places: just before the beginning of the loop (Line 7) and at the bottom of the loop body (Line 12).

```
 1 class ConditionControlled2
 2 {
 3    public static void main(String[] args)
 4    {
 5       int x = 1, square;
 6
 7       while (true)
 8       {
 9          square = x*x;                    // compute and save x squared
10          if (square >= 5000) break;  //   exit test
11          System.out.println(x + " squared = " + square);
12          x++;
13       }
14    }
15 }
```

Figure 4.7

```
 1 class ConditionControlled3
 2 {
 3    public static void main(String[] args)
 4    {
 5       int x = 1, square;
 6       boolean keepGoing = true;
 7
 8       while (keepGoing)
 9       {
10          square = x * x;
11          if (square >= 5000)        // exit test
12             keepGoing = false;      // causes exit from loop
13          else
14          {
15             System.out.println(x + " squared = " + square);
16             x++;
17          }
18       }
19    }
20 }
```

Figure 4.8

```
 1 class ConditionControlled4
 2 {
 3    public static void main(String[] args)
 4    {
 5       int x = 1, square;
 6
 7       square = x*x;                      // "priming" statement
 8       while (square < 5000)
 9       {
10          System.out.println(x + " squared = " + square);
11          x++;
12          square = x*x;          // compute square once per iteration
13       }
14    }
15 }
```

Figure 4.9

However, for each value of x, x is squared only once. For the first value of x, Line 7 computes its square. For all subsequent values of x, Line 12 computes their squares. We call Line 7 the **priming statement** because it "primes" square (i.e., it assigns it a value so it can be meaningfully tested on Line 8).

4.7 Keyboard Input

Most programs input data, process that data, and output the results. We have already seen programs that process data (for example, the programs that use arithmetic expressions to perform computations on numbers) and output results (for example, the programs with the println statement). However, we have yet to see a program that inputs data. So let's now examine a program that does that. The program in Fig. 4.10 sums the integers from 1 up to whatever integer the user enters on the keyboard. For example, here is a run of the program in which the user enters 10:

```
Enter integer greater than 0    (message displayed by program)
10                              (integer entered by the user)
Sum of 1 to 10 = 55             (sum displayed by program)
```

```
1 import java.util.Scanner;
2 class KeyboardInput
3 {
4    public static void main(String[] args)
5    {
6       int count = 1, sum = 0, n;
7
8       // create scanner object that represents keyboard
9       Scanner kb = new Scanner(System.in);
10
11      // prompt user of program for an integer greater than 0
12      System.out.println("Enter integer greater than 0");
13
14      // read in an integer from the keyboard, assign to n
15      n = kb.nextInt();
16
17      //now sum the integers from 1 to n
18      while (count <= n)
19      {
20         sum = sum + count;    // add count to sum
21         count++;              // add 1 to count
22      }
23
24      // display the sum
25      System.out.println("Sum of 1 to " + n + " = " + sum);
26   }
27 }
```

Figure 4.10

Here is another run. For this run, the user enters 20:

```
Enter integer greater than 0
20
Sum of 1 to 20 = 210
```

This program is a generalization of the program in Fig. 4.4. This new program sums integers from 1 to the integer the user enters on the keyboard. If the user enters 10, the program sums the integers from 1 to 10. But if the user enters 20, it sums the integers from 1 to 20. Our new program is more flexible than the program in Fig. 4.4 because it allows the user to specify the upper integer in the sum. The program in Fig. 4.4 sums integers from 1 to 10 only.

The program in Fig. 4.10 makes use of the predefined class named Scanner to read from the keyboard. Predefined classes in Java are grouped into **packages**. The Scanner class is in the java.util package. To use the Scanner class, we must inform the Java compiler in which package Scanner resides. We do this with the import statement on Line 1. By specifying java.util.Scanner in the import statement, we are indicating that Scanner is in the java.util package. Incidentally, back in Chapter 1, we used the predefined class String in the program in Fig. 1.3. String is in the java.lang package. All the classes in java.lang are automatically imported into every Java program. Thus, we did not need an import statement for String.

Line 9 creates a Scanner object:

```
9        Scanner kb = new Scanner(System.in);
```

The argument, System.in, represents the keyboard (System.in is a reference to an object that represents the keyboard). Accordingly, Line 9 creates a Scanner object that inputs from the keyboard, and assigns kb its reference. Line 12 informs the user that a keyboard input is required:

```
12       System.out.println("Enter integer greater than 0");
```

The next statement,

```
15       n = kb.nextInt();
```

invokes the nextInt method in the Scanner object pointed to by kb. nextInt causes the program to pause until the user enters an integer on the keyboard. When the user enters an integer and hits the return key, nextInt then returns the value entered to the right side of the assignment statement above. This value is then assigned to n. Thus, the net effect of Line 15 it to read in an integer from the keyboard and assign its value to n. Next, the while loop sums the integers from 1 to n. After the loop completes, the println statement on Line 25 displays the values in n and sum:

```
25       System.out.println("Sum of 1 to " + n + " = " + sum);
```

Laboratory 4 Prep

1. Which of the `if` statements that follow is legal? Compile a test program to check your answers.

```
if (count <= 10)
{
}
else
    System.out.println("hello");

if (count <= 10)

else
    System.out.println("hello");

if (count <= 10)
    ;
else
    System.out.println("hello");
```

A semicolon by itself is the **null statement**. It is a legal statement in Java. When executed, it does nothing. Braces that do not contain any statements act like a `null` statement.

2. Write a multibranch `if` statement that displays the English word for the integer value in the variable x for any value between 0 and 5. For other integer values, your `if` statement should display other. For example, if x is 2, then your `if` statement should display two. If x is -20, your `if` statement should display other.

3. Write the statement that reads in an integer from the keyboard using the `Scanner` object pointed to by p, and assigns the value read in to an `int` variable x.

4. Write a `while` loop that computes the sum of the odd integers from 1 to 999 inclusive. Increment the variable that is acting as a counter by 2 each time the loop body is executed.

5. List the first 10 operations that occur when the code in Fig. 4.7 is executed. Do the same for the code in Fig. 4.9. How do the two sequences compare?

Laboratory 4

1. Run the following program (it contains an infinite loop):

```
class C4e1
{
    public static void main(String[] args)
```

```
    {
        int x = 1;
        while (x == 1)
            System.out.println("Infinite loop");
    }
}
```

Determine the keyboard sequence for your computer system that will end the infinite loop. Try ctrl-c, ctrl-d, ctrl-z, and ctrl-break. You can also terminate the program by closing the terminal/command-mode session running the program.

2. What is the effect of the following statement. Try it for values of n equal to 0 to 10. n has type int.

```
switch(n)       // n is the controlling expression
{
    case 0:
    case 1:
    case 7:     System.out.println("dog");
                break;
    case 3:     System.out.println("cat");
    case 4:     System.out.println("bird");
                break;
    case 6:     System.out.println("elephant");
                break;
    default:    System.out.println("default");
}
```

The break statement has two uses: to break out of a loop and to break out of a switch statement. The constants used for each case should have an integer type or a type that is represented with integers (for example, char). The type of the controlling expression should match the type of the case constants. The default case is optional. The controlling expression can be a complex expression. For example, we could have used n + 1 in place of n in the preceding example.

Remove the break statements in the preceding code. With this change, what is displayed for each value of n from 0 to 10. In what sequence are the instructions executed without the break statements?

3. Test the following statement in a program. Try it for y equals 1 and z equals 2. Also try it for y equals 10 and z equals 8. What is its effect?

```
x =     y < z ? 10 : 20;
        ---------------
               ↑
```

this is a **conditional expression**

LABORATORY

The `?:` pair is called the **conditional operator**. The conditional operator has three operands:

```
operand1 ? operand2 : operand3
```

operand1 is a true/false expression. If operand1 is `true`, the value of the entire expression is given by operand2. If operand1 is `false`, the value of the entire expression is given by operand3. operand2 and operand3 can be expressions. In the preceding example, y < z, 10, and 20 are operand1, operand2, and operand3, respectively. If y < z is `true`, 10 is assigned to x. Otherwise, 20 is assigned to x.

4. Write a program that reads in two integers and displays their sum. (*Hint:* Invoke `nextInt` twice.)

5. Write a program that displays all the integers from 1 to 1000 that are not evenly divisible by 13. (*Hint:* x is not evenly divisible by 13 if the expression x%13 != 0 is true. Recall that % is the remainder operator.)

6. Run the following program:

```
class C4e6
{
    public static void main(String[] args)
    {
        int i = 1;
        while (i < 5) ;      // put semicolon after parentheses
        {
            System.out.println(i);
            i++;             // adds 1 to i
        }
    }
}
```

What happens? A lone semicolon is a valid statement in Java. It is called the `null` **statement**. A `null` statement does nothing when executed. The semicolon after the right parenthesis in the `while` statement functions as the *entire* body of the `while` statement. Now remove this semicolon, compile and run. What happens?

7. Write a program that computes the value of 7 factorial. 7 factorial is equal to 7 × 6 × 5 × ... × 1. Initialize a variable named `factorial` to 7. Then using a loop, multiply `factorial` by the integers 6 down to 2. Use type `long` for your computations. What is the largest factorial a variable of type `long` can hold?

8. What does the following program display? Run it to check your answer.

```
class C4e8
{
    public static void main(String[] args)
```

```
    {
        int i, j;
        i = 1;
        while (i < 10)
        {
            j = 1;
            while (j < 5)
            {
                System.out.print(i + "," + j + "  ");
                j++;
            }
            System.out.println();      // go to next line
            i++;
        }
    }
}
```

This program has a loop within a loop. This structure is called a **nested loop**.

9. Suppose you are performing calculations on a calculator that displays only three digits. If you enter 12.3, +, 0.04, and = , the calculator will add 12.3 and 0.04. But because the calculator maintains only three digits, it gets the result 12.3 (which is 12.34 truncated to three digits). *Adding* 0.04 *has no effect.* Now suppose you enter 0.01, +, 0.04, and =. The calculator in this case displays 0.05, the correct answer. The problem in the first case is **roundoff error** that results because of the finite precision with which numbers are represented within a calculator. This error can be significant if the difference in the value of the numbers to be added is large. In the extreme case, adding the smaller number to the larger number has no effect on the larger number, as illustrated by our first case. An important observation: Computations on a calculator or a computer do not necessarily yield the correct answers, *even if the correct operations are performed.*

In the following program, the two loops perform the same computation but in a different order. Why do they yield different answers? If so, which one yields the better answer?

```
class C4e9
{
    public static void main(String[] args)
    {
        float sum1 = 0.0f, sum2 = 0.0f;
        int i;

        i = 1;
        while (i <= 100)    // sum from large to small
```

LABORATORY

```
        {
            sum1 = sum1 + 1.0f/i;
            i++;
        }
        System.out.println("sum1 = " + sum1);
        i = 100;
        while (i >= 1)      // sum from small to large
        {
            sum2 = sum2 + 1.0f/i;
            i--;
        }
        System.out.println("sum2 = " + sum2);
    }
}
```

10. What is the effect of the `continue` statement in the following loop:

```
int i = 1;
while (i <= 10)
{
    System.out.println("before continue i = " + ++i);
    if (i%3 == 0) continue; // execute continue when i multiple of 3
    System.out.println("after continue i = " + i);
}
```

Homework 4

1. Write a program that displays the cubes of all the integers that are greater than n but less than m, where n and m are values entered via the keyboard. Test your program for n = 10, m = 10000.

2. Write a program that repeatedly reads an integer and displays its square. Your program should terminate only if the user enters 0.

3. Write a program that computes and displays the value of

$$0.1 + (0.1)^2 + (0.1)^3 + \ldots + (0.1)^n$$

Your program should prompt for and read from the keyboard the value of n. For this program, you should use a variable `sum` to accumulate the sum. Also use a variable `term`. Initialize `term` to 0.1 (which is the first term in the summation). Each time through the loop, execute

```
sum = sum + term;
```

Follow this statement with a statement that changes the value in the variable `term` to the value of the next term in the summation. Get the next term from the current term by multiplying the current term by 0.1. Use type double for sum and term. Test your program for n equals 1, 15, 50, and 100.

4. Write a program that computes the value of

```
+ 1.0/(1!) + 1.0/(2!) + 1.0/(3!) + ... + 1.0/(n!)
```

Your program should prompt for and read from the keyboard the value of n. Use the technique described in Homework Exercise 3 (i.e., compute each term from the previous term). Also include the following statement in your program:

```
System.out.println("e = " + Math.E);
```

Use type double for your computations. Run your program for n = 1, 10, 20, 50, and 100.

5. Display all the values in the following sequence that are less than max:

```
1, 2×1, 3×2×1, 4×3×2×1, ...
```

Your program should prompt for and read the value of max. Use a loop with an interior exit test constructed with an if statement and a break statement. Obtain each value to be displayed from the previous value displayed by multiplying the previous value by the appropriate factor. For example, get the second value by multiplying the first value by 2; get the third value by multiplying the second value by 3. In general, get the ith value by multiplying the $(i-1)$st value by i. Test your program with values for max equal to -1, 1, 2, 3, 10, 100, and 1000.

6. Same as Homework Exercise 5 but use the structure illustrated in Fig. 4.8.

7. Same as Homework Exercise 5 but use the structure illustrated in Fig. 4.9.

8. Write a program that displays

```
1
1 2
1 2 3
1 2 3 4
1 2 3 4 5
1 2 3 4 5 6
1 2 3 4 5 6 7
1 2 3 4 5 6 7 8
1 2 3 4 5 6 7 8 9
1 2 3 4 5 6 7 8 9 10
```

Use nested loops (i.e., a loop within a loop). The outer loop body should execute 10 times. Each time the inner loop is activated, it should display one line of numbers. (*Hint:* Use the print statement to display each number. Use the println statement with no arguments to go to the next line.)

9. Write a program that reads the number of terms to sum and then sums that number of terms in the series

   4 − 4/3 + 4/5 − 4/7 + 4/9 + . . .

   For example, if the user enters 100, then your program should sum the first 100 terms of the series. Use type double for all your computations. Run your program for the following inputs: 1, 10, 100, and 1000. Your program should display the computed value and the value of Math.PI.

10. Write a program that contains a loop that executes 20 times. Each time the loop body executes, it should compute the square root of x and assign the result back to x. Initialize x to 5.0. Do the square roots seem to converge on a value? Use Math.sqrt (a predefined method in the Math class) to compute square roots. Run your program a second time using an initial value of 0.5 for x.

CHAPTER 5

Calling Methods

OBJECTIVES

- Learn how to call a method
- Understand the argument-passing mechanism
- Learn how to return a value
- Understand the overloading of method names
- Distinguish between external and internal calls and accesses

5.1 Why Use Methods

Before writing a program for a large problem, we typically break up the large problem into several smaller ones. We then, in turn, break up each of the smaller problems into several even smaller problems. We continue this process until we are left with a collection of problems each of which is easily managed by a single, small method. We call this process **stepwise refinement**. For example, suppose you had to write a program that required 10,000 lines of code. It would be crazy to use one method for all 10,000 lines. To work with this method—for example, to debug it—you would have to remember the details of all 10,000 lines. But, if instead you used stepwise refinement to break up the program into, let's say, 200 small methods, each performing one function, you could then work on the program method by method. In this approach, each method would be quite small, and, therefore, easy to write and debug. Moreover, once you write and test a method, you could then use it in your program without having to remember the details of its implementation.

5.2 How to Call a Method

A method can **invoke** or **call** (i.e., initiate the execution of) another method. A method call consists of, at a minimum, the method name followed by a pair of parentheses and a semicolon. For example, the following statement calls the f method:

```
f();
```

Calling a method causes its execution. After the called method completes its execution, it returns to the statement that follows the statement that called it. For example, in the program in Fig. 5.1, main calls f on Line 6. When f completes, it returns to Line 7 in main.

Execution then continues in main from Line 7. Thus, the lines in this program are executed in the following order: 5, 6, 12, and 7, displaying

```
before call
in f
after call
```

The order in which the two methods appear within the class in Fig. 5.1 is not significant. main is always executed first.

Before a method in an object can be called, the object, obviously, has to be constructed. However, static methods—that is, methods marked with the reserved word static—exist independently of objects. Thus, they can be called without first creating any objects.

```
 1 class Call1
 2 {
 3     public static void main(String[] args)
 4     {
 5         System.out.println("before call");
 6 ┌──── f();                                        // call f
 7 │       System.out.println("after call");  ◄──────┐
 8 │     }                                           │
 9 │     //--------------------------------          │
10 └─► public static void f()                        │
11     {                                             │
12         System.out.println("in f");               │
13     }                                             │
14 }          └─────────────────────────────────────┘
```

Figure 5.1

Note that f in Fig. 5.1 is static. Thus, main can call f without having to first create an object.

Because main is always the first method to be executed, it has to be static. If it were not, then before it could be executed, an object containing it would have to be constructed. But this implies some other method executes first—the method that constructs the object containing main.

When we call a method, we can pass it values that it can then use. For example, consider the call of the displaySum method in Fig. 5.2:

```
6         displaySum(x, x + 5, 20);
                     ▲    ▲    ▲
                     └────┴────┘
                      Arguments
```

Here, we are passing displaySum three values: 1 (which is the value of x), 6 (which is the value of x + 5), and 20. The items whose values are passed are called **arguments**. The call of displaySum shown has three arguments: x, x + 5, and 20.

If a method call has arguments, then the called method must be set up to receive the values of those arguments. To receive the value of each argument, the called method must have a special variable—a **parameter**—for each argument. Parameters are declared

```
 1 class Call2
 2 {
 3    public static void main(String[] args)
 4    {
 5        int x = 1;
 6        displaySum(x, x + 5, 20);      // 3 arguments
 7        System.out.println("All done");
 8    }
 9    //-----------------------------------
10    public static void displaySum(int a, int b, int c)  // 3 params
11    {
12        int sum;
13        sum = a + b + c;
14        System.out.println("sum = " + sum);
15    }
16 }
```

Figure 5.2

within the parentheses in the header of the called method. For example, the header of the displaySum method declares three parameters—a, b, and c—one for each argument:

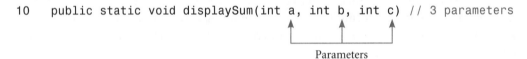

```
10   public static void displaySum(int a, int b, int c) // 3 parameters
```

Parameters

Because each parameter variable receives the value of its corresponding argument, its type has to be compatible with the type of its argument. For example, the type of the first argument in the call of displaySum on Line 6 is int; its corresponding parameter, a, has the same type.

When displaySum is called on Line 6, the following six actions occur:

1. The parameters a, b, and c are created.
2. The values of the arguments—1, 6, and 20—are **passed** to their corresponding parameters. That is, 1, 6, and 20 are automatically assigned to a, b, and c, respectively.
3. The local variable sum is created (Line 12). It has no initial value.
4. The body of the displaySum method is executed. Line 13 computes the sum of a, b, and c, and assigns the result to sum. Line 14 displays the value in sum.
5. The local variable sum and the parameters a, b, and c are destroyed.
6. Control returns to the statement that follows the call of the displaySum method (Line 7).

When displaySum finishes, the local variable sum and the parameters a, b, and c are all destroyed. If displaySum is called a second time, its parameters and local variable are created again. They are then destroyed again when displaySum finishes. Because sum, a, b, and c are destroyed when displaySum returns to its caller, *their values are not retained from one call to the next.* That is, each time displaySum is called, a, b, and c get new values (the values passed to them by the calling statement), and sum is recreated with no initial value (it does not start with the value in sum from the previous call). When the program in Fig. 5.2 is executed, it displays

```
sum = 27
All done
```

Parameters and local variables are local to their method. We can use them only in the method in which they are declared. For example, in the program in Fig. 5.2, we can use a, b, c, and sum only within the displaySum method. This restriction makes sense: a, b, c, and sum are created when displaySum starts executing, and they are destroyed when displaySum finishes. Thus, they exist only when displaySum is executing. For this reason, it would be impossible to refer to the a, b, c, or sum variables local to displaySum from anywhere outside displaySum.

Because parameters are local, we have a lot of flexibility in how we name them—we don't have to worry about some other method using the same names. For example, suppose we change the parameters in the displaySum method in Fig. 5.2 to x, y, and z, to get the program in Fig. 5.3.

```
 1 class Call3
 2 {
 3     public static void main(String[] args)
 4     {
 5         int x = 1;
 6         displaySum(x, x + 5, 20);
 7         System.out.println("All done");
 8     }
 9     //-----------------------------------
10     public static void displaySum(int x, int y, int z)
11     {
12         int sum;
13         sum = x + y + z;      // x does not conflict with x in main
14         System.out.println("sum = " + sum);
15     }
16 }
```

Figure 5.3

The parameter x in the Fig. 5.3 version of `displaySum` does *not* conflict with the local variable x in `main` because both x's are local to their methods. The scopes of the two x's (i.e., where they can be used) do not overlap. Thus, there is never any ambiguity when either x is used.

5.3 Argument-Parameter Type Mismatch

Recall from Section 3.2 that an `int` value can be assigned to a `double` variable, but not vice versa unless the `double` value is first cast to `int`. For example, if i has type `int` and d type `double`, then the following statement is legal:

```
d = i;        // legal to assign int to double
```

but not the following statement:

```
i = d;        // illegal to assign double to int without a cast
```

unless we first cast the `double` to `int`:

```
i = (int)d;   // legal with cast
```

Some assignments are not legal even with a cast. For example, you cannot assign a `String` to an `int` variable, even with a cast. The `String` and `int` types are incompatible.

The argument-parameter mechanism in method calls is an assignment operation. For example, when a method whose header is

```
public static void g(int i)
```

is called with

```
g(20);
```

the argument, 20, is assigned to its corresponding parameter i. Because the argument-parameter mechanism performs an assignment operation, we have the same restrictions on this mechanism that we have on the assignment statement. For example, we cannot call the preceding g method with

```
g(d);
```

because d (a `double`) cannot be assigned to i (an `int`). However, we can call g with

```
g((int)d);
```

because the cast makes the assignment legal.

5.4 Returning a Value

In Fig. 5.3, the displaySum method is passed three values. displaySum then computes and *displays* the sum of these three values. Alternatively, we can write a method that computes and *returns* the sum to the caller. The calling method can then use the returned value in whatever way it wants. It might, for example, display it or use it in a computation. getSum in Fig. 5.4. uses this approach.

main calls getSum with

```
6          y = getSum(x, x + 5, 20);     // assigns returned value
```

When getSum returns a value, that value is then used as if it occupied the position of the method call. Because the method call here is on the right side of an assignment statement, the value returned is assigned to y, the variable on the left side of the assignment statement. main then displays the value in y with

```
7          System.out.println("sum = " + y);
```

Let's see how getSum returns a value. On Line 14, getSum computes the sum of a, b, and c and assigns the result to its local variable sum. It then executes the following return statement:

```
15         return sum;        // returns value in sum
```

```
1 class ReturnValue1
2 {
3    public static void main(String[] args)
4    {
5        int x = 1, y;
6        y = getSum(x, x + 5, 20);    // assigns returned value
7        System.out.println("sum = " + y);
8        System.out.println("All done");
9    }
10   //------------------------------------
11   public static int getSum(int a, int b, int c)
12   {
13       int sum;
14       sum = a + b + c;
15       return sum;        // returns value in sum
16   }
17 }
```

Figure 5.4

This statement forces a return to the calling method. Thus, the parameters and local variable in getSum are destroyed, and control goes back to the calling method. This return statement, however, also causes the value of sum to be returned to the calling method (main in this example).

Because getSum returns an int value, we have to specify int as the return type in its header. The return type must immediately precede the method name. Notice on Line 11, the return type int immediately precedes the method name getSum:

return type

```
11      public static int getSum(int a, int b, int c)
```

Because getSum returns a value that we want, it would not make sense to have a statement that consisted of just the call of getSum:

```
getSum(x, x + 5, 20);                 // serves no purpose
```

This statement does not use the value returned by getSum. Thus, it does not serve any useful purpose (however, it is legal, and it will cause the execution of getSum). It also does not make sense to use a method call as if it returned a value if, in fact, it does not return one. For example, it does not make sense to call displaySum in Fig. 5.3 with

```
y = displaySum(x, x + 5, 20);     // illegal
```

because displaySum does not return a value so there is no value to assign to y.

Fig. 5.5 shows another version of getSum. In this version, the sum of a, b, and c is computed right in the return statement (see Line 12). Thus, we do not need a local variable

```
 1 class ReturnValue2
 2 {
 3    public static void main(String[] args)
 4    {
 5       int x = 1
 6       System.out.println("sum = " + getSum(x, x + 5, 20));
 7       System.out.println("All done");
 8    }
 9    //----------------------------------
10    public static int getSum(int a, int b, int c)
11    {
12       return a + b + c;    // both computes and returns sum
13    }
14 }
```

Figure 5.5

sum to hold the result. main calls getSum from within the println statement (see Line 6). Thus, we do not need a local variable in main to hold the returned value. Here, the value returned by getSum is immediately concatenated to "sum = " and displayed by the println statement.

If you are asked to write a method that *returns* a value, be sure your method does, indeed, return a value. *It must include a return statement that returns some value.* Your method should not simply display a value. Displaying a value and returning a value *are two different operations.* Compare displaySum in Fig. 5.2 with getSum in Fig. 5.5.

5.5 Overloading Method Names

In Chapter 2, we saw that the "+" operator is overloaded. That is, it has more than one meaning. The meaning of any particular instance of "+" depends on its context. For example, if "+" is surrounded by arithmetic operands, then "+" means add. But if "+" is surrounded by strings, then "+" means concatenate. Method names can be similarly overloaded. For example, in the program in Fig. 5.6, we have five methods all with the name o.

```
1 class Overloading
 2 {
 3    public static void main(String[] args)
 4    {
 5       o();          // calls o on line 12
 6       o(2);         // calls o on line 17
 7       o(2.0);       // calls o on line 22
 8       o(2, 2.0);    // calls o on line 27
 9       o(2.0, 2);    // calls o on line 32
10    }
11    //-----------------------------------
12    public static void o()
13    {
14       System.out.println("No args");
15    }
16    //-----------------------------------
17    public static void o(int i)
18    {
19       System.out.println("i = " + i);
20    }
21    //-----------------------------------
22    public static void o(double d)
```

Figure 5.6   (continues)

```
23    {
24        System.out.println("d = " + d);;
25    }
26    //----------------------------------
27    public static void o(int i, double d)
28    {
29        System.out.println("i = " + i + "    d = " + d);
30    }
31    //----------------------------------
32    public static void o(double d, int i)
33    {
34        System.out.println("d = " + d + " i = " + i);
35    }
36 }
```

Figure 5.6   (continued)

Note that the o methods have different parameter lists. These parameter lists differ in type, number, and/or order. Because of this, the calls of o are not ambiguous. The argument list in each call determines uniquely which o should be called. For example, the call

```
6        o(2);    // calls o on line 17
```

calls the method that starts with

```
17    public static void o(int i)
```

because the argument list in the call (a single int) matches the parameter list in this and only this method. When the program in Fig. 5.6 is executed, it displays

```
No args
i = 2
d = 2.0
i = 2    d = 2.0
d = 2.0 i = 2
```

Notice that the methods on Lines 27 and 32 have the same parameters but in a different order. Thus, the order of the arguments in the calls determines which of these two methods is called (see Lines 8 and 9).

5.6   External and Internal Calls and Accesses

A program can consist of one or more classes. In a program with multiple classes, a call of a static method can be **external** (from one class to a method in another class) or **internal** (from one class to a method in the same class). Similarly, accesses of variables can be external (from one class to a variable in another class) or internal (from one class to a variable in the same class). In this section, we will discuss external and internal calls and accesses of static methods and variables only. We will discuss nonstatic methods and variables in the next chapter.

A **static method** is a method whose header is marked with the reserved word static. Static methods exist independently of objects. That is, we do not have to construct objects to use static methods. Unlike nonstatic methods, static methods are not contained within objects.

Consider the program in Fig. 5.7. Notice it consists of two classes: One starting on Line 1 and Two starting on Line 11.

```
 1 class One
 2 {
 3    public static void main(String[] args)
 4    {
 5       Two.add();                            // external call
 6       System.out.println("x = " + Two.x);   // external access
 7    }
 8
 9 }
10 //=================================================
11 class Two
12 {
13    public static int x = 1;      // x is a static variable
14    //---------------------------------
15    public static void add()
16    {
17       int y = 2;               // y is a local variable
18       x = x + y;               // internal access of x
19       display();               // internal call
20    }
21    //---------------------------------
22    private static void display()
23    {
24       System.out.println("x = " + x); // internal access of x
25    }
26 }
```

Figure 5.7

The call of `display` on Line 19 is an internal call

```
19        display();                    // internal call
```

The call and the called method are in the same class (`Two`). Now compare this call with the call on Line 5:

```
5         Two.add();                    // external call
```

This statement is in a method in the `One` class. However, the method called is in the `Two` class. Thus, this is an external call. External calls of static methods must be prefixed with the name of the class that contains the called method. The class name and the method name should be separated by a period. The first part of this call (the class name `Two`) **qualifies** the call. That is, it provides additional information on the call. Specifically, it indicates that the method to be called is in the `Two` class. If Line 5 were simply

```
add();                      // illegal external call
```

then the call would be ambiguous. There might be many classes that have an `add` method. This call does not specify which `add` method among possibly many to call. We do not run into this problem with the internal call of `display` on Line 19. Because there is a `display` method in the same class as the call, the compiler assumes the call is to this `display` method. In other words, the compiler translates the statement on Line 19 as if it were written this way:

```
Two.display();
```

A variable that is marked with the reserved word `static` is called a **static variable** or a **class variable**. Static variables are declared in a class *outside* the methods of that class (it would be illegal to declare a static variable *inside* a method). For example, x on Line 13 in Fig. 5.7 is a static variable. Note that x is marked with `static` and declared outside the `add` and `display` methods in the `Two` class. Compare x on Line 13 with y on Line 17. y is not a static variable. It is declared inside the `add` method. Thus, y is a local variable.

Static methods and variables in a class come into existence when the class is first loaded into memory, and remain in existence until the program ends. The methods `main`, `add`, and `display`, and the variable x in the program in Fig. 5.7 are all static. Thus, they come into existence as soon as their respective classes are loaded into memory. In contrast, the local variable y comes into existence only when the method that declares it—the `add` method—is called.

A static variable is directly accessible by all the methods in its class. We say that a static variable is **global** to the class. What one method places in a static variable can be accessed by another method in the same class. For example, the value assigned to x by the add method (see Line 18 in Fig. 5.7) can be accessed by the display method (see Line 24). In contrast, local variables are accessible only within the method in which they are declared.

Like an external call of a static method, an external access of a static variable requires qualification with the class name. For example, on Line 6 in Fig. 5.7, main accesses the static variable x in the Two class:

```
6          System.out.println("x = " + Two.x);   // external access
```

Note that x is qualified with the class name Two.

Internal accesses of variables (accesses of a variable in one class from the same class) do not have to be qualified. The compiler translates unqualified internal accesses of static members of a class as if they were qualified with the class name of the containing class. The compiler, for example, translates Line 18 in Fig. 5.7 as if it were written this way:

```
Two.x = Two.x + y;
```

If a method or a variable of a class is marked with public, it is "available to the public." That is, it can be accessed from any class. However, if it is marked with private, it can be accessed from only within its own class. For example, the display method in Fig. 5.7 is private (see Line 22). It can be accessed only from within its own class. Thus, the following statement would be *illegal* if it appeared in main:

```
Two.display();
```

The compiler would flag it with the error message

```
display() has private access in Two
```

main, however, has indirect access to display via the add method. main can call add because add is public. Because add is in the same class as display, add can then call display.

public and private are called **access specifiers** because they specify the level of access a class member can have. In the Two class in Fig. 5.7, x and add have public access; display has private access.

Generally, each class in a multiple-class program should be in a separate file. The name of each file should match—including the case—the name of the class it contains. For example, the program in Fig. 5.7 should be in two files: the One class should be in a file named One.java; the Two class should be in a file named Two.java. Because the One class uses the Two class, the compile of the One class will automatically trigger the compile of the Two class. Thus, to compile this program, we enter only one command:

```
javac One.java
```

This command compiles both One.java and Two.java and produces the corresponding class files, One.class and Two.class. To run the program, we invoke the java interpreter, specifying only the class that contains the main method:

```
java One
```

The collection of source code available for this textbook contains every program in this textbook, *each in a single file* whose name matches the name of the class that contains the main method. Thus, for multiple-class programs, each class is *not* in a separate file. We packaged the programs in this nonstandard way to make accessing them as easy as possible: To get a program, you simply obtain the *one* file that contains it. For example, to get the program in Fig. 5.7 (both the One and Two classes), you simply get the file named One.java. To compile and run the program in this file, you should enter the same commands you would if the classes were in separate files. That is, you should enter

```
javac One.java
java One
```

Laboratory 5 Prep

1. Is this a legal overloading of p1?

```
public static void p1(int x)
{
    ...
}
public static void p1(int y)
{
    ...
}
```

   Compile a test program to check your answer. (*Hint:* Which method would the following statement call?)

```
p1(5);
```

2. Is the following method legal? Explain. Compile a test program to check your answer.

```
public static void p2(int x)
{
    int x = 1;
    System.out.println(x);
}
```

3. Is the following method legal? Explain. Compile a test program to check your answer.

```
public static void p3(int x)
{
    {
        int x = 1;
        System.out.println(x);
    }
}
```

4. Is the following method legal? Explain. Compile a test program to check your answer.

```
public static void p4(int a, b, c)
{
    System.out.println(a + b + c);
}
```

5. Write the statement that calls the static method p5 in the class P5, passing it 5. Assume the call is external.

LABORATORY

Laboratory 5

1. Is it legal to call

```
public static void rabbit(double x)
{
    System.out.println("hello");
}
```

with

```
rabbit(5);
```

Is it legal to call

```
public static void hare(int x)
{
    System.out.println("hello");
}
```

with

```
hare(5.0);
```

Compile a test program to check your answers.

2. Write a program with a main method and a max method. max should *return* the largest of the three values it is passed. main should call max three times. On the first call, it should pass max 1, 2, and 3; on the second call, it should pass 2, 3, and 1; on the third call, it should pass 3, 1, and 2. For each call, main should display the value returned, appropriately labeled.

3. Can you call goose with

```
goose(5.0f);
```

if you have overloaded goose as follows:

```
public static void goose(int x)
{
    ...
}
public static void goose(double x)
{
    ...
}
```

Run a test program to check your answer. What happens?

The parameter `5.0f` in the method call of `f` is a `float` constant. Neither parameter in the two `goose` methods matches this type. When the compiler translates a method call, it generates code that calls the method whose parameter list is the best compatible match with the argument list. An exact match is not required.

4. Is this a legal overloading of the method name `pig`:

```
public void pig()
{
    System.out.println("hello");
}
public int pig()
{
    return 5;
}
```

Compile a test program to check your answer.

5. We call the operators "||" and "|" in the following program **logical operators** because they operate on true/false values and yield results that are true/false.

```
class C5e5
{
    public static void main(String[] args)
    {
        if (f() || g())                 // short circuited OR
            System.out.println("first if");
        if (f() | g())                  // not short circuited
            System.out.println("second if");
    }
    public static boolean f()
    {
        System.out.println("in f");
        return true;
    }
    public static boolean g()
    {
        System.out.println("in g");
        return true;
    }
}
```

Java has two logical OR operators: "||" (with two vertical bars) and "|" (with one vertical bar). "||" is the **short-circuit** or **lazy** logical OR. That is, if the value of the operation can be determined from the left operand alone, the right operand is not evaluated. "|" is not short circuited—that is, both operands are always evaluated. Run the preceding program. Explain why the two `if` statements in the preceding code behave differently?

LABORATORY

Java also has two logical AND operators: "&&" (short circuited) and "&" (not short circuited). When the operators "|", "||", "&", and "&&" have true/false operands, they function as **logical operators**. That is, they operate on true/false values and they yield true/false results. However, "|" and "&" (but not "||" and "&&") can also have operands of an integer type, in which case they function as **bitwise operators**. For more information on the bitwise operators, see Lab Exercise 6.

6. The "|" and "&" operators are overloaded. If their operands have true/false values, they function as logical operators (i.e., they operate on true/false values and they yield results that are true/false). But if their operands are an integer type (i.e., byte, short, int, or long), they function as bitwise operators. In a bitwise operation, the corresponding bits in the two operands are operated on, yielding the values given by the following tables:

bit 1	bit 2	|		bit 1	bit 2	&
0	0	0		0	0	0
0	1	1		0	1	0
1	0	1		1	0	0
1	1	1		1	1	1

Include the following code in a program and run:

```java
int x = 12, y = 10, z1, z2;
System.out.println("x  = " + Integer.toBinaryString(x)); // display x
System.out.println("y  = " + Integer.toBinaryString(y)); // display y
z1 = x | y;    // bitwise OR
System.out.println("z1 = " + Integer.toBinaryString(z1));// display z1
z2 = x & y;    // bitwise AND
System.out.println("z2 = " + Integer.toBinaryString(z2));// display z2
```

Examine the values of x, y, z1, and z2 that are displayed. Confirm that the bitwise OR and AND operators work as specified by the preceding tables.

7. Does the following program compile without errors? If so, does it run without errors? What is unusual about this program?

```java
class C5e7
{
    public static void main(String[] args)
    {
        f();
    }
    public static int f()
    {
        return 1;
    }
}
```

8. Does the following program compile without errors? If so, does it run without errors? What is unusual about this program?

```
class C5e8
{
    public static void main(String[] args)
    {
        int x;
        x = stingy();
    }
    public static void stingy()
    {
        System.out.println("hello");
    }
}
```

9. Change Line 13 of `C5e9.java` (a copy of Fig. 5.7) to

```
public static int x;
```

Compile and run the program. From the output displayed, deduce the initial value of x. Change Line 17 to

```
int y;
```

Compile. What happens? Why? Reset Line 17 to

```
int y = 2;
```

Then change `public` on Line 15 to `private`. Compile. What happens? Why?

10. Compile the following program to determine what is wrong with it:

```
class C5e10
{
    public static void main(String[] args)
    {
        static int x = 3;
        System.out.println(x);
    }
}
```

11. Write a program in which `main` prompts for and reads in from the keyboard an integer. It should then call `f` passing it the value read in. `f` should display the letter `f` and then call `g`, passing it one less than the value in its parameter. On return from `g`, `f` should display `hello`. If the value passed to `g` is negative, `g` should immediately return to its caller. Otherwise `g` should display the letter `g` and then call `f`, passing it one less than the value in its parameter. Before you run your program, predict what its output will be when the integer entered is 2.

12. Is it legal in a method to return a value of type int if the return type in the method's header is double? Is it legal in a method to return a value of type double if the return type in the method's header is int? Compile a test program to check your answers.

Homework 5

1. Write a program in which main prompts for and reads three integers, and then calls a sort method, passing sort the three integers read in. sort should display the three values in ascending order. Test your program with several different triplets of integers to make sure it works for all cases.

2. Write a program in which main calls Math.cos *and* myCos twice, once passing them Math.PI/3.0 and once passing them Math.PI/6.0. Math.cos and Math.PI are both available in the predefined Math class. myCos is a method you should write. main should display the values returned by both methods. myCos should compute and return the value of

$$1.0 - x^2/(2!) + x^4/(4!) - x^6/(6!) + \ldots + x^{96}/(96!) - x^{98}/(98!)$$

where x is the double parameter that receives the value passed to myCos. Compute the value of each term by multiplying the value of the previous term by some appropriate factor (see Homework Exercises 3 and 4 in Chapter 4).

3. Write a program that generates and displays 30 random numbers between 0 and 1. Your program should contain a main method, a myRand method, and a static variable seed. Each time myRand is called, it should return a random double value between 0 and 1. main should call myRand 30 times, each time displaying the number that myRand returns. myRand should use the following **algorithm** (i.e., step-by-step procedure) to generate each random number:

   a. Square the sum of Math.PI and seed. Put the result back into seed.

   b. Assign seed to an int variable x (you will need a cast).

   c. Subtract x from seed. Put the result back into seed.

   d. Return the value in seed.

   Initialize seed to 0.123456789. What is the effect of Steps (b) and (c) on seed? How well does your myRand method work? Do the numbers it generates look like true random numbers? Compute the average of 10,000 numbers generated by your rand method. Is it close to 0.5? Generate 10,000 numbers and count the number of numbers between 0.1 and 0.2 and between 0.4 and 0.5. Are the two counts close to 1000? Why can we not use a local variable within the myRand method for seed?

4. Suppose you want to determine the square root of x. Set root to 1.0. If root is less than the square root of x, then x/root has to be greater than the square root of x. If root is greater than the square root of x, then x/root has to be less than the square root of x. Thus, regardless of the value of root, root and x/root bound the square root of x. That is, the square root of x is somewhere between root and x/root. By averaging root and x/root, we can get a better estimate of the square root of x than is in root. We can then assign this better estimate to root. If we repeat this process many times in a loop, the value in root will converge on the square root of x. Using this technique, implement a method that *returns* the square root of the value it is passed. Call your method mySqrt. Use your method *and* the Math.sqrt method to determine the square roots of 5.0E-100, 5.0, 500.0, 50000.0, 5000000.0, 500000000.0, and 5.0E300. When your program starts, it should prompt for and read from the keyboard the number of times the loop that computes the square root should iterate. The larger the number entered (up to some limit), the more accurate the calculated square root. Math.sqrt is a static method in the predefined Math class. How many times does your method have to iterate to get an accurate value of the square root. Is there some way to get a starting value for root better than 1.0?

At the machine language level, the computer can perform only the basic math operations, such as add, subtract, multiply, and divide. This exercise and Homework Exercise 2 illustrate how a computer can be programmed to perform more sophisticated mathematical operations, such as square root and cosine.

5. Suppose a dart board is a square with dimensions 1×1, on which we draw a quarter circle with radius 1 and with the origin located at the lower left corner of the dart board. The area on the dart board that is inside the quarter circle is the "hit" area. The area on the dart board outside the quarter circle is the "miss" area. If we throw randomly at the dart board, the ratio of hits to throws will be roughly equal to the ratio of the hit area ($\pi r^2/4 = \pi 1^2/4 = \pi/4$) to the total area ($1 \times 1 = 1$). Write a program that simulates randomly throwing a dart one million times at this dart board. Estimate a value for π from the hits-to-throws ratio. (*Hint:* To "throw" a dart, generate two random double values, each between 0.0 and 1.0. Treat these values as the (x, y) coordinates of the point on the dart board on which the dart lands. To determine if a throw is a hit, check if the distance of the hit from the origin is less than or equal to 1. If it is, then the throw is a hit; otherwise, it is a miss. This problem is particularly interesting because we are using a random process to determine the universal constant π.)

To generate random numbers, use the predefined Random class. Place the following statement at the beginning of your program:

```
import java.util.Random;
```

LABORATORY

To create a Random object, use

```
Random r = new Random();
```

To generate a random double value between 0.0 and 1.0 and assign it to x, use

```
x = r.nextDouble();
```

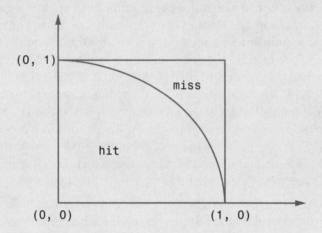

Sample Exam 1 (Chapters 1–5)

Each question is worth 20%   Name _____

1. What is displayed when the following instructions are executed:

```
System.out.print("yes");
System.out.print("no");
System.out.println("maybe");
System.out.println(10/3);
System.out.println("10/3");
System.out.println(10%3);
System.out.println("bert" + 3 + 5);
System.out.println("bert" + (3 + 5));
System.out.println(3 + 5 + "bert");
System.out.println(100*10/10*10);
```

2. Write a Java program that displays hello 10 times, each on a separate line. Use a loop.

3. Write a Java program that displays the odd numbers between 1 and 999, inclusive except for the odd numbers between 223 and 333, inclusive. Use only one loop.

4. Write a Java program that contains a `main` method and two `getGrade` methods. One version of `getGrade` has a single `int` parameter; the other has two `int` parameters. The first version of `getGrade` returns the letter grade that corresponds to the test score it is passed. Test scores and their corresponding letter grades are as follows:

```
Test Score     Letter Grade
  90–100            A
  80–89             B
  70–79             C
  65–69             D
  0–64              F
```

For example, the call of `getGrade` in the following statement should return (not display) the `char` value `'B'`:

```
char grade = getGrade(81);
```

The second version of `getGrade` is passed two test scores. It returns the grade that corresponds to the average of the two test scores it is passed. It should

a. determine the average of the two numbers it is passed;

b. call the first version of `getGrade`, passing it the average to get the corresponding letter grade; and

c. return the letter grade it gets in Step (b).

`main` should call `getGrade` three times, once passing it 64, once passing it 99, and once passing it both 73 and 91. For each call, `main` should display the score or scores and the corresponding letter grade obtained from `getGrade`. The display produced by `main` should look like this:

```
64 gets the grade F
99 gets the grade A
73 and 91 gets the grade B
```

5. Write a program that prompts for and then reads in a non-negative two-digit integer. Your program should then call a method named `displayDigits` passing it the integer read in. `displayDigits` should display each digit of the integer it is passed on a separate line. For example, if `displayDigits` is passed 57, `displayDigits` should display

```
First digit  = 5
Second digit = 7
```

(*Hint:* Use the "`/`" and "`%`" operators to isolate the individual digits.)

Constructing Objects: Part 1

6.1 Object-Oriented Programming

Java is an **object-oriented** (OO) programming language. Programs written in Java typically construct objects. However, in the preceding chapters, we barely used the OO features of Java so that we could first present the fundamentals of programming. Now that you know these fundamentals, we can concentrate our study on Java's OO features.

To perform a task on a computer, we need the methods that perform the required task. But we also need the data on which those methods operate. An object encapsulates both of these components—methods and data—into a single unit. Thus, an object provides us everything we need to perform some task on a computer.

6.2 Constructing an Object from a Class

A Java class is like a blueprint for a house. A blueprint, of course, is not a house. Rather, it is a specification of a house. It specifies the structure of a house. Similarly, a Java class is a specification. It specifies the structure of an object.

One can construct multiple houses from one blueprint. All the houses will have the same structure. For example, the number of the rooms in each house will be the same. However, the houses will not necessarily be identical. For example, in one house, the living room might contain a TV; in another, the living room might contain a computer. Similarly, objects created from the same Java class share a common structure but are not necessarily identical. For example, two objects from the same class might have different data. One might have the number 10, the other 20.

We call an object constructed from a class an **instance** of that class. To **instantiate** a class means to construct an object from the class.

Classes and their corresponding objects can contain three types of members:

1. Variables (also called **data fields**).
2. Constructors. Constructors are special methods that are generally used to initialize a newly created object. The name of a constructor must match the class name. Constructors can be overloaded. That is, multiple constructors—all with the same name—are allowed in a class, as long as they can be distinguished by their parameter lists.
3. Methods.

For example, the OOP1 class in Fig. 6.1 contains two variables (x on Line 3 and y on Line 4), one constructor (OOP1 on Lines 6–9), and two methods (xDisplay on Lines 11–14 and yDisplay on Lines 16–19). Note that the name of the constructor matches the class name (OOP1). The members of a class may appear in any order, but we will always list the variables first, then the constructors, and finally the methods.

Variables and methods marked public can be directly accessed from both inside and outside their classes. Objects interact with each other through their public methods. Variables and methods marked private can be accessed directly only from inside their classes. Generally, we make variables and the **helper methods** (methods called only internally by other methods in the same class) private.

Static variables and **static methods** exist independently of objects. Moreover, there is one and only one set of static variables and methods per class. For this reason, static variables and static methods are often called **class variables** and **class methods**, respectively. In Fig. 6.1, x (Line 3) is a static variable, and xDisplay (Line 11) is a static method.

Nonstatic variables and **nonstatic methods** do not exist independently of objects. To use nonstatic variables and methods, we first have to create an instance of the class that contains them. Each instance of a class (i.e., each object constructed from a class) has its own set of nonstatic variables and methods. For this reason, nonstatic variables and

```
1 class OOP1  ←──────────────────→  class name same as constructor name
2 {
3      private static int x = 3;          // static variable
4      private int y;                     // instance variable
5      //----------------------------------
6      public OOP1(int yy)                // constructor
7      {
8          y = yy;
9      }
10     //----------------------------------
11     public static void xDisplay()      // static method
12     {
13         System.out.println(x);         // displays 3
14     }
15     //----------------------------------
16     public void yDisplay()             // instance method
17     {
18         System.out.println(y);
19     }
20 }
21 //===================================================
```

Figure 6.1   (continues)

```
22 class TestOOP1
23 {
24    public static void main(String[] args)
25    {
26       OOP1.xDisplay();              // call before creating objects
27
28       OOP1 n;                       // declare reference n
29       n = new OOP1(10);             // create object
30       OOP1 m = new OOP1(20);        // declare m and create object
31
32       n.yDisplay();                 // displays 10
33       m.yDisplay();                 // displays 20
34    }
35 }
```

Figure 6.1 (continued)

methods are often called **instance variables** and **instance methods**, respectively. In Fig. 6.1, y (Line 4) is an instance variable, and yDisplay (Line 16) is an instance method.

Assuming the program in Fig. 6.1 is in the file TestOOP1.java, we compile it by entering

```
javac TestOOP1.java
```

The compiler will then compile both the TestOOP1 and OOP1 classes, producing the corresponding class files, TestOOP1.class and OOP1.class. To execute the program, we invoke the java interpreter with

```
java TestOOP1
```

In this command, we specify only the name of the class that contains the main method.

Let's go through the execution of the program in Fig. 6.1. As always, main is executed first. As execution starts, both xDisplay and x in the OOP1 class already exist because they are static (see Fig. 6.2a). Thus, main can immediately invoke xDisplay to display the value of x. main calls xDisplay with

```
26       OOP1.xDisplay();              // call before creating objects
```

which displays 3, the value of x. Because this is an external call of a static method, the call has to be qualified with OOP1, the name of the class that contains xDisplay. Next, main declares a local variable n with

```
28       OOP1 n;                       // declare reference n
```

This statement declares n to have type OOP1. This is a perfectly legitimate statement. In Java, a type can be any class as well as any of the primitive types. A variable whose type is a class is called a **reference variable**. n initially contains garbage. However, the next statement,

```
29          n = new OOP1(10);          // create object
```

constructs a new object from the OOP1 class and assigns n the **reference** to this object (see Fig. 6.2b). A reference is, in effect, a pointer to an object.

The right side of the assignment statement on Line 29 contains two items: the operator new and the call of the OOP1 constructor. The new operator triggers the creation of a new object and returns a reference to it. This reference is assigned to n. The call of the constructor initializes the new object. This call passes 10 to the parameter yy in the constructor. The constructor then assigns yy to the instance variable y. Thus, the constructor in this case initializes y to 10.

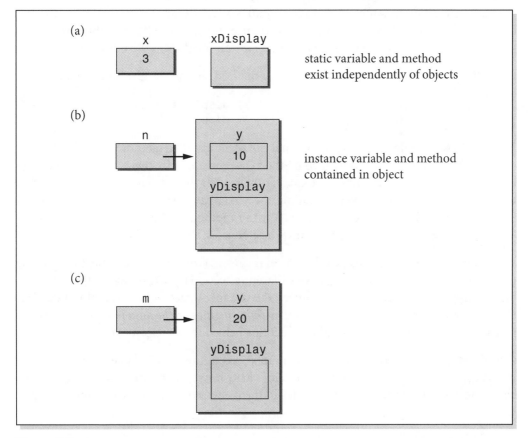

Figure 6.2

On Line 30, we both declare a reference variable and create an object in one statement:

```
30      OOP1 m = new OOP1(20);          // declare m and create object
```

Here, we are declaring the reference m, creating a new OOP1 object, initializing its y variable to 20, and assigning m the reference to the new object, all in a single statement (see Fig. 6.2c). At this point in the execution of our program, we have

1. The x static variable and the xDisplay static method (see Fig. 6.2a).
2. n and the "n object" (i.e., the object to which n points). The n object contains a y instance variable and the yDisplay instance method (see Fig. 6.2b).
3. m and the "m object" (i.e., the object to which m points). The m object contains a y instance variable and the yDisplay instance method (see Fig. 6.2c).

The n and m objects each have their own y instance variable and yDisplay instance method. Each time we instantiate an object from the OOP1 class, we get another y instance variable and yDisplay instance method in the newly created object. However, we have a completely different situation with x and xDisplay. Because they are static, there is only one x and one xDisplay for the class (hence the names "class variable" and "class method"), regardless of the number of objects instantiated from the OOP1 class.

On Lines 32 and 33, we invoke the yDisplay methods in the n and m objects with

```
32      n.yDisplay();                   // displays 10
33      m.yDisplay();                   // displays 20
```

Because these are external calls (an external call of an instance method is a call from outside the object that contains the called method), we must qualify them. However, because the calls are to *instance* methods, we qualify them with the *references* to the objects that contain them. On Line 32, we are calling the yDisplay method in the object pointed to by n; on Line 33, we are calling the yDisplay method in the object pointed to by m. Clearly, if these calls were not qualified with references, they would be ambiguous.

Although the code for yDisplay methods in the n and m objects is the same, they operate on different data, and, therefore, have different effects. The yDisplay method in the n object displays the value of y in that object; the yDisplay method in the m object displays the value of y in that object. *Each instance method operates on the data in its own object* (we will see the actual mechanism used to effect this behavior in Section 6.4).

It is legal for main to invoke the yDisplay methods in the n and m objects and the static xDisplay method because they are public. main, however, cannot directly access the class variable x or the y instance variables in the n and m objects because x and y are private. Thus, if we were to include any of the following statements in `main`, we would get compile-time errors:

```
OOP1.x = 4;          // illegal in main because x is private
n.y = 30;            // illegal in main because y is private
m.y = 40;            // illegal in main because y is private
```

In the first statement, we are attempting to assign 4 to the x class variable in the OOP1 class. In the second statement, we are attempting to assign 30 to the y in the n object. In the third statement, we are attempting to assign 40 to the y in the m object. All three statements, however, would be legal if x and y were public. Note that we qualify an external access to a class variable with a class name, but we qualify an external access to an instance variable with a reference.

A class can have zero or more constructors. The OOP1 class in Fig. 6.1 contains one constructor on Lines 6–9. The header of a constructor consists of three items:

1. The reserved word `public`
2. Its name, which must be the same as the class name
3. Its parameter list within parentheses

Unlike the header of an ordinary method, the header of a constructor does *not* include a return type. Thus, it would be illegal to start a constructor for OOP1 with

```
public void OOP1()           // illegal because of void
```

A constructor can be used only during the construction of an object. Thus, we cannot use the constructor in Fig. 6.1 to change the value of y once the object has been created.

Let's summarize the important features of classes and objects:

*   Static variables and methods exist independently of objects.
*   An external access to a static variable or an external call to a static method must be qualified with the class name.
*   Nonstatic variables and methods are contained in objects.
*   An external access of a nonstatic variable in an object or an external call of a nonstatic method in an object must be qualified with the reference to the object.
*   External access is not permitted if the variable or method to be accessed is marked as private.
*   A constructor always has the same name as its class.
*   The header for a constructor does not include a return type.

- Static variables are also called class variables. Static methods are also called class methods.
- Nonstatic fields are also call instance variables. Nonstatic methods are also called instance methods.

6.3 Constructors

The OOP2 class in Fig. 6.3 has no constructor. However, every class must have a constructor. For this reason, the compiler will automatically include a **default constructor** in the bytecode it generates when it translates this class. The bytecode produced is as if the following constructor were in the class:

```
public OOP2()
{
}
```

The compiler inserts a default constructor into the bytecode it generates *only if the source code for the class contains no constructors.*

```
 1 class OOP2
 2 {
 3    private int q;
 4    //---------------------------------
 5    public void set(int qq)
 6    {
 7       q = qq;
 8    {
 9    //---------------------------------
10    public int get()
11    {
12       return q;
13    }
14 }
15 //================================================
16 class TestOOP2
17 {
18    public static void main(String[] args)
19    {
20       OOP2 r = new OOP2();
21       r.set(10);                  // sets q to 10
22       System.out.println(r.get());   // displays 10
23    }
24 }
```

Figure 6.3

The default constructor has no parameters. Thus, when we call it, we cannot pass it any arguments. Accordingly, when we call the constructor on Line 20, we do not pass it any arguments:

```
20        OOP2 r = new OOP2();
```

                  ↑
                └──── No arguments

If we were to use the following statement, we would get a compile-time error:

```
OOP2 r = new OOP2(5);    // illegal because no matching constructor
```

To make this statement legal, we would have to include in the OOP2 class a one-parameter constructor, such as:

```
public OOP2(int qq)
{
    q = qq;
}
```

However, if we did this, the compiler would then *not* insert the default constructor (the compiler inserts the default constructor only if the class has no constructors). Thus, Line 20 would become illegal (because it needs a constructor with no parameters). Then, to make Line 20 legal, we would have to include a constructor with no parameters. It could be one with an empty body, like the default constructor. Or it could be one that contains some initialization statements, such as the following constructor:

```
public OOP2()
{
    q = 100;
}
```

To summarize: If you include any constructors in a class, then those are the only constructors the class has. If you include no constructors, then and only then will the compiler insert a default constructor. The default constructor has no parameters. Thus, calls of the default constructor must have no arguments.

The set method in OOP2 sets the instance variable q to the value of the argument passed to set. For example, when Line 21 is executed,

```
21        r.set(10);                          // sets q to 10
```

the set method in the object to which r points is called. The parameter qq in set is created and the argument 10 in the call of set is automatically assigned to qq. The body of set is then executed:

```
7         q = qq;
```

This statement assigns the value of qq to the instance variable q. set is an example of a mutator method. A **mutator method** is a method that sets or changes the value of one or more instance variables.

The get method in OOP2 returns the value of the instance variable q. In the statement in main that calls get,

```
22          System.out.println(r.get());    // displays 10
```

the value returned by get is displayed by the println statement. get is an example of an accessor method. An **accessor method** is a method that returns the value of an instance variable. Note that although q in OOP2 is private, we have access to it through the public methods set and get.

6.4 `this`

The program in Fig. 6.4 constructs and initializes two objects with the following statements:

```
26          OOP3 r1 = new OOP3(10);
27          OOP3 r2 = new OOP3(20);
```

The x instance variable in the r1 object is initialized to 10 by the action of the constructor; similarly, the x instance variable in the r2 object is initialized to 20.

When main calls divide with

```
28          r1.divide(2);                   // r1 and 2 passed
```

it passes 2 to divide. This value is received by y, the parameter in the divide method. But 2 is not the only item passed to divide. *The value of qualifying reference* r1 *is also passed*, even though it does not appear in the argument list in the call. This reference is received by a special parameter named this, which divide can access (see Fig. 6.5a). Every instance method creates a this parameter when it is called to receive the qualifying reference used in its call. Thus, divide has two parameters: this, which receives the reference in r1 (so this also points to the object), and y, which receives 2.

main calls divide a second time with:

```
29          r2.divide(5);                   // r2 and 5 passed
```

```
 1 class OOP3
 2 {
 3    private int x;
 4    //---------------------------------
 5    public OOP3(int xx)
 6    {
 7       x = xx;
 8    }
 9    //---------------------------------
10    public void divide(int y)
11    {
12       x = x/y;    // translated as if this.x = this.x/y;
13       display(); // passes its this parameter
14    }
15    //---------------------------------
16    private void display()
17    {
18       System.out.println(x); // x translated as if this.x
19    }
20 }
21 //===============================================
22 class TestOOP3
23 {
24    public static void main(String[] args)
25    {
26       OOP3 r1 = new OOP3(10);
27       OOP3 r2 = new OOP3(20);
28       r1.divide(2);            // r1 and 2 passed
29       r2.divide(5);            // r2 and 5 passed
30    }
31 }
```

Figure 6.4

As in the previous call of divide, the value of the qualifying reference (r2 in this case) is passed to the this parameter in divide. The argument 5 is passed to the parameter y (see Fig. 6.5b).

Let's summarize what we have learned about calls of instance methods:

When an instance method is called, the value of the qualifying reference is passed to the called method, along with the values of the arguments, if any. The value of the reference is received by the this parameter in the called method.

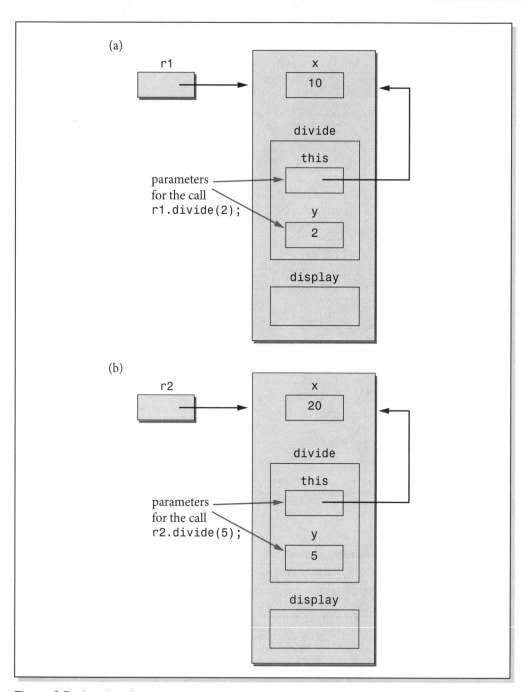

Figure 6.5 (continues)

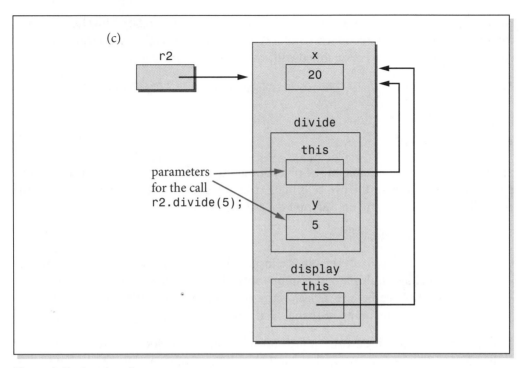

Figure 6.5 (continued)

We can now answer the following question that may have been puzzling you:

The divide methods in the r1 and r2 objects are identical (they both come from the same class). How then can they have different effects? Specifically, why does the divide in the r1 object divide the x in the r1 object, and the identical divide method in the r2 object divide the x in the r2 object? Should not the two divide methods have identical effects because they are *identical*?

The reason why the two divide methods have different effects is because the references passed to their this parameters differ for the two calls. For the call

```
28        r1.divide(2);              // r1 and 2 passed
```

the this parameter in divide contains a pointer to the r1 object (see Fig. 6.5a). For the call

```
29        r2.divide(5);              // r2 and 5 passed
```

the `this` parameter contains a pointer to the r2 object (see Fig. 6.5b). Now here is a very important point for you to understand: The compiler translates any internal use of an instance variable as if it were qualified with `this`. Thus, it translates

```
12          x = x/y;    // translated as if this.x = this.x/y;
```

as if it were written as

```
this.x = this.x/y;
```

`this.x` accesses the x variable in the object pointed to by `this`. Thus, because the `this` parameters in `divide` for the two calls of `divide` in Fig. 6.4 point to different objects, the two calls of `divide` operate on different data. Puzzle solved!

But now consider this great idea:

> The `divide` methods in all the objects instantiated from the OOP2 class are identical. Why then have multiple copies in memory—one in each object—of the `divide` method? Multiple copies are a clear waste of memory space. Why not have just a single copy of `divide` in memory that all the objects can share?

This, indeed, is a great idea. It is, in fact, precisely what Java does. A reference does not really point to a block of memory that contains an object's data and methods. It points to just the object's data (see Fig. 6.6). Only one copy of each method in a class is loaded into memory. These methods are shared by all the objects of the class.

The representation of the r1 and r2 objects in Fig. 6.5 is the **conceptual view** of these objects. It does not show how objects are actually represented in memory. The representa-

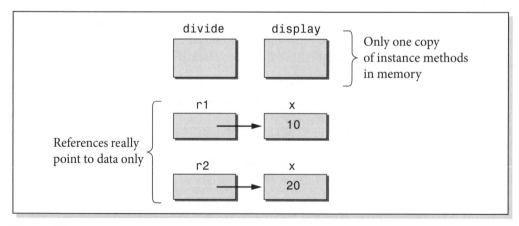

Figure 6.6

tion of the r1 and r2 objects in Fig. 6.6 shows the **actual view**. It shows how these objects are actually represented inside the computer.

The conceptual view of objects is a good way for us to think of objects. It captures the essence of an object—an entity containing data along with the methods that operate on that data. By viewing objects conceptually, we can more easily design and implement programs. In this book, we will represent objects using the conceptual view. But be sure to understand that this view is not an accurate representation of objects inside the computer. *A reference really points to only an object's data.*

Now let's consider what happens when `divide` in Fig. 6.4 calls `display` with

```
13        display(); // passes its this parameter
```

Because `display` is an instance method, it too creates a `this` parameter when it is called. When `display` is called, its `this` parameter must be passed the reference to the object (otherwise `display` would not be able to access the instance variables in the object). Where does this reference come from? It comes from the `divide` method. The compiler translates the call of `display` in the `divide` method on Line 13 as if it were written this way:

```
this.display();
```

The qualifying reference here is the `this` parameter *in the* `divide` *method*. Thus, the `this` parameter in the `divide` method is passed to the `this` parameter in the `display` method. When `display` executes, its `this` parameter, like the `this` parameter for `divide`, points to the object (see Fig. 6.5c). Now consider what happens when the `display` method executes

```
18        System.out.println(x); // x translated as if this.x
```

Because `x` is an instance variable, the compiler translates this statement as if it were written this way:

```
System.out.println(this.x);
```

When `divide` is called with r1 as the qualifying reference, a copy of the reference in r1 ultimately ends up in the `this` parameter of `display`. Thus, Line 18 displays the x data in the r1 object. But when `divide` is called with the r2 as the qualifying reference, a copy of the reference in r2 ultimately ends up in the `this` parameter of `display`. Thus, Line 18 then displays the x data in the r2 object.

Let's summarize all that we have learned about calls of instance methods:

- An external call of an instance method must be qualified with a reference.
- An internal call of an instance method is translated as if it were qualified with `this`. Thus, every call of an instance method is qualified, either explicitly or implicitly.
- The qualifying reference in a call of an instance method is passed to the `this` parameter of the called method.
- Internal accesses of instance variables are translated as if they were qualified with `this`. Thus, they access the data the `this` parameter points to.

6.5 Case Study

The program in Fig. 6.7 illustrates some important features of objects. It creates objects, each of which represents a single integer number. Now consider the statement on Line 27 in `main`:

```
27        Number n3 = n1.add(n2);
```

This call of the `add` method adds the integers in *two* objects, and returns the reference of a new `Number` object that contains the sum. But this call has only *one* argument—n2—so how can it add *two* integers? There are two correct answers to this question. One answer is based on a conceptual view on the calling mechanism, and one is based on the actual view.

Let's consider the conceptual view first: We are calling the `add` method in the n1 object. This instance of the `add` method has access to the x variable in its own object (the n1 object). Thus, the left x on Line 12 accesses the x variable in the n1 object:

```
12        return new Number(x + r.x);
```

Line 12 also accesses r.x—the x variable to which r points. But n2 is passed to r in the call on Line 27. Thus r.x is the x variable in the n2 object.

Now the actual view. As we learned in the preceding section, `add` is actually passed two arguments: n1, which is received by the `this` parameter, and n2, which is received by the r parameter. Thus n1 and `this` point to one object, and n2 and r point to the second object. The compiler translates Line 12 as if it were written this way:

```
return new Number(this.x + r.x);
```

Thus, this statement adds `this.x`, the x variable in the `this` object (which is also the n1 object) and r.x , the x variable in the r object (which is also the n2 object).

```
 1 class Number
 2 {
 3    private int x;
 4    //----------------------------------
 5    public Number(int xx)
 6    {
 7       x = xx;
 8    }
 9    //----------------------------------
10    public Number add(Number r)
11    {
12       return new Number(x + r.x);
13    }
14    //----------------------------------
15    public String toString()
16    {
17       return "" + x;        // return value in x as String
18    }
19 }
20 //================================================
21 class TestNumber
22 {
23    public static void main(String[] args)
24    {
25       Number n1 = new Number(10);
26       Number n2 = new Number(20);
27       Number n3 = n1.add(n2);
28       System.out.println("n3 = " + n3.toString());
29    }
30 }
```

Figure 6.7

Another curious feature of the program in Fig. 6.7 is that it seems to violate the privacy of x.

The add method in the n1 object accesses r.x on line 12—this is the private x data in the n2 object. Is this not a violation of the privacy of x in n2? Because x is marked with private (see Line 3), it can be directly accessed from only within the Number *class*. But the access of r.x on Line 12 is inside the Number class, so it is legal. Here, one object is accessing private data in another object. But the classes of both objects are the same. Thus, the privacy restriction is *not* violated.

Classes often contain a `toString` method that returns *in string form* the data in an object. The `toString` method in the `Number` class in Fig. 6.8 performs this function. Line 17 converts a copy of the value of x to string form and returns this string:

```
17          return "" + x;       // return value in x as String
```

The left operand of the plus sign is the null string, `""`. This is the string that contains no characters. It, nevertheless, is a legitimate `String` constant. Because its left operand is a string, the plus sign designates the concatenation operation. The concatenation operation forces the right side (specifically, a copy of the value in x) to be converted to a string. The null string and the converted string are then concatenated, yielding a string that contains the value of x. Because the null string contains no characters, it does not add any characters to the beginning of the resulting string. Its function is simply to trigger the conversion of the value of x to a string. Without it (i.e., if we simply returned x), we would get a compile-time error because you cannot return an `int` value when the return type of a method is `String`.

6.6 Garbage Collection

Suppose we execute the following statement, where Egg is some class:

```
Egg e1 = new Egg();
Egg e2 = new Egg();
```

Then we get two Egg objects, one pointed to by e1, the other pointed to by e2 (see Fig. 6.8a).

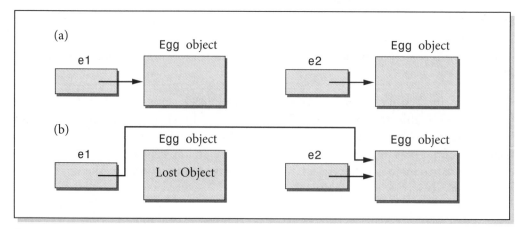

Figure 6.8

Now suppose we execute

```
e1 = e2;
```

This statement assigns to e1 a copy of the reference in e2. As a result, both e1 and e2 now point to the same object, and the original e1 object has no reference pointing to it (see Fig. 6.8b). Thus, we can no longer get to the original e1 object. It has become a **lost object**. Unfortunately, it is still sitting in memory taking up valuable space. However, if the Java interpreter runs out of memory when a Java program is executing, the interpreter will automatically go into **garbage collection mode**. In this mode, it locates and reclaims the memory occupied by lost objects. When the interpreter finishes the garbage collection process, it continues with the execution of the program, using the memory obtained from the garbage-collecting process.

6.7 Accessing Instance Variables and Methods from a Static Method

The OOP4 class in Fig. 6.9 contains two static items (the variable x and the method addOne) and two instance items (the variable y and the method display). We have specified the initial values of x and y right in their declarations (see Lines 3 and 4).

```
 1 class OOP4
 2 {
 3    private static int x = 1;     // static variable
 4    public int y = 2;             // instance variable
 5    //----------------------------------
 6    public static void addOne()   // static method
 7    {
 8       x++;                       // legal
 9       y++;                       // illegal
10       display();                 // illegal
11    }
12    //----------------------------------
13    public void display()         // instance method
14    {
15       System.out.println(x);     // legal
16       System.out.println(y);     // legal
17    }
18 }
19 //================================================
```

Figure 6.9 (continues)

```
20 class TestOOP4
21 {
22    public static void main(String[] args)
23    {
24       OOP4.addOne();
25       OOP4 p = new OOP4();
26       p.display();              // legal
27       System.out.println(p.y);  // legal
28    }
29 }
```

Figure 6.9 (continued)

Because addOne is static, it exists independently of any object. main in Fig. 6.9 can call addOne as soon as it starts executing. addOne then increments x with

```
8       x++;                      // legal
```

Because x is static, it already exists and can be accessed. Thus, this statement is perfectly legal. However, on Line 9, addOne attempts to access y:

```
9       y++;                      // illegal
```

But y is an instance variable. At this point in the execution of the program, there are no y variables in existence. So there is no y that can be incremented. The statement on Line 9 is illegal. But even if there were y instance variables in existence, this statement would still be illegal. Instance variables are accessed via references. But the addOne method has no access to any references (because it is static, a reference is not passed to it when it is called). The compiler will flag Line 9 with the message,

```
non-static variable y cannot be referenced from a static context.
```

For the same reason, the call of display on Line 10 is also illegal:

```
10      display();                // illegal
```

display is an instance method. Thus, it becomes available only when an OOP4 object is created. Moreover, when display is called, it must be provided with a reference for its this parameter. But it is not possible for this call to provide display with the required reference for the following reason: When addOne is called, it is not passed a reference because it is a static method. Thus, it, in turn, has no reference to pass to display. In contrast, the call of display on Line 26 is legal:

```
26      p.display();              // legal
```

This call occurs after an OOP4 object has been created to which p points. The reference in p is passed to the this parameter in the display method. display then uses it to access the instance data to be displayed. Line 27 is also legal because main is accessing y via the reference variable p (and y is public):

```
27       System.out.println(p.y);   // legal
```

Here is an important rule to remember:

> From a static method, you cannot call an instance method or access an instance variable unless it is via a reference to an object that contains that method or variable. However, from an instance method, you can call a static method or access a static variable (see Line 15 in Fig. 6.9).

main in Fig. 6.9 is a static class. But its call of the instance method display (Line 26) and its access of the instance variable y (Line 27) are legal because they are via the reference variable p.

6.8 Private Versus Public Data

Normally, all the data in an object should be private. Private data cannot be accessed directly from outside a class. However, it can be accessed indirectly through public methods. This approach has two important advantages:

1. Public methods that access data often have checks to ensure the integrity of the data. For example, a well-designed method that sets a variable to a test grade in an object would check that the grade is reasonable (i.e., between 0 and 100). Requiring that the variable is set only through this set method (by making the variable private) ensures that integrity checks are performed whenever the variable is set. If, on the other hand, the variable were public, then it could be set directly without any integrity checks.

2. The public methods that access data hide the implementation details of the data. For example, suppose an object holds a collection of numbers. If it has a public method average that returns the average of the numbers, you can simply call this method to get the average. You do not have to know anything about how the numbers are stored in the object. If the format of the data were changed, the implementation of the public methods that access the data would have to change. However, you would still get the average by calling the public average method. Thus, you would not have to change how you interact with the object. If, on the other hand, you computed the average by making direct accesses to the data, you would have to know

how the data is stored. Moreover, you would have to makes changes in your Java code to accommodate any changes in the format of the data. The public methods that access private data in an object provide an unchanging interface to the users of the class. This approach to data access is called **encapsulation** and **information hiding**.

6.9 Named Constants Versus Literal Constants

Suppose we are writing a program that processes the data for a group of 100 employees of a company. The literal constant 100 will probably appear multiple times in our program. For example, to compute the average salary, we would divide the sum of the salaries by 100:

```
averageSalary = sumOfSalaries/100;
```

To display the salary of each employee, we would use a loop whose exit condition included 100:

```
int employeeNumber = 1;
while (employeeNumber <= 100)
{
    .
    .
    .
    employeeNumber++;
}
```

Suppose we use a variable initialized to 100 in our program instead of the literal constant 100. For example, suppose we define a variable named numberOfEmployees using

```
public static int numberOfEmployees = 100;
```

We could then replace all the occurrences of 100 with numberOfEmployees. For example, we would compute the average salary with the same preceding assignment statement as before but with 100 replaced with numberOfEmployees:

```
averageSalary = sumOfSalaries/numberOfEmployees;
```

Three advantages of this approach are

1. The variable name conveys a meaning that the literal constant does not. For example, the literal constant 100 might be 100 employees, 100 chickens, or 100 ice cream

cones. However, the variable name `numberOfEmployees` tells us exactly what it represents.

2. Using a variable makes it easy to modify the program if the constant should change. For example, suppose the company hires three more people. In the program in which we used the literal constant `100` repeatedly, we would have to replace every occurrence of `100` with `103`. However, in the version with the `numberOfEmployees` variable, we would have to change only one `100`—the `100` in the declaration of that variable.

3. If the constant requires many keystrokes, it is easier to enter the variable name than the constant. For example, entering `PI` is easier than entering `3.141592654`.

One danger of using a variable to hold a constant is that the programmer might accidentally assign the variable a new value. Then, of course, any use of that variable would provide an incorrect value. Why would a programmer assign a new value to a variable that is holding a constant? Because all programmers make mistakes. To ensure that this problem cannot occur, we can use a **named constant** instead of a variable to hold a constant. A named constant is a variable whose value is fixed. If you attempt to assign it a new value, you will get a compile-time error.

To create a named constant as a field in a class, simply insert the reserved word `final` before the type in your declaration. For example, the statement

```
public static final int NUMBEROFEMPLOYEES = 100;
```

creates the named constant `NUMBEROFEMPLOYEES` whose value is `final` (i.e., fixed) at `100`. By convention, all the letters in the name of a named constant should be uppercase. That way, you can easily distinguish named constants from the variables in your program. Both `NUMBEROFEMPLOYEES` and `100` are constants. `NUMBEROFEMPLOYEES` is a name that represents a value, so we called it a *named* constant. `100`, on the other hand, is the constant itself, so we call it a *literal* constant.

Named constants do not have to be static. However, it makes sense to make them static if they are declared outside methods. Otherwise, you will get a copy of the constant for each object you create. Why create multiple copies of the same constant when a single static constant will do? Moreover, if a constant is static, it can be accessed by both instance methods and static methods. But if a constant is not static, it cannot be accessed by static methods.

If a named constant is needed only within a method, you should create a named constant that is local to that method. To do this, simply declare and initialize it as you would a local variable but precede the declaration with the reserved word `final`. Do not include the reserved word `static` (it is illegal on local variables). For example, in the following code, we declare a named constant `NUMBEROFSTUDENTS` within the `f` method:

```
public void f()
{
   final int NUMBEROFSTUDENTS = 20;
   ...
}
```

6.10 Summary of Constants and Variables

Let's review the categories of constants and variables we have in Java. We have two categories of constants:

1. Literal constants like `123`, `3.5`, `3.5f`, `'x'`, `"hello"`, `true`, and `false`.
2. Named constants. For example, the following statement creates the named constant `PI`:

   ```
   public static final double PI = 3.141592654;
   ```

We have four categories of variables:

1. Local variables

   These are variables declared within a method. Local variables are created when the method that contains them is called, and destroyed when the method returns to its caller.

   ```
   class C1
   {
      ...
      public void f()
      {
         int w;          // w is a local variable
         ...
      }
   }
   ```

2. Parameters

   These are special variables in a method that receive the values of the arguments in a method call. Parameters are created when the method that contains them is called, and destroyed when the method returns to the caller.

```
class C2
{
   ...
   public void g(int x)      // x is a parameter
   {
      ...
   }
}
```

3. Static variables (also called class variables)

    These are variables created from the static fields in a class when the class is first loaded into memory. Because static variables are associated with a class and not an object, we often call static variables **class variables**. There is only one set of static variables for a class regardless of the number of objects instantiated from the class. Static variables exist independently of objects.

```
class C3
{
   private static int y;     // y is static variable
      ...
}
```

4. Nonstatic variables (also called instance variables)

    These are variables created from nonstatic fields in a class when a class is instantiated. Because a new set of nonstatic variables is created every time an instance of a class is created, we often call nonstatic variables **instance variables**.

```
class C4
{
   private int z;      // z is nonstatic variable
      ...
}
```

We can refer to local constants, local variables, and parameters only within the methods in which they are declared. We can refer to instance and static variables in a class from any method in the same class with one exception: We cannot refer to instance variables from a static method unless it is via a reference.

We can refer to instance variables and static variables from outside a class if they are not private. For external access, however, we have to specify a reference (for instance variables) or the class name (for static variables).

Laboratory 6 Prep

1. What is the scope of a private static variable?
2. What two items are passed to f in the following call:

   ```
   r.f(23);
   ```

3. Under what circumstances, if any, can a static method call an instance method?
4. Why should a named constant that is not inside a method be static?
5. When do class variables come into existence? When do instance variables come into existence?

Laboratory 6

1. What are the errors in the following class? Compile the class to check your answers.

   ```
   class C6e1
   {
       private int x;
       //-----------------------------------
       public void f()
       {
           int y;
           System.out.println(x);
           System.out.println(y);
           static int z = 3;
           System.out.println(z);
       }
   }
   ```

2. Write a class that contains

   ```
   private final int x = 10;
   ```

   and the method

   ```
   public void f()
   {
       x = 5;
   }
   ```

   What happens when you compile the class? Explain.

3. Compile and run the following C6e3 program. It displays the default values for instance variables of various types. Run the program to determine the default value corresponding to each type.

```java
class DefaultValues
{
    private byte b;
    private short s;
    private int i;
    private long l;
    private float f;
    private double d;
    private char c;
    private boolean boo;
    //-------------------------
    public void displayVariables()
    {
        System.out.println(b);
        System.out.println(s);
        System.out.println(i);
        System.out.println(l);
        System.out.println(f);
        System.out.println(d);
        System.out.println(c);
        System.out.println(boo);
    }
}
//=========================================
class C6e3
{
    public static void main(String[] args)
    {
        DefaultValues v = new DefaultValues();
        v.displayVariables();
    }
}
```

4. Add the following constructor to your `DefaultValues` class from Lab Exercise 3:

```java
public DefaultValues(int x)
{
    i = x;
}
```

Make no other changes. Why does your new program fail? Fix the problem.

5. Compile the following class. What happens? What is wrong with the program?

```java
class C6e5
{
    private int x;
    public static void main(String[] args)
```

LABORATORY

```
    {
        x = 1;
        g();
    }
    //-----------------------------------
    public void g()
    {
        System.out.println(x);
    }
}
```

6. Does the following program work? Compare this program with the program in Lab Exercise 5.

```
class C6e6
{
    private int x;
    public static void main(String[] args)
    {
        C6e6 r = new C6e6();
        r.x = 1;
        r.g();
    }
    //-----------------------------------
    public void g()
    {
        System.out.println(x);
    }
}
```

7. Does the following program work? Compare its structure with the program in Lab Exercise 6.

```
class Variation
{
    private int x;
    public void g()
    {
        System.out.println(x);
    }
}
//=================================================
class C6e7
{
    public static void main(String[] args)
    {
        Variation r = new Variation();
        r.x = 1;
```

```
            r.g();

    }
}
```

8. Write a class that contains an instance variable x. This class should also contain a method that has a parameter x. Does the class compile without error? When the method is executing, two x variables exist: the instance variable and the parameter. Your method should assign 99 to x. Which x—the instance variable or the local variable—is assigned 99? Check your answer by adding a second method that displays the instance variable x. Use it to determine if the instance variable is assigned 99 by the first method.

9. The set method in the following program assigns 5 to the local variable x declared within set. Run this program. The call of display will display 1, indicating that the assignment to x within set was to the local x, not to the instance variable x.

```
class WhichX
{
    private int x;
    //---------------------------------
    public WhichX(int a)
    {
        x = a;
    }
    //---------------------------------
    public void set()
    {
        int x;
        x = 5;        // assigns 5 to local x not instance variable x
    }
    //---------------------------------
    public void display()
    {
        System.out.println(x);  // displays instance variable x
    }
}
//=================================================
class C6e9
{
    public static void main(String[] args)
    {
        WhichX r = new WhichX(1);
        r.display();
        r.set();
        r.display();
    }
}
```

Now change the assignment statement in the `set` method to

```
this.x = 5;
```

Compile and run. Which x is assigned 5 now? Whenever we qualify a variable with `this` in an instance method, the variable is treated as an instance variable in the object, even if there is a local variable or parameter with the same name. In the preceding `set` method,

```
x = 5;
```

assigns 5 to the local x. But if we change this statement to

```
this.x = 5;
```

it would then assign 5 to the instance variable x. It is convenient to name a parameter used to initialize an instance variable with the same name as the instance variable. If we do this, we have to use `this` to distinguish between the instance variable and the parameter. For example, we can replace the constructor in the preceding program with the following:

```
public WhichX(int x)    // parameter has same name as variable
{
    this.x = x;    // x is the parameter, this.x is instance variable
}
```

Here both the parameter and the instance variable are named x. Within the constructor, we refer to the instance variable using `this.x`, and we refer to the parameter using x alone. Thus, the statement

```
this.x = x;
```

assigns the parameter x to the instance variable x.

10. Move the main method in the `TestOOP1` class in Fig. 6.1 into the `OOP1` class. Delete the `TestOOP1` class. Now the complete program is in the `OOP1` class. Enter

```
javac OOP1
java OOP1
```

Does the new program work the same way the original program works? In the new program, only `main` and x are initially available because they are static. `main` creates the n and m objects as in the original program and then proceeds as in the original program. The only difference is that `main` is now in the `OOP1` class.

Homework 6

1. Create a class named Point. It should have instance variables x and y of type double whose values define the location of a point on the *x-y* plane. Include a constructor with no parameters that assigns 0.0 to x and y. Include a second constructor with two parameters that sets the values of x and y to whatever values you pass the constructor. Your class should have a method named distanceFromOrigin that returns the distance of the point defined by x and y from the origin (i.e., the point (0.0, 0.0)). Your class should also have a second method toString that returns a string representing the values of x and y. For example, if *x* and *y* are both 1.0, then toString should return the string "(1.0, 1.0)". Test your program with the following main method:

```
public static void main(String[] args)
{
    Point p = new Point();
    System.out.println(p.toString() + " is this far from origin: " +
                    p.distanceFromOrigin());
    p = new Point(3, 4);
    System.out.println(p.toString() + " is this far from origin: " +
                    p.distanceFromOrigin());
}
```

(*Hint:* The distance of the point (x, y) from (0.0, 0.0) is the square root of the sum of the squares of x and y. To determine the square root of a double value, call the method Math.sqrt, passing it the value for which you need the square root. This method will then return the square root as a double value. For example, to find the square root of the value in sum and assign it to d, use

```
d = Math.sqrt(sum);
```

sqrt is a static method in the Math class. Thus, it is called via the name of its class.)

2. Add a method distance to your program for Homework Exercise 1. The distance method should have one parameter of type Point. It should return the distance between the point in the object containing the called method and the point it is passed. For example, in the following code, distance returns the distance between the p1 and p2 points:

```
Point p1 = new Point(1.0, -2.0);
Point p2 = new Point(5.0, 6,0);
System.out.println(p1.distance(p2));
```

Write a program that tests your new Point class. Use the distance method to determine the distance between the point (1.0, -2.0) and (5.0, 6.0). (*Hint:* To compute the distance between two points, square the difference of the two x values, square the difference of the two y values, add these two squares, and take the square root of the result.)

3. Draw a picture of the structure the following program creates. What will eventually happen when it is executed?

```
class Node
{
    public Node link;
    public long count;
}
//=====================================================
class C6h3
{
    public static void main(String[] args)
    {
        long i = 1;
        Node first = null, p;
        while (true)
        {
            p = new Node();
            p.count = i++;
            p.link = first;
            first = p;
        }
    }
}
```

Change the while loop in the C6h3 class to

```
while(true)
{
    p = new Node();
    p.count = i++;
}
```

What impact does this change have on the ultimate behavior of the program?

4. A **rational number** is any number that can be expressed as the ratio of two integers. A rational number can be represented by two integers: the numerator and the dominator. Create a RationalNumber class according to the following specifications:

Data fields: `int numerator, int denominator`

Constructor: `public RationalNumber(int n, int d)`

Instance Methods: `public RationalNumber add(RationalNumber r)`

Adds the rational number in the object containing the called method and the rational number in the r object. Returns a new `RationalNumber` object that contains the sum.

`public RationalNumber multiply(RationalNumber r)`

Multiplies the rational number in the object containing the called method and the rational number in the r object. Returns a new `RationalNumber` object that contains the product.

`public void reduce()`

Reduces the rational number to lowest terms. Does not create a new object.

`public String toString()`

Returns a string represesenting the value of the rational number. The string returned should include the slash character between the numerator and denominator. For example, if numerator and denominator are 5 and 7, respectively, then `to-String` returns the string `"5/7"`.

Write a program that uses your `RationalNumber` class. Your program should add 3/7 and 7/3 and display the result. It should also multiply 3/7 and 7/3, put the result in reduced form, and display the result.

CHAPTER 7

Constructing Objects: Part 2

OBJECTIVES

- Learn different techniques to initialize instance variables
- Understand the ramifications of passing a reference versus a primitive type
- Learn how to create a copy constructor
- Understand shallow versus deep copies
- Understand and fix privacy leaks

7.1 Initializing Instance Variables

Instance variables can be initialized by a constructor. For example, in Fig. 7.1, the fields x and y are initialized to 0 and 1, respectively, by the constructor.

What happens if an instance variable is not explicitly initialized? Then its initial value is the default value it is given when it is created by the Java interpreter. The default value for arithmetic instance variables is zero. Thus, if we omitted Line 7 in Fig. 7.1, x would still have an initial value of zero. Figure 7.2 shows the default values corresponding to every

```
1 class Initialize1
2 {
3     private int x, y;
4     //--------------------------------
5     public Initialize1()
6     {
7         x = 0;          // initialize instance variables
8         y = 1;
9     }
10    //--------------------------------
11    public void displaySum()
12    {
13        System.out.println(x + y);
14    }
15 }
```

Figure 7.1

Type	Default value of instance variable
byte	0
short	0
int	0
long	0
float	0.0f
double	0.0
char	space
boolean	false
any class	null

Figure 7.2

possible type. null is the default value for reference variables. null can be assigned to any reference variable, regardless of its type. null, however, does not point anywhere.

Although Line 7 in Fig. 7.1 is unnecessary, most programmers would prefer to include it for two reasons:

1. Not everyone knows that instance variables not explicitly initialized get default values. Explicit initialization makes clear what the initial values will be.
2. If Java were changed so that instance variables were given different default values or not given default values at all, classes that relied on the current default values would no longer compile to the correct bytecode.

Note that local variables (i.e., variables declared inside a method) do *not* have default initial values. For example, in the following method, the local variable z has no initial value:

```java
public void f()
{
    int z;                      // uninitialized local variable
    System.out.println(z);    // compile-time error
}
```

Thus, it makes no sense to display the value of z with a println statement unless z is first given a value. The compiler will flag the println statement in this method with the message, variable z might not have been initialized.

Another approach to initialization is to initialize fields in the declarations of those fields. For example, in Fig. 7.3, we are initializing y to 1 in its declaration.

x is initialized to 0 by default. y is explicitly initialized to 1. If 0 and 1 are the initial values we want for x and y, respectively, we do not need to define a constructor for this class. But

```
                                    Default constructor

1 class Initialize2
2 {
3     private int x, y = 1;                    public Initialize2
4     //-------------------------------        {
5     public void displaySum()                 }
6     {
7         System.out.println(x + y);
8     }
9 }
```

Figure 7.3

every class must have a constructor. Thus, if you do not include one, the compiler inserts a default constructor into the bytecode it generates. It translates the class in Fig. 7.3 as if it contained the default constructor.

The default constructor inserted by the compiler has no parameters. Thus, we should pass it no arguments when we call it. For example, to create an object from the Initialize2 class, and assign its reference to r, use

```
Initialize2 r = new Initialize2();
```

In Fig. 7.3, we are initializing the y field in the statement that declares it. Because we can do this, you may be wondering why have constructors. Can we not simply initialize fields in their declarations and do away with constructors? No, we cannot, because constructors provide a flexibility that initializations in declarations cannot. For example, in Fig. 7.4, the constructor initializes the x and y fields. The constructor is parameterized so we can specify the initial values of x and y when we call the constructor. For example, the statement

```
Initialize3 p = new Initialize3(2, 3);
```

constructs an object and initializes x and y to 2 and 3, respectively. Similarly, the statement

```
Initialize3 q = new Initialize3(4, 5);
```

constructs another object and initializes x and y to 4 and 5, respectively. Because of the constructor, we can specify the initial values of x and y when we construct the object.

```
 1 class Initialize3
 2 {
 3     private int x, y;
 4     //-----------------------------------
 5     public Initialize3(int xx, int yy)
 6     {
 7         x = xx;      // init instance variable x with parameter xx
 8         y = yy;      // init instance variable y with parameter yy
 9     }
10     //-----------------------------------
11     public void displaySum()
12     {
13         System.out.println(x + y);
14     }
15 }
```

Figure 7.4

If, however, we initialize x and y in their declarations, then their initial values are fixed. We cannot specify the initial values we want when we construct the object. For example, in Fig. 7.3, the initial values of x and y are always 0 and 1, respectively.

7.2   Passing Primitive Types Versus Passing References

When we call a method, the values of the arguments in the call are automatically assigned to their corresponding parameters in the called method. The arguments and parameters are distinct. Thus, if the called method changes the values of its parameters, it has no effect on the corresponding arguments. For example, on Line 22 in Fig. 7.5a, main calls the change method. Note that the change method is overloaded. The call on Line 22 calls the change method that starts on Line 30.

```
(a)

 1  class SideEffect
 2  {
 3     private int x = 1;
 4     //---------------------------------
 5     public void xSet(int xx)
 6     {
 7        x = xx;
 8     }
 9     //---------------------------------
10     public int xGet()
12     {
13        return x;
14     }
15  }
16  //=================================================
17  class TestSideEffect
18  {
19     public static void main(String[] args)
20     {
21        int p = 1;                          // p is 1 here
22        change(p);
23        System.out.println(p);              // p is still 1
24
25        SideEffect r = new SideEffect();    // x is 1 here
```

Figure 7.5   (continues)

```
26          change(r);
27          System.out.println(r.xGet());       // x is 2 here
28      }
29      //-----------------------------------
30      public static void change(int q)
31      {
32          q = 2;                              // does not affect p
33      }
34      //-----------------------------------
35      public static void change(SideEffect t)
36      {
37          t.xSet(2);                          // assigns 2 to x
38      }
39 }
```

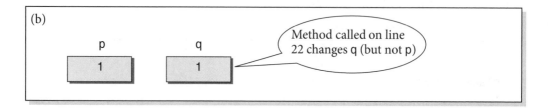

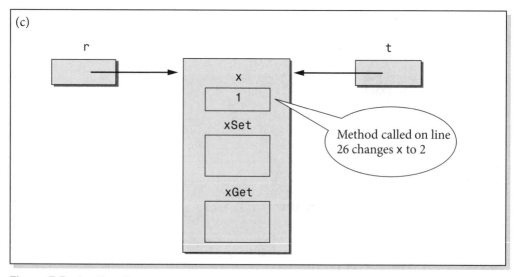

Figure 7.5   (continued)

When this call is executed, the value of p (which is 1) is assigned to the parameter q in change. p and q are separate slots in memory (see Fig. 7.5b). Thus, when change assigns 2 to q on Line 32, only q is affected. The value in p stays at 1.

Now consider what happens when on Line 26 main calls change, passing it the reference r. This call calls the change method that starts on Line 35. The value in the argument r (which is a pointer to an object) is passed to its corresponding parameter t. Thus, r and t point to the same object (see Fig. 7.5c). The change method can now access this object via t. On Line 37, it calls the xSet method, the effect of which is to set to 2 the x instance variable in the object. change cannot change the argument r by changing t because r and t are separate slots. Any change to t will not affect r. However, change *can change the object to which* r *points* because its parameter t points to the same object.

The two calls of change in Fig. 7.5 illustrate a fundamental difference between passing a value whose type is primitive and passing a reference. When a call passes an argument with a primitive type, the called method cannot affect the argument. When a call passes a reference, the called method similarly cannot affect the argument. However, *it can affect the object to which that reference points.*

7.3 Copy Constructor

Constructors can be overloaded. The program in Fig. 7.6 has two constructors. The call of the constructor on Line 20 calls the constructor that starts on Line 5; the call of the constructor on Line 21 calls the copy constructor that starts on Line 10.

```
 1 class Con1
 2 {
 3     private int x;
 4     //---------------------------------
 5     public Con1(int xx)        // first constructor
 6     {
 7         x = xx;
 8     }
 9     //---------------------------------
10     public Con1(Con1 original) // copy constructor
11     {
12         x = original.x;
13     }
14 }
```

Figure 7.6 (continues)

```
15 //====================================================
16 class TestCon1
17 {
18    public static void main(String[] args)
19    {
20        Con1 c1 = new Con1(5);    // calls first constructor
21        Con1 c2 = new Con1(c1);   // calls second constructor
22    }
23 }
```

Figure 7.6 (continued)

The first constructor initializes the x variable in the new object with the value it is passed. Thus, the statement

20   `Con1 c1 = new Con1(5);    // calls first constructor`

creates an object whose x variable is initialized to 5. The second constructor also initializes x. But it is not passed the initial value of x. Instead, it is passed a reference to a Con1 object:

21   `Con1 c2 = new Con1(c1);   // calls second constructor`

This constructor initializes the x field in the new object by assigning it the value of the x field from the Con1 object it is passed. The effect is to create a copy of the object it is passed. After this statement is executed, we have two identical objects, one pointed to by c1 and one pointed to by c2 (see Fig. 7.7).

A constructor that creates a copy of the object it is passed is called a **copy constructor**.

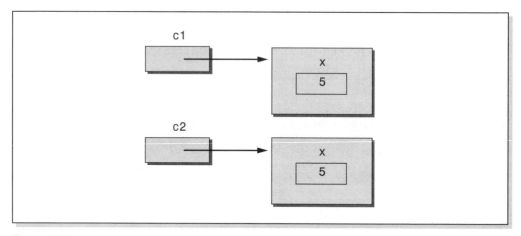

Figure 7.7

Let's examine the copy constructor in Fig. 7.6 (Lines 10–13). When it is executed, the x instance variable in the new object has already been created. The copy constructor has to initialize this x to the value of x in the object to be copied. Note that the parameter in the copy constructor is original:

```
10      public Con1(Con1 original) // copy constructor
```

Thus, original receives the reference to the object to be copied. To create an identical copy of this object, the copy constructor simply executes

```
12          x = original.x;
```

This statement assigns original.x (the value of x in the object to be copied) to x (the x in the new object). Although x is private, both accesses of x are legal because they are from inside the Con1 class.

The copy constructor in Fig. 7.6 simply copies the x field in the original object to the corresponding field in the new object. Unfortunately, the job of the copy constructor is not always this simple. For example, consider the Con2 class in Fig. 7.8.

Suppose we create a Con2 object with

```
Con2 p1 = new Con2();
```

We get the structure in Fig. 7.9a. The Con2 object contains a reference that points to a D object. We use the phrase "**has a**" to describe this relationship: We say a Con2 object has a D object. Let's now create a copy of the p1 object using the copy constructor using

```
Con2 p2 = Con2(p1);        // use copy constructor
```

```
 1 class Con2
 2 {
 3     private D r;                 // r is a reference
 4     //----------------------------------
 5     public Con2()
 6     {
 7         r = new D();
 8     }
 9     //----------------------------------
10     public Con2(Con2 original)  // copy constructor
11     {
12         r = original.r;    // bad—replace with r = new D(original.r);
13     }
14 }
```

Figure 7.8

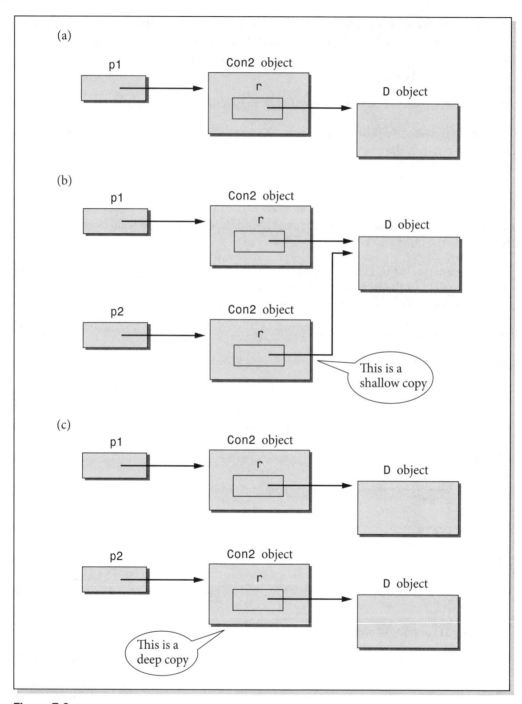

Figure 7.9

Because the copy constructor in Fig. 7.8 simply copies the r field from the object to be copied to the r field of the new object, we get the structure in Fig. 7.9b.

The p1 and p2 objects are identical, but they are not independent. Their r fields point to the *same* D object. Thus, if we change the D object in the structure to which p1 points, we are simultaneously changing the D object in the structure to which p2 points, and vice versa.

A copy constructor should create a completely independent copy. Changes in the original should not affect the copy and vice versa. If D has its own copy constructor, we can fix our copy constructor by simply replacing Line 12 in Fig. 7.8 with

```
r = new D(original.r);
```

Here, we are constructing a new D object using the copy constructor for D. We are passing it the reference to the original D object. The new D object will be identical to the original. We then assign its reference to the r field in the new Con2 object. Thus, we no longer have a shared D object (see Fig. 7.9c). The Con2 structure created by our new copy constructor is completely independent of the original.

An **immutable object** is one that cannot be changed once it is created. Suppose D objects were immutable. Then the p2 object in Fig. 7.9b would be a perfectly satisfactory copy of the p1 object. Although it shares a D object with the p1 object, it would not be able to affect the p1 object, and vice versa, because the common object is immutable.

The Con3 class program in Fig. 7.10a has two instance variables: r and x. Because r has type String, and a String object is immutable, the copy constructor does not have to create a copy of the String object to which r in the original object points. Instead, it can simply copy r in the original object to r in the new object with

```
14        r = original.r;              // simple copy ok
```

The x field has a primitive type. So it, too, can simply be copied from the original object to the new one with

```
15        x = original.x               // simple copy for primitives
```

When the program in Fig. 7.10a executes, it creates the structure shown in Fig. 7.10b. The two Con3 objects share a common String object.

A copy of an object obtained from the original by simply copying the fields in the original is called a **shallow copy**. For example, the copy constructor in Fig. 7.8 creates a shallow

(a)

```
 1 class Con3
 2 {
 3     private String r;
 4     private int x;
 5     //---------------------------------
 6     public Con3(String rr, int xx)
 7     {
 8         r = rr;
 9         x = xx;
10     }
11     //---------------------------------
12     public Con3(Con3 original)    // copy constructor
13
14         r = original.r;           // simple copy ok
15         x = original.x;           // simple copy ok for primitives
16     }
17 }
18 //===================================================
19 class TestCon3
20 {   public static void main(String[] args) {
21         Con3 m1 = new Con3("hello", 7);
22         Con3 m2 = new Con3(m1);
23 }                                              }
```

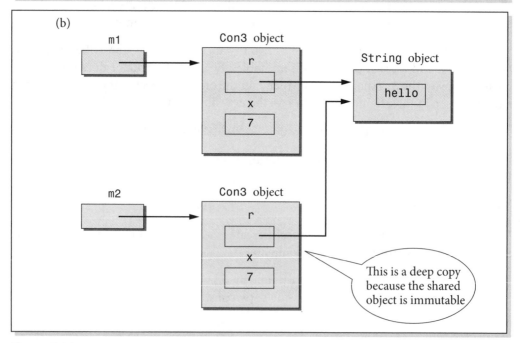

Figure 7.10

copy. If the entire structure associated with a copy shares no references with the original except to immutable objects, it is called a **deep copy**. By replacing

```
12        r = original.r;                        // bad
```

in the copy constructor in Fig. 7.8 with

```
r = new D(original.r);
```

we get a copy constructor that creates a deep copy (assuming the copy constructor for D also creates a deep copy). The copy constructor in Fig. 7.10a also creates a deep copy because the shared String object is immutable. Unless special conditions dictate otherwise, a copy constructor should make a deep copy of the object it is passed.

7.4 Fixing Privacy Leaks Using Copy Constructors

The Leaks class in Fig. 7.11 looks like a reasonable class. It has one field (r), two constructors including a copy constructor, an accessor method (rGet), and a mutator method (rSet).

```
1 class Leaks
2 {
3     private D r;
4     //-----------------------------------
5     public Leaks(D rr)
6     {
7         r = new D();
8     }
9     //-----------------------------------
10    public Leaks(Leaks original) // copy constructor
11    {
12        r = original.r;               // bad: creates shallow copy
13    }
14    //-----------------------------------
15    public D rGet()
16    {
17        return r;                // bad: gives direct access to r object
18    }
19    //-----------------------------------
20    public void rSet(D rr)
21    {
22        r = rr;                  // bad: gives direct access to r object
23    }
24 }
```

Figure 7.11

However, the lines in Fig. 7.11 that are commented with "bad" (Lines 12, 17, and 22) all have a serious shortcoming associated with them. We will use calls to copy constructors to fix these shortcomings.

From our discussion in the preceding section, we already know what is wrong with Line 12 in the copy constructor: it creates a shallow copy because it simply copies the reference variable in the original object to the reference variable in the new object. Thus, the r field in the new object points to the same D object as the r field in the original object. To fix this problem, we replace Line 12 with

```
r = new D(original.r);
```

Then r in the new object will point to a new D object, rather than sharing the D object with the original Leaks object.

The second problem in Fig. 7.11 occurs in the accessor method rGet. Suppose p points to a Leaks object, and we execute

```
D d = p.rGet();
```

The rGet method returns the reference in r in the Leaks object, which is then assigned to d. Thus, both r in the Leaks object and d point to the same D object (see Fig. 7.12a).

We now can use d to directly access the object to which it and the Leaks object point. Thus, although r is private in the Leaks class, *the object to which it points is not secure—* that is, we can access it from outside the Leaks class via d. We call this problem a **privacy leak**. To fix it, replace Line 17 in Fig. 7.11 with

```
return new D(r);
```

Then, rather than returning the reference in r, rGet returns a reference to a copy of the D object created by the copy constructor for D (see Fig. 7.12b). Thus, if we execute

```
D d = p.rGet();
```

and then use d, we do not access the D object to which the `private` field r in the p object points.

The third problem in Fig. 7.11 occurs in the mutator method rSet. Suppose p points to a Leaks object. If we execute

```
D d = new D();
p.rSet(d);
```

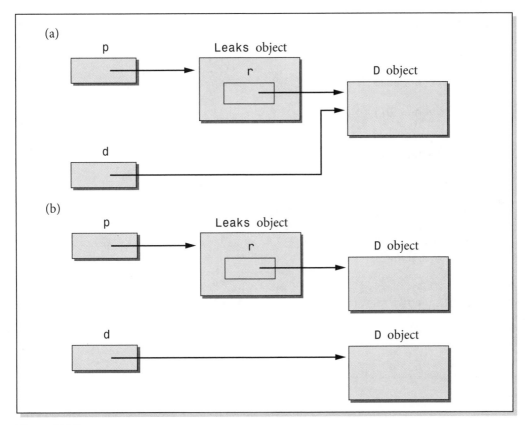

Figure 7.12

then rSet assigns d to the r field in the Leaks object to which p points. Thus, both d and r point to the same D object (see Fig. 7.12a). We now can use d to directly access the object to which the p object points. Here again, we have a privacy leak: although r is private in the Leaks class, the object to which it points is not secure. That is, we can access it from outside the Leaks class via d. To fix this problem, we again use the copy constructor for D: We replace Line 22 in the mutator method with

```
r = new D(rr);
```

Then r and d will point to different objects (see Fig. 7.12b). Thus, we will not be able to access the D object associated with the p object via d.

Fig. 7.11 modified with all our corrections appears in Fig. 7.13.

```
 1 class NoLeaks
 2 {
 3    private D r;
 4    //-----------------------------------
 5    public NoLeaks(D rr)
 6    {
 7       r = new D();
 8    }
 9    //-----------------------------------
10    public NoLeaks(NoLeaks original)   // copy constructor
11    {
12       r = new D(original.r);          // now ok
13    }
14    //-----------------------------------
15    public D rGet()
16    {
17       return new D(r);                // now ok
18    }
19    //-----------------------------------
20    public void rSet(D rr)
21    {
22       r = new D(rr);                  // now ok
23    }
24 }
```

Figure 7.13

Laboratory 7 Prep

1. How do instance variables differ from local variables with respect to default values?

2. Can an instance variable be initialized in its declaration?

3. Suppose x is a local variable with type int. Can the following call affect the value of x? Explain.

```
f(x);
```

4. Suppose all the fields of a class are private and have primitive types. Is it possible for the class to have privacy leaks?

5. Why does Line 14 in Fig. 7.10a not invoke the copy constructor for String?

Laboratory 7

1. What is displayed when the following program is executed. Determine your answer first by inspection. Then check your answer by running the program.

```java
class Counter
{
    private static int count1;
    private int count2;
    //------------------------------------
    public Counter()
    {
        count1++;   // add 1 to count1
        count2++;   // add 1 to count2
    }
    //------------------------------------
    public display()
    {
        System.out.println("count1 = " + count1);
        System.out.println("count2 = " + count2);
    }
}
//==================================================
class C7e1
{
    public static void main(String[] args)
    {
        int i = 1;
        Counter r = new Counter();
```

LABORATORY

```
        while (i++ <= 100)
            r = new Counter();
        r.display();
    }
}
```

2. What is wrong with the following constructor?

```
public C7e2()
{
    C7e2 r;
    r = new C7e2();
}
```

Run a test program to check your answer.

3. Is it legal to initialize a static variable in a constructor for a class? Run a test program to check your answer. Why would it generally not be a good idea to initialize static variables in a constructor?

4. Create a `MyRectangle` class according to these specifications (x are y are the coordinates of the upper left corner of the rectangle):

Fields:

```
private double x;
private double y;
private double width;
private double height;
```

Constructors

```
public MyRectangle(double newX, double newY,
        double newWidth, double newHeight)
```

Assigns newX, newY, newWidth, and newHeight to x, y, width, and height, respectively.

```
public MyRectange(MyRectangle r)
```

Copy constructor

Instances methods:

```
public void set(double newX, double newY,
                double newWidth, double newHeight)
```

Assigns newX, newY, newWidth, and newHeight to x, y, width, and height, respectively.

```
public String toString()
```

Returns a string with the values of x, y, width, and height in the following format:

```
x = ___    y = ___    width = ___    height = ___
```

```
public double area()
```

Returns the area of the rectangle.

```
public void move(double xChange, double yChange)
```

Adds xChange to x, and adds yChange to y

Also write a class TestMyRectangle that tests your MyRectangle class. The main method of TestMyRectangle should

a) Create an object from your MyRectangle class in which all the fields are initially zero.

b) Display the initial values of x, y, width, and heigth.

c) Set x to 2.0, y to 3.0, width to 4.5, and height to 5.1.

d) Display x, y, width, and height.

e) Display the area.

f) Move the rectangle to the right 2.5 units and down 3.0 units.

g) Display x, y, width, and height.

h) Display the area.

i) Create a second MyRectangle object by calling the copy constructor.

j) Display x, y, width, and height of the new object.

Homework 7

1. Write a Clock class according to the following specifications:

Fields:

```
private int seconds;
private int minutes;
private int hours;
```

Constructors:

```
public Clock(int s, int m, int h)
```

Initializes the instance variables seconds, minutes, and hours to the parameters s, m, and h, respectively.

```
public Clock(Clock r)
```

Copy constructor

Instance methods:

```
public void setTime(int s, int m, int h)
```

Sets the instance variables seconds, minutes, and hours to the parameters s, m, and h, respectively.

```
public void tick()
```

Adds 1 to seconds. seconds wraps around at 60 seconds to 0, in which case tick adds 1 to minutes. minutes similarly wraps around at 60 minutes to 0, in which case tick adds 1 to hours. hours similarly wraps around at 24 hours to 0.

```
public String toString()
```

returns a string containing the values of seconds, minutes, and hours in the following format:

```
seconds = ___  minutes = ___  hours   = ___
```

```
private void incrementMinutes()
```

Adds 1 to minutes. minutes and hours wrap around at 60 and 24, respectively.

```
private void incrementHours()
```

Add 1 to hours. hours wraps around at 24 hours to 0.

Use named constants to hold the wrap-around values for seconds, minutes, and hours (60, 60, and 24). Write a test program that constructs a Clock object, sets seconds, minutes, and hours to 58, 59, and 23, respectively. Then call tick four times. Display the time after each call of tick. Then create a copy with the copy constructor. Display the time in the new clock.

2. Same as Homework Exercise 1 but add a changeMode method that changes the mode: 12 hour to 24 hour, or 24 hour to 12 hour. In either the 24- or 12-hour mode, the clock should record hours as a number from 0 to 23. However, in the 12-hour mode, the toString method should return the time as a 12-hour time, labeled with a.m., p.m., noon, or midnight, as required. Initially, a Clock object should be in the 24-hour mode. Write a test program that checks all the features of your enhanced clock.

For example, make sure it correctly progresses from a.m. to noon to p.m., and from p.m. to midnight to a.m. when in either 12-hour or 24-hour mode.

3. Create classes C1, C2, and C3 as follows:

   C1 has an instance variable r1 whose type in C2.

   C2 has an instance variable r2 whose type is C3.

   C3 has an instance variable x whose type is int.

   Each class should have a parameterless constructor. The C1 constructor should create a C2 object and assign r1 its reference. Similarly, the C2 constructor should create a C3 object and assign r2 its reference. The C3 constructor should initialize x to 7. Each class should also have a copy constructor. Your main method should create a C1 object and then create a copy using the copy constructor for C1. main should then change the value of x associated with the first C1 object from 7 to 11 (add set methods to your classes to allow this). It should then display the x value associated with both C1 objects.

4. Create a MinimalChange class that has two instance methods: deposit and change. deposit accepts and accumulates deposits. Amounts are passed to the deposit method in units of cents. For example, to deposit $5.25, you would pass the deposit method 525. change returns in string form the current balance using the *minimum* pieces of currency. For example, if the current balance is $26.61, then change would return one twenty-dollar bill, one five-dollar bill, one one-dollar bill, two quarters, one dime, and one penny. change also sets the deposit amount to zero. Assume the change method has an unlimited supply of pennies, nickels, dimes, quarters, one-, five-, ten-, and twenty-dollar bills. Test change on the following balances: $0.00, $0.01, $0.09, $0.10, $0.57, $4.99, $31.33, and $1234.56.

5. Create an ExamResults class that has four instance methods: record, average, max, min, and count. record enters a grade (an integer between 0 and 100). average, max, min, and count report on the grades entered so far. average, min, and count return the average, minimum, and maximum grades, respectively. count returns the number of grades entered. record should perform an integrity check on the grade it is passed (it should check that the grade is between 0 and 100). Write a program to test your class. Assume grades are integers. However, average should return the average grade as a double value.

Using Predefined Classes

8.1 Java Class Library

A class is a functional unit of a Java program. It provides us not only with methods that perform some task but also data fields on which the methods operate.

When we create a Java program, we usually do not have to write all the classes we need. We can often use classes that someone else has already written. Indeed, one of the beauties of Java is that there are so many predefined classes we can use. Thus, when we create a program, much of the work is often already done for us in the form of these predefined classes. The library of predefined classes that comes with Java is called the **Java Class Library** or the **Application Programming Interface** (API).

Classes in Java are organized into groups called **packages**. Each package has a name. The packages that we use in this chapter are the java.lang and java.util packages. These two packages each contain many classes. In this chapter, we will examine only a few of the classes in each of these packages. In the java.lang package, we will examine the String, StringBuffer, Math, and the "wrapper" classes (i.e., classes that "wrap" the primitive types). In the java.util package, we will examine the Random and Scanner classes.

There are so many classes available in Java that it is not possible to remember how to use all of them. Fortunately, you do not have to do this. Whenever you need information on a class, you should simply consult a Java class reference. To access a class reference online, go to http://www.java.sun.com and follow the links to the APIs. Alternatively, use a search engine to search for the class name plus the word "java." There is, however, a small subset of classes you should learn to use. In this chapter and in Chapters 9, 12, and 13, we describe these classes and their most commonly used methods.

8.2 import Statement

All the classes in the java.lang package are available to us via their class names when we write a Java program. That is, if we need them, we simply use their class names in our programs. However, the classes in the other packages are not similarly available. To use them, we have to indicate to the compiler in which package they are located. We do this with an import statement at the beginning of our program. For example, to use the Random class, we need the following import statement:

```
import java.util.Random;
```

This statement indicates that the Random class is in the java.util package. When we then use the name Random in our program, the compiler will know that we want the

Random class in the `java.util` package. `java.util.Random` is the **fully qualified name** of the Random class in the `java.util` package. It indicates not only the class (Random) but also the package to which the class belongs (`java.util`).

The preceding `import` statement imports only one class. Alternatively, we can import all the classes in a package. To do this, use an asterisk in place of the class name in the `import` statement. For example, to import all the classes in the `java.util` package, use

```
import java.util.*;
```

An alternative to using `import` statements is to use fully qualified class names in our program. For example, if we use `java.util.Random` in place of `Random` in our program, we would then not need an `import` statement for the `Random` class. Using fully qualified names, however, is generally less convenient than using an `import` statement.

8.3 String Class

Let's review and expand on what we learned about the `String` class in Chapter 1. The `String` class is in the package `java.lang`. All the classes in this package are automatically available to us—we do not need to import them or use their fully qualified names.

As we learned in Chapter 6, to construct an object from a class, we use the `new` operator and a call of a constructor for that class. For example, let's create a `String` object that contains the string `hello`. We first create the reference variable:

```
String s;
```

We then trigger the construction of the object with the `new` operator and a call of a constructor, passing it `"hello"`:

```
s = new String("hello");
```

Alternatively, we can combine both statements into one:

```
String s = new String("hello");
```

Either way, we get the object shown in Fig. 8.1. It contains the string `"hello"` (without the quotes) plus a collection of methods that operate on that string.

We will discuss only the most important methods in the `String` class. For complete information on the `String` class, consult a Java class reference.

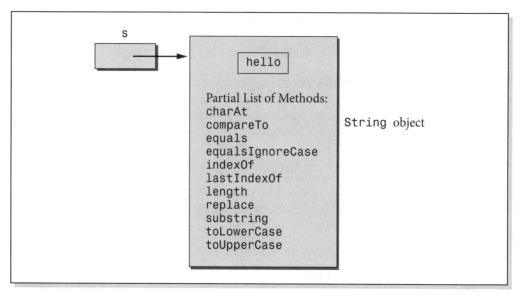

Figure 8.1

Strings are used so often in Java programs that Java allows a String object to be created without an explicit call of a String constructor. To create a String object, we can simply write the string constant. For example, instead of

```
s = new String("hello");
```

we can simply use

```
s = "hello";
```

In both cases, a reference to a String object containing hello is assigned to s. Don't be confused by the second assignment statement shown. It is not assigning the string itself to s—it is assigning the reference to the string to s (see Fig. 8.1).

If we call println and pass it a value with a primitive type, println displays the value it is passed. For example, if x is an int variable that contains 5, and we execute

```
System.out.println(x);
```

println displays the value it is passed (5 in this example). However, println behaves differently if we pass it a reference to a String object: *it displays the string to which the reference points—not the reference itself.* For example, if we execute

```
String s = "hello";
System.out.println(s);
```

then `println` displays `hello`—not the reference in `s` that is passed to `println`.

Let's examine some of the methods in a `String` object. Suppose `s` points to a `String` object that contains `hello`. Each character in the string `hello` has an index that indicates its position in the string. Indices start at zero. Thus, `h` in `hello` has the index 0; `e` has the index 1, and so on. The `charAt` method returns a copy of the character at the specified index. For example, to get a copy of the character at index 1 (the letter `e`) and assign it to the `char` variable `c`, use

```
c = s.charAt(1);       // returns char in s string at index 1
```

We can determine the lexicographic order of two strings using the `compareTo` method. Lexicographic order is essentially alphabetical order extended to include all characters. Suppose `s1` and `s2` point to two `String` objects. If we call the `compareTo` method in the `s1` object with

```
s1.compareTo(s2)
```

then this method has access to two strings:

1. the `s1` string because the `compareTo` method that is called here is in the `s1` object so it has access to the string data in that object.
2. the `s2` string because `s2` is the argument passed to `compareTo`.

`compareTo` compares these two strings and takes one of the following actions depending on the result of the comparison:

- If the `s1` string precedes lexicographically the `s2` string, `compareTo` returns a negative `int` value.
- If the `s1` string equals the `s2` string, `compareTo` returns 0.
- If the `s1` string follows lexicographically the `s2` string, `compareTo` returns a positive `int` value.

For example, the following code displays the `s1` and `s2` strings in lexicographic order:

```
if (s1.compareTo(s2) < 0)
{
    System.out.println(s1);
    System.out.println(s2);
}
else
{
    System.out.println(s2);
    System.out.println(s1);
}
```

The equals method compares two strings for equality. Its return type is boolean. It returns true if the strings are equal, and false otherwise. For example, to display whether the s1 and s2 strings are equal, we can use

```
if (s1.equals(s2))
    System.out.println("They are equal");
else
    System.out.println("They are not equal");
```

It would be incorrect to test two String objects for equality with the "==" operator. For example, suppose s1 and s2 point to different objects. Then the code

```
if (s1 == s2)
    System.out.println("They are equal");
else
    System.out.println("They are not equal");
```

would necessarily display They are not equal regardless of the contents of the two String objects. The expression s1 == s2 compares the two references, not the two objects to which they point. Thus, if s1 and s2 point to different objects, s1 == s2 evaluates to false.

equalsIgnoreCase works exactly like equals except that the comparison is case insensitive. For example, when comparing hello and Hello, equals returns false but equalsIgnoreCase returns true.

indexOf returns the index of the starting point of the first occurrence of the specified substring. For example, if s points to a String object containing hello, the following statement would assign 3, the starting index of the substring lo in the string hello, to i:

```
int i = s.indexOf("lo");   // assign starting index of lo
```

lastIndexOf works the same way as indexOf except that it returns the index of the last occurrence of the specified substring.

replace replaces all occurrences of one character with another. It creates a new String object to hold the modified string. The original String object is unchanged (remember, String objects are immutable). For example, suppose s1 is a reference that points to a String object that contains meet. If we then execute

```
s2 = s1.replace('e', 'o');   // replace 'e' with 'o'
```

replace creates a new String object that contains moot and returns its reference. This reference is then assigned to s2, whose type should be String (see Fig. 8.2a). The String object to which s1 points still contains meet. Now suppose we execute

```
s1 = s1.replace('m', 'B');   // replace 'm' with 'B'
```

Here again, `replace` creates a new `String` object. This time, however, the reference to the new object is assigned to `s1`, overlaying the reference to the original object (see Fig. 8.2b). If there are no other references to the original object, it is lost—we can no longer access it.

`substring` extracts a copy of the substring that starts at the specified index. It creates a new `String` object to hold the substring. For example, if `s1` points to a `String` object containing `hello`, the following statement would extract `ello` from `hello` (1 is the index of `e` in `hello`), create a new object containing the substring, and assign its reference to `s2`:

```
s2 = s1.substring(1);      // extracts substring from index 1 to end
```

If a second index is specified in a call of `substring`, the substring starting at the first index and ending just before the second index is extracted. For example, the call of `substring` in the following statement extracts the substring that consists of the characters at indices 1, 2, and 3 (but not 4):

```
s2 = s1.substring(1, 4);   // extracts substring from index 1 through 3
```

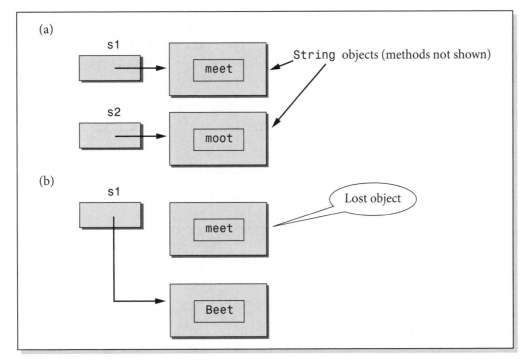

Figure 8.2

length returns the number of characters in the string. For example, if s points to a String object that contains hello, the call of length in the following statement returns 5, which is assigned to i:

```
i = s.length();
```

Note that length does not take any arguments.

We already discussed toUpperCase in Chapter 1. A String object also has a toLower-Case method that works in the same way. Both methods create new objects that contain the modified string. They do not modify the original string. For example, suppose s1 points to a String object that contains Hello. Then the following statement creates a new String object that contains hello, the lowercase version of the original string, and assigns its reference to s2:

```
s2 = s1.toLowerCase();
```

8.4 StringBuffer Class

The StringBuffer class is similar to the String class: objects of both types hold a single string, and both classes are in the java.lang package. The big difference between these two classes is that a String object is immutable but a StringBuffer object is not. Once we create a String object, we cannot change it. But when we create a Stringbuffer object, we can perform a variety of modifications on the string it contains.

The program in Fig. 8.3 illustrates the use of a StringBuffer object.

```
 1 class StringBufferExample
 2 {
 3    public static void main(String[] args)
 4    {
 5       String s;
 6       StringBuffer sb;
 7       s = "hello";
 8       sb = "hello";                          // illegal
 9       sb = new StringBuffer("hello");        // construct object
10       s = sb.toString();                     // extract string
11
12       // would work if sb were a String
13       System.out.println(sb);                // displays hello
14       System.out.println(sb.charAt(0));      // displays h
15       System.out.println(sb.length());       // displays 5
```

Figure 8.3 (continues)

```
16        System.out.println(sb.substring(1));     // displays ello
17        System.out.println(sb.substring(1, 3));  // displays el
18        System.out.println(sb.indexOf("lo"));    // displays 3
19
20        // StringBuffer and String do append differently
21        sb.append("bye");                         // hellobye
22        s = s + "bye";                            // hellobye
23
24        // would not work if sb were a String
25        sb.insert(5, " / ");                      // hello / bye
26        sb.setCharAt(0, 'm');                     // mello / bye
27        sb.deleteCharAt(6);                       // mello  bye
28        sb.delete(2, 4);                          // meo   bye
29        sb.replace(3, 8, "w");                    // meow
30        sb.reverse();                             // woem
31    }
32 }
```

Figure 8.3   (continued)

On Line 7, we implicitly trigger the construction of a String object simply by specifying a String constant:

```
7       s = "hello";
```

However, we cannot similarly assign a String constant to a StringBuffer reference. Thus, the following statement is illegal (sb is a StringBuffer reference):

```
8       sb = "hello;                        // illegal
```

This restriction makes sense: "hello" has type String; sb has type StringBuffer. Although the two types are similar, they are, nevertheless, incompatible. We cannot directly assign one to the other. To create a StringBuffer object that contains hello, we have to use the new operator and the StringBuffer constructor:

```
9       sb = new StringBuffer("hello");
```

To extract the string in the sb StringBuffer object, use its toString method:

```
10      s = sb.toString();                  // extract string
```

A Stringbuffer object has a charAt, length, substring, and indexOf method that work just like the identically named methods in a String object. Thus, the following statements work as they would work if the type of sb were String:

```
12      // would work if sb were a String
13      System.out.println(sb);             // displays hello
```

```
14         System.out.println(sb.charAt(0));      // displays h
15         System.out.println(sb.length());       // displays 5
16         System.out.println(sb.substring(1));    // displays ello
17         System.out.println(sb.substring(1, 3)); // displays el
18         System.out.println(sb.indexOf("lo"));   // displays 3
```

Now let's see what we can do with a `Stringbuffer` object that we *cannot* do with a `String` object. We can append a string to the end of the string in the sb object with the append method:

```
21         sb.append("bye");                      // hellobye
```

We can get a similar effect with a string using concatenation:

```
22         s = s + "bye";                         // hellobye
```

Although these two statements have a similar effect (the sb and s objects now both hold the string `hellobye`), they are fundamentally different. When we concatenate `bye` to the string in the s object, a new object containing the concatenated string is created. The reference to this new object is then assigned to s. The original `String` object (the one containing `hello`) still exists (see Fig. 8.4). When we use append to append `bye` to the string in the sb object, `bye` is appended to the string currently in the sb object—a new object is *not* created.

We can use the `insert` method to insert a string at the specified index in a `StringBuffer` object. All the characters from the specified index to the right are shifted to the right to make room for the inserted string. The following statement inserts `" / "` into the sb string at index 5:

```
25         sb.insert(5, " / ");                   // hello / bye
```

We can change any character in a `StringBuffer` object at the specified index with `setCharAt`. The following statement overlays the initial `'h'` with `'m'`:

```
26         sb.setCharAt(0, 'm');                  // mello / bye
```

We can also delete any character at a specified index. All the characters to the right of the deletion point are shifted left one position to fill the hole left by the deletion. The following statement deletes the character at index 6 (the slash):

```
27         sb.deleteCharAt(6);                    // mello  bye
```

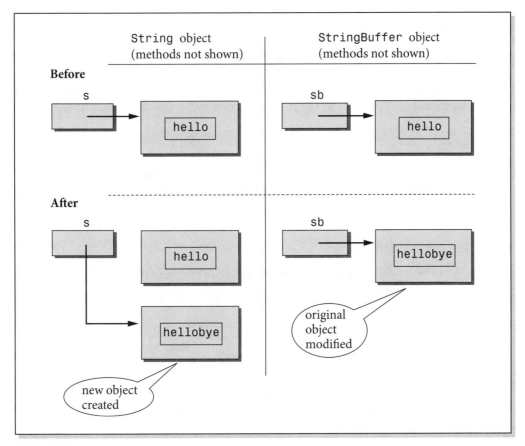

Figure 8.4

We can also delete a substring. For example, to delete all characters from index 2 up to but not including 4, use

```
28      sb.delete(2, 4);                              // meo  bye
```

We can replace a substring. For example, to replace the substring from indices 3 through 7 with "w", use

```
29      sb.replace(3, 8, "w");                        // meow
```

We can reverse the entire string in a StringBuffer object:

```
30      sb.reverse();                                 // woem
```

8.5 Math Class

The Math class in is the java.lang package so we do not need to import it or use its fully qualified name. Unlike most classes, all the methods in the Math class are static. Thus, to access the Math class, we do not create any objects. We simply call its static methods via the class name Math. For example, the following code computes the square root of 2.5:

```
double root;
root = Math.sqrt(2.5);
```

The Math class has two static constants: E (the base of natural logarithms) and PI (the ratio of the circumference of a circle to its diameter). For example, the following code computes the area of a circle whose radius is 5:

```
double area;
area = Math.PI*5.0*5.0;
```

Math.E and Math.PI are accurate to 20 digits. They are certainly more convenient to use than the actual 20-digit literal constants. Fig. 8.5 lists some of the commonly used methods in the Math class.

Method	Returns
public static double abs(int x)	absolute value
public static double abs(long x)	absolute value
public static double abs(float x)	absolute value
public static double abs(double x)	absolute value
public static double ceil(double x)	smallest whole number $\geq x$
public static double floor(double x)	largest whole number $\leq x$
public static long round(double x)	x rounded to nearest long
public static double sin(double x)	$\sin(x)$, x in radians
public static double cos(double x)	$\cos(x)$, x in radians
public static double tan(double x)	$\tan(x)$, x in radians
public static double exp(double x)	e^x
public static double pow(double x, double y)	x^y
public static double sqrt(double x)	square root of x
public static double max(int x, int y)	larger of x and y
public static double max(double x, double y)	larger of x and y
public static double min(int x, int y)	smaller of x and y
public static double min(double x, double y)	smaller of x and y

Figure 8.5

8.6   Random Class

The Random class allows us to generate pseudorandom numbers of type int, long, float, or double. We call these numbers **pseudorandom** ("pseudo" means false) because they are not truly random. They are generated by methods that are capable of generating the same sequence of numbers repeatedly. However, the numbers generated have essentially the same characteristics as true random numbers. A good question to ask at this point is why would we ever need random numbers in a program? Random numbers, in fact, can be very useful. They allow us to model many real-life processes.

Figure 8.6 tells us what we need to know to use the Random class. It does not tell us how the Random class is implemented, but we do not need to know that information to use the class. You can get this type of information on any Java class at the java.sun.com website (click on the link to the APIs).

Constructors

```
public Random()
```

   Constructs a Random object using the time of day as the seed.

```
public Random(long s)
```

   Constructs a Random object using the value of the parameter s as the seed.

Methods

```
public boolean nextBoolean()
```

   Returns true or false, uniformly distributed.

```
public double nextDouble()
```

   Returns a double pseudorandom number between 0.0 (inclusive) and 1.0 (exclusive). The numbers are uniformly distributed.

```
public float nextFloat()
```

   Returns a float pseudorandom number between 0.0 (inclusive) and 1.0 (exclusive). The numbers are uniformly distributed.

```
public double nextGaussian()
```

   Returns a double pseudorandom number with a mean of 0.0 and a standard deviation of 1.0. The numbers have a Gaussian (i.e., bell-shaped) distribution.

Figure 8.6   (continues)

```
public int nextInt()
```

   Returns an int pseudorandom number. The numbers are uniformly distributed.

```
public int nextInt(int n)
```

   Returns an int pseudorandom number of type int between 0 and $n - 1$, inclusive.
   The numbers are uniformly distributed over the interval 0 to $n - 1$.

```
public long nextLong()
```

   Returns a long pseudorandom number of type long. The numbers are uniformly
   distributed.

```
public void setSeed(long s)
```

   Sets the seed to s.

Figure 8.6   (continued)

Random number generators need a **seed** number to start the number-generating process.
This seed determines the sequence of numbers generated. If we generate two sequences,
each starting with the same seed, the two sequences will be identical.

When we construct a Random object, we can optionally pass the constructor the seed. If
we do not, then the time of day is used as the seed.

To make the Random class available to our program, we have to indicate to the Java compiler that the Random class is in the java.util package. We do this with

```
import java.util.Random;
```

Figure 8.7 contains a program that creates and uses two Random objects. It calls next-
Double (which returns a random double value) and nextInt (which returns a random
int value).

```
1 import java.util.Random;
2 class TestRandom
3 {
4     public static void main(String[] args)
5     {
6             Random r1 = new Random(7777777);    // set seed to 7777777
7             System.out.println("r1 object");
8             System.out.println(r1.nextDouble());
```

Figure 8.7   (continues)

```
 9          System.out.println(r1.nextDouble());
10
11          System.out.println(r1.nextInt());
12          System.out.println(r1.nextInt());
13
14          System.out.println(r1.nextInt(2));
15          System.out.println(r1.nextInt(2));
16
17          Random r2 = new Random(7777777);   // set seed to 7777777
18          System.out.println("r2 object");
29          System.out.println(r2.nextDouble());
20          System.out.println(r2.nextDouble());
21
22          System.out.println(r2.nextInt());
23          System.out.println(r2.nextInt());
24
25          System.out.println(r2.nextInt(2));
26          System.out.println(r2.nextInt(2));
27      }
28 }
```

Figure 8.7 (continued)

This program produces the following output:

```
r1 object
0.7748014570608913
0.24105795048444711
875655393
495956042
0
1
r2 object
0.7748014570608913
0.24105795048444711
875655393
495956042
0
1
```

Notice that the r2 object produces the same sequence as the r1 object. This duplication is no coincidence. It results because we used the same seed (7777777) when we constructed both objects (see Lines 6 and 17).

If we pass nextInt an int value, it restricts the range of the random number returned to 0 up to but not including the number passed. For example, if we call nextInt, passing it 2, we will then get back either 0 or 1. We can use such a call to model the tossing of a coin.

0 can represent tails; 1, heads. For example, using the r1 Random object, we can model a single toss of a coin with

```
coinToss = r1.nextInt(2);
```

To model the tossing of a die ("die" is the singular form of "dice"), we can pass 6 to next-Int and then add 1:

```
dieThrow = r1.nextInt(6) + 1;
```

nextInt here returns 0, 1, 2, 3, 4, or 5. So when we add 1, we get 1, 2, 3, 4, 5, or 6—the six possible outcomes when we throw a die.

Let's now model exam grades. Assume grades run from 60 to 100. There are 41 grades in this range starting with 60. To generate one grade, use

```
grade = r1.nextInt(41) + 60;
```

Because we are passing 41 to nextInt, it returns an integer between 0 and 40. By adding 60, we get an integer between 60 and 100—precisely the range we want for our grades. Notice that the number we add to the value returned by nextInt determines the lowest possible number. The number we pass to nextInt determines the number of distinct numbers possible (see Fig. 8.8).

The grades that the preceding assignment statement generates are **uniformly distributed**. That is, each number between 60 and 100 is equally likely to occur. Exam grades, however, typically have a distribution that is bell-shaped. That is, the grades in the middle of the range occur more often than at the ends. To model a bell-shaped curve, we can simply generate two numbers, each uniformly distributed between 60 and 100 and take the average:

```
grade = (r1.nextInt(41) + 60 + r1.nextInt(41) + 60)/2;
```

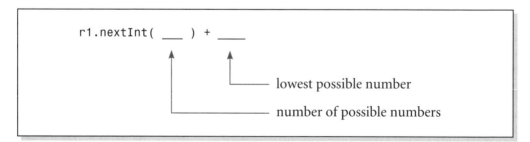

Figure 8.8

or equivalently

```
grade = (r1.nextInt(41) + r1.nextInt(41))/2 + 60;
```

For this assignment statement to produce a 100 grade, both calls of nextInt have to return 40. So getting a 100 grade is not very likely. In contrast, there are many values the two calls of nextInt can return that yield a number in the center region of the range. For example, to generate an 80 grade, the two calls could return 20 and 20, or a 19 and a 21, or 21 and 19, or 18 and 22, and so on. Because there are more ways to generate an 80, it is more likely to occur.

8.7   Scanner Class

Using the Scanner class, we can perform input from either the keyboard or a file. In this chapter, we use it for keyboard input only. In Chapter 12, we will use it for file input.

To make the Scanner class available, we import it with

```
import java.util.Scanner;
```

To create a Scanner object for keyboard input, we first create a Scanner reference variable:

```
Scanner kb;
```

We then use the new operator and call the Scanner constructor, passing it System.in:

```
kb = new Scanner(System.in);
```

Alternatively, we can combine these two statements into one:

```
Scanner kb = new Scanner(System.in);
```

Because System.in represents the keyboard, the Scanner constructor creates an object that inputs from the keyboard. kb is assigned the reference to this Scanner object. We can then call the various methods in this Scanner object via kb. For example, when the following code is executed

```
double x;
x = kb.nextDouble();
```

the program pauses, waiting for you to enter a double value on the keyboard (unless you have already entered one that has yet to be processed). Once you have entered this value, the program recommences, starting with the assignment of the value you entered to x. Similarly, for

```
int i;
i = kb.nextInt();
```

the program pauses, waiting for you to enter an int value. Once you have entered this value, the program recommences with the assignment of the value entered to i. The Scanner class also has nextByte, nextShort, nextLong, nextFloat, and nextBoolean methods (but no nextChar) that work like nextInt and nextDouble.

nextDouble and nextInt return arithmetic values. nextLine and next—two more methods in a Scanner object—return strings. nextLine returns the entire line entered (assuming you have not already consumed part of the line with other method calls, such as nextInt). For example, when the following statement is executed,

```
s = kb.nextLine();
```

the program pauses and waits for you to enter a line. You signal the end of the line by hitting the Enter key on your keyboard. Suppose you type in (starting with three spaces)

```
   hello 7    goodbye
```

and then hit the Enter key. nextLine will return the reference to the string "   hello 7   goodbye". If you use next instead of nextLine, you get just the next section of the keyboard input delimited by whitespace. For example, if the following statement is executed,

```
s = kb.next();
```

and you enter

```
   hello 7    goodbye
```

next will return the reference to "hello". Subsequent calls of next will return the references to "7" and then "goodbye". All the spaces are discarded. nextLine, in contrast, returns everything you enter on a line.

Whenever nextDouble is executed, you should enter a value compatible with the type double. This could be either a double or an integer-type constant. If you enter an integer, it is converted to type double. If you enter an incompatible value (such as "hello"), your program will fail. nextDouble does not skip over keyboard input that cannot be converted to a double value.

Before calling nextDouble, you can check if the next item in the input stream is compatible with nextDouble. To do this, use the method hasNextDouble. It returns true if the next item from the keyboard is a double or assignable to a double, and false otherwise. For example, the following code uses hasNextDouble to check the next item from the keyboard. It then executes nextDouble only if that item is assignable to a variable of type double:

```
double x;
if (kb.hasNextDouble())     // test if input okay for nextDouble
   x = kb.nextDouble();
```

The Scanner class has a hasNext method for each of its next methods. For example, it has a hasNext method, a hasNextLine method, a hasNextInt method, and so on.

Whenever a program wants input from the keyboard, it should display a **prompt message** that specifies what information the user should enter. For example, if we want the user to input the number of employees, we should place

```
System.out.println("Enter number of employees");
```

or some similar statement just before the statement that performs the input.

Let's examine the complete program in Fig. 8.9 that performs keyboard input.

```
1 import java.util.Scanner;
2 class Average
3 {
4    public static void main(String[] args)
5    {
6       Scanner kb = new Scanner(System.in);
7       double sum = 0.0;
8       int numberOfGrades, i = 1;
9
10      System.out.println("Enter number of grades");
11      numberOfGrades = kb.nextInt();
12      System.out.println("Enter grades");
13
14      while (i <= numberOfGrades)
15      {
16         sum = sum + kb.nextDouble();
17         i++;
18      }
19
20      System.out.println("Average = " + sum/numberOfGrades);
21   }
22 }
```

Figure 8.9

It contains a count-controlled loop (Lines 14–18). Its body executes once for each grade. The number of grades is prompted for and read in with

```
10          System.out.println("Enter number of grades");
11          numberOfGrades = kb.nextInt();
```

Each time the loop body is executed, the statement

```
16              sum = sum + kb.nextDouble();
```

reads in a grade from the keyboard and adds it to sum. The prompt message for the grades,

```
12          System.out.println("Enter grades");
```

appears before the loop. Thus, it is executed only once. Grades must be entered with each separated from the next by at least one space or the end-of-line marker (which corresponds to the Enter key on the keyboard). Thus, you can enter each grade on a separate line or enter them all on one line with intervening spaces. After the loop finishes, the sum of the grades is divided by the number of grades to determine the average grade:

```
20          System.out.println("Average = " + sum/numberOfGrades);
```

When the program calls nextDouble for the first time (see Line 16), the program pauses until you make an entry on the keyboard. If you enter more than one grade, the extra grades are saved. As long as there are saved values yet to be consumed by nextDouble, the execution of nextDouble will not cause the program to pause. It, instead, simply consumes the saved value that is next in line.

The program in Fig. 8.9 works for any number of grades because the user enters this number. The number entered determines the number of times the loop body is executed. A less flexible approach would be to write the program to process a specific number of grades. For example, suppose we delete the lines that input the number of grades and start the while loop with

```
while (i <= 20)
```

Then the program would work *only* for a set of 20 grades. Clearly, the loop in Fig. 8.9 is better. But we can do even better. The loop in Fig. 8.9 requires the user to count the number of grades and enter this count. We can use a different loop that requires the user only to inform the program when all the grades have been entered. With this loop, the user does not have to know the number of grades. Here is our improved loop:

```
double sum = 0.0;
int numberOfGrades = 0;
while (true)
{
   double x;
   x = kb.nextDouble();
   if (x < 0.0) break;     // exit loop if x is sentinel
   sum = sum + x;
   numberOfGrades++;       // count grade that was entered
}
```

The new loop executes until the user enters a negative number. A negative number for this program is a **sentinel**. A sentinel is not regular data. It is an input that signals to the program some change of status. Here, the sentinel—any negative number—signals the end of data. The program responds by immediately exiting the loop through the action of the `break` statement. The immediate exit is necessary because the sentinel is not data to be included in the computation of the average grade. Thus, we do not want to add it to `sum`. The variable `numberOfGrades` in this loop counts the number of grades entered. The program—not the user—determines the number of students.

8.8 Wrapper Classes

`byte`, `short`, `int`, `long`, `float`, `double`, `char`, and `boolean` are primitive types.

Classes are also types. In Java, there are some situations in which we must use a class type rather than a primitive type. We will see this in Chapters 9 and 17 when we discuss generic classes. What should we do in these situations if we want to use a primitive type? The answer is to use a wrapper class. A **wrapper class** is a special class that "wraps" (i.e., contains) a value that has a primitive type. Thus, in those situations in which we want to use a primitive type but a class type is required, we can simply use a wrapper class. The wrapper class satisfies the requirement that we use a class but it contains the primitive type that we want. Wrapper classes also include a variety of useful constants and methods. Wrapper classes are all immutable. Once we create an object from a wrapper class, we cannot change it. The wrapper classes are in the `java.lang` package so we do not need to import them or use their fully qualified names.

For each primitive type, there is a corresponding wrapper class (see Fig. 8.10). The names of the wrapper classes all start with a capital letter and are unabbreviated. For example, the wrapper class for `int` is `Integer`.

Primitive type	Corresponding wrapper class
byte	Byte
short	Short
int	Integer
long	Long
float	Float
double	Double
char	Character
boolean	Boolean

Figure 8.10

To create an object from a wrapper class, we call its constructor, passing it the primitive value to be wrapped. For example, the following code creates an `Integer` object containing 7, and then assigns r the reference to that object:

```
Integer r;
r = new Integer(7);    // create Integer object that wraps 7
```

Alternatively, we can combine both statements into one:

```
Integer r = new Integer(7);
```

Figure 8.11 shows the structure that results.

Because `parseInt` is a static method in the `Integer` class, it is independent of any objects. For this reason, we show it outside the object box in Fig. 8.11. The field containing

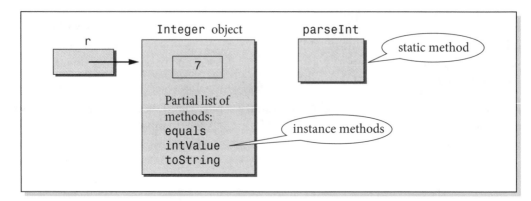

Figure 8.11

the int data within an Integer object is private. Thus, we cannot access it directly. However, the public method intValue will extract a copy of it for us. For example, the following code assigns the int data in the r Integer object to i:

```
int i;
i = r.intValue();
```

Recent versions of Java support a capability called **auto-boxing** and **auto-unboxing**. With auto-boxing, we do not have to use the new operator or explicitly call the Integer constructor to create an Integer object. Auto-boxing automatically constructs an Integer object when one is needed. For example, if r has the type Integer, then the statement

```
r = 7;
```

auto-boxes 7 (i.e., it constructs an Integer object that wraps 7) and assigns its reference to r. Thus, this statement has the same effect as

```
r = new Integer(7);
```

With auto-unboxing, we do not have to use intValue to access the data in an Integer object. Auto-unboxing extracts a copy of the embedded primitive data when the primitive data is needed. For example, if i is type int and r is a reference to an Integer object, the statement

```
i = r;
```

auto-unboxes the int data in the object and assigns it to i. That is, it extracts a copy of the integer in the object and assigns it to i. Thus, this statement has the same effect as

```
i = r.intValue();
```

auto-boxing and auto-unboxing can also occur when an argument value is passed to a parameter in a method call. For example, suppose an int value is passed to an Integer parameter. In this case, the int value is auto-boxed into an Integer object. Its reference is then assigned to the Integer parameter. Auto-unboxing can similarly occur during argument passing. For example, if an Integer reference is passed to an int parameter, the argument is unboxed. That is, the int value it contains is extracted and assigned to the int parameter.

The toString method converts the data embedded in a wrapper object to a string. For example, in the following code,

```
Integer r;
String s;
r = 123;
s = r.toString();
```

toString converts the int data 123 in the r object to the string "123" whose reference is then assigned to s. Recall that "123" (the string) is quite different from 123 (the int). The string is stored as a sequence of codes representing the characters '1', '2', and '3'. The int constant is represented by the single binary number that is equivalent to 123 decimal.

The equals method in the wrapper classes tests two wrapper objects for equality. For example, suppose r1 and r2 are references to Integer objects. Then

```
if (r1.equals(r2))
   System.out.println("Objects are equal");
```

tests if the integer data in the r1 object is equal to the integer data in the r2 object. For example, if both objects contain the value 7, then the equals method would return true. Note that it would be incorrect to perform this test with

```
if (r1 == r2))
   System.out.println("Objects are equal");
```

r1 == r2 tests if the two references—not the objects to which they point—are equal.

The static method parseInt in the Integer class converts a string to type int. Because it is a static method, we call parseInt via its class name. For example, if s points to "123", then the following statement converts the string in the s object to the int value 123, which is then assigned to i.

```
int i = Integer.parseInt(s);
```

Here are some of the features that are common to all the wrapper classes:

- They support auto-boxing and auto-unboxing.
- They have a toString, an equals, and a compareTo method. The compareTo method in the wrapper classes works like the compareTo method in the String class. Specifically, it returns an integer that is either less than zero, zero, or greater than zero to indicate the result of the comparison.
- They are immutable. Once an object is created from a wrapper class, it cannot be changed.
- They have a method comparable to intValue in Integer but named differently. For example, Double has doubleValue. These methods return the primitive data in the wrapper object. However, we normally do not have to use them because auto-unboxing extracts the primitive data in a wrapper object for us.

All the wrapper classes for the arithmetic types have a "parse" method. Like parseInt, these methods convert a string to a primitive type. For example, in the following code,

```
public static boolean isDigit(char c)
public static boolean isLetter(char c)
public static boolean isLetterOrDigit(char c)
public static boolean isLowerCase(char c)
public static boolean isUpperCase(char c)
public static boolean isWhitespace(char c)
public static char    toLowerCase(char c)
public static char    toUpperCase(char c)
```

Figure 8.12

parseDouble converts the string in the s object to the corresponding double value, which is then assigned to the double variable d:

```
String s = "1.234";
double d = Double.parseDouble(s)
```

Because the parse methods in the wrapper classes are static, they are accessed via their class names.

The Character wrapper class has a collection of static methods that are useful for processing characters (see Fig. 8.12). For example, if c has type char, then Character. isWhitespace(c) returns true if c contains a whitespace character (invisible characters such as space, tab, and newline), and false otherwise.

The wrapper classes corresponding to arithmetic types have named static constants MAX_ VAL and MIN_VAL that contain the maximum and minimum possible values for their types. For example, Byte.MIN_VAL is −128 (the smallest value of type byte), and Byte. MAX_VAL is 127 (the largest value of type byte).

8.9 System and System.out

We have been using System.out since Chapter 1. What exactly is System.out? System is a predefined class. out is a static field in the System class. Thus, to access this field, we specify System.out—the class name (System) and the static field (out) separated by a dot. out is a reference variable that points to a PrintStream object (PrintStream is another predefined class). This object contains the println and print methods that output to the computer screen. println and print are overloaded. The object to which System.out points actually contains 10 versions of println and 9 versions of print (see Fig. 8.13).

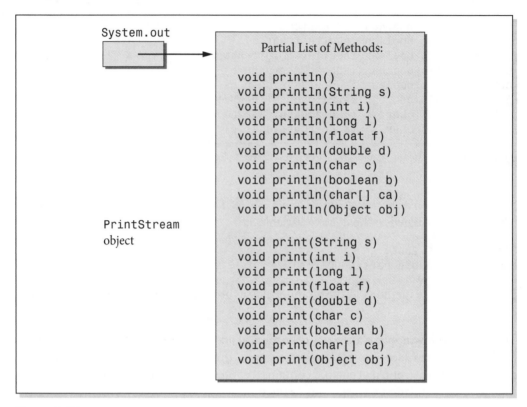

Figure 8.13

Object is a predefined class in the java.lang package. We will discuss this class in Chapter 10. For now, all you need to know is that a reference variable whose type is Object is universal. That is, it can be assigned a reference of any type. For example, if we declare obj with

```
Object obj;
```

we can assign it an Integer reference,

```
obj = new Integer(7);
```

or a Double reference,

```
obj = new Double(3.5);
```

or a String reference,

```
obj = "hello";
```

or any other type of reference. This universality is true only for Object reference variables.

Suppose a method f has a parameter obj whose type is Object:

```
public void f(Object obj)
{
    ...
}
```

Because of the universality of obj, we can pass f any reference, regardless of its type. For example, suppose we define r and t with

```
Integer r = new Integer(7);
Double t = new Double(3.5);
```

It would be legal to pass f either r or t:

```
f(r);      // legal call, passing Integer reference to obj
f(t);      // legal call, passing Double reference to obj
```

In both calls, the argument (r or t) is assigned to the parameter obj. Because obj has type Object, these assignments are legal.

Now, getting back to the System.out, note that in Fig. 8.13, one of the println methods and one of the print methods have a parameter whose type is Object. Thus, these methods can be passed any reference, regardless of its type. For each primitive type, the System.out class has a compatible println and print method. Thus, when you call println or print, you can pass it anything, regardless of its type.

LABORATORY

Laboratory 8 Prep

1. Why is it better to get random numbers from the Random class than to get them from the famous book, *10,000 Random Numbers Arranged in Ascending Order,* in the order given?

2. Give a statement that displays a random integer between 10 and 100 (inclusive). Assume r is a reference to a Random object.

3. Suppose s1 and s2 point to String objects. Give the statement that displays ASCENDING if the s2 string follows the s1 string lexicographically.

4. Write a statement that reads in one double value using kb, where kb is a reference to a Scanner object.

5. Give the statement that converts the string "1.23456" to a double value and assigns the result to a double variable.

Laboratory 8

1. Compile the program in C8e1.java to confirm it compiles correctly. Remove the import statement and recompile. What happens? Now compile without the import statement but use the fully-qualified name for Random (java.util.Random) in the program. What happens?

2. What is displayed by the following program? Run it to check your answer.

```java
class C8e2
{
    public static void main(String[] args)
    {
        String s1, s2, s3, s4;
        s1 = "hello";
        s2 = "hello";
        if (s1 == s2)
            System.out.println("s1 == s2");
        s3 = new String("hello");
        s4 = new String("hello");
        if (s3 == s4)
            System.out.println("s3 == s4");
    }
}
```

From this example, can you conclude that the construction of the strings that occurs as a result of

```java
s1 = "hello";
s2 = "hello";
```

is exactly the same as the construction of strings that occurs as a result of

```
s3 = new String("hello"):
s4 = new String("hello")
```

3. What are the possible values assigned to x by

```
x = (r.nextInt(5) + r.nextInt(5))/2;
```

where x is type int and r is a reference to a Random object. Write a program that executes the preceding statement one million times and counts the number of times each integer between 0 and 4 (inclusive) is assigned to x. Your program should display the final counts. Use a switch statement (see Lab Exercise 2 in Chapter 4). Based on your results, does it appear that 0, 1, 2, 3, and 4 are equally likely?

4. Same as Lab Exercise 3 but count the integers −7 to 7 for the following statement:

```
x = (int)(5.0 * r.nextGaussian());
```

5. The following code demonstrates the auto-boxing and unboxing between Integer and int:

```
Integer i;
int j;
i = 5;    // 5 is auto-boxed in an Integer object
j = i;    // int in i is auto-unboxed and assigned to j
```

But does auto-boxing and unboxing work between Object and int? Is the following code legal:

```
Object obj;
int j;
obj = 5;      // is 5 auto-boxed?
obj = new Integer(5);
j = obj;      // is the integer in the obj object auto-unboxed?
```

Run a test program to check your answer.

6. Write a program that reads in a string from the keyboard, and then determines and displays the number of occurrences of vowels (a, A, e, E, i, I, o, O, u, and U).

7. Write a program that displays hello repeatedly as long as the user enters 0 after each display. Entering any nonzero integer terminates the program. Sample session:

```
hello
enter non-zero integer to stop
0
hello
enter non-zero integer to stop
0
```

```
hello
enter non-zero integer to stop
1      ◄──── program terminates at this point
```

This program naturally calls for a loop with the following structure:

```
display "hello"
prompt for number
read number
if number is not zero, exit loop.
```

Notice the loop has a **trailing exit test** (i.e., the exit test is at the bottom of the loop). Because the while loop has a leading exit test, implement the loop you need for this exercise using a do-while loop (it has a trailing exit test). Its form is

```
do
    statement
while (true/false expression);
```

where the embedded statement can be either a simple statement or a compound statement (i.e., a sequence of statements enclosed with braces). The exit occurs at the bottom of the loop if the true/false expression is false.

8. If a variable is declared within a do-while loop, does its scope (i.e., where it can be used) extend to the true/false expression? For example, is the following loop legal:

```
do
{
    int i = 1;
    System.out.println(i);
    i++;
} while (i <= 5);
```

Run a test program to check your answer.

9. Write a program that reads in an integer by executing the nextInt method in a Scanner object. What happens if you enter a noninteger rather than an integer when nextInt executes? Try entering "hello", 3.5, and 3.0. What happens if you enter an integer that is too big, such as 999999999999999?

10. Write a program that displays 30 random integers between 10 and 15 inclusive.

11. Write a program that prompts for and reads in a double number and then determines and displays its square root. Your program should do this repeatedly until the user enters a negative number. Use Math.sqrt to compute square roots. Use the class

name C8e11 for your program. The output your program creates should look like the following sample session:

```
Enter double
9.0
Square root of 9.0 = 3.0
Enter double
100.0
Square root of 100.0 = 10.0
Enter double
-3.0        ◄─── program terminates at this point
```

After you have tested your program, create a file named lab8e11.txt with a text editor. The file should contain the data 9.0, 100.0, and 23.0 (do *not* include the commas). Then run your program by entering

```
java C8e11 < lab8e11.txt
```

The angle bracket here **redirects** input so that it is from the specified file rather than the keyboard.

12. What happens if you pass a negative number to Math.sqrt? Run a test program to find out.

13. Write a program that prompts for and reads in the radius of a circle and then displays its area. Use the constant Math.PI in the Math class for π.

14. Is the following a legal statement:

```
i = r1 + r2;
```

where i is an int variable and r1 and r2 are Integer references that point to Integer objects? Run a test program to check your answer.

15. Write a program in which main passes f references to two Integer objects. f should return the sum of the two integers in the Integer objects. Its return type should be int. main and should display the value returned by f.

16. Write a program that prompts the user for an integer. Your program should read in the integer and display positive, negative, or zero, according to the value of the number. The output your program creates should look like the following sample session:

```
Enter integer
3
3 is positive     ◄─── program terminates at this point
```

LABORATORY

17. Suppose two packages `java.a` and `java.b` each have an XXX class. If you want to use both XXX classes in your program, how would you do it? Would you use `import` statements?

18. Do the wrapper classes have constructors with no parameters? For example, is the following code legal:

```
Integer i = new Integer();
```

Run a test program to check your answer.

19. Can a `String` object be concatenated to a `StringBuffer` object? For example, if `sb` points to a `Stringbuffer` object, is the following statement legal:

```
System.out.println(sb + "xyz");
```

Run a test program to check your answer.

20. Can a `StringBuffer` object be cast to a `String`? For example, if `s` and `sb` have type `String` and `StringBuffer`, respectively, is the following statement legal:

```
s = (String)sb;
```

Run a test program to check your answer.

21. Write a program that prompts for an integer, reads in an integer with `nextInt`, prompts for a string, and reads in a string with `nextLine`, in that order. Your program should then display the integer and the string on separate lines, in that order. (*Hint:* When your program reads in the integer, it consumes only the integer, not the end-of-line marker at the end of the current input line. If `nextLine` is then executed, it returns the empty string terminated by the end-of-line marker. It does not read in the next line.)

22. Write a program that displays the current time and date. Use the `Date` class. Consult a Java class reference to determine how to use `Date`.

23. Incorporate the following code in a program and execute:

```
System.out.println(Integer.toBinaryString(257));
```

It displays 257 in binary. Do you now see why the following code assigns 1 to b?

```
int i = 257;
byte b = (byte)i;
```

24. Suppose r1 and r2 have type `Integer`. Do r1 and r2 point to the same object if the following statements are executed?

```
r1 = 5;
r2 = 5;
```

Do r1 and r2 point to the same object if the following statements are executed?

```
r1 = new Integer(10);
r2 = new Integer(10);
```

Run a test program to check your answers.

Homework 8

1. Write a `Graph` class that has methods `countIt` and `graphIt`. `countIt` should use five counters (c0, c1, c2, c3, and c4) to count the number of 0's, 1's, 2's, 3's, and 4's it is passed. Use a `switch` statement to determine which counter to increment (see Lab Exercise 2 in Chapter 4). `graphIt` should display the final counts in the form of a bar graph, with one bar for each count. Each bar should consist of a horizontal line of consecutive asterisks. If the largest count is greater than 50, scale the size of the bars so that the largest bar has 50 asterisks.

   Write a program that uses your `Graph` class. It should generate one million random integers all of which are 0, 1, 2, 3, or 4. For each integer, your program should call `countIt` in a `Graph` object. After all the integers have been counted, your program should call `graphIt`.

2. Write a program that estimates the probability of getting three heads when three coins are tossed. Let 0 represent tails, 1 heads. Simulate the tossing of a coin by generating a random integer equal to 0 or 1. To toss three coins, generate three random integers. A sum of 3 indicates three heads has occurred. Toss three coins one million times. Determine the fraction of times the outcome is three heads. This fraction approximates the theoretical probability of getting three heads when tossing three coins.

3. Write a program in which you read a line from the keyboard, and then display the line with its characters reversed. Display both the original and the reversed strings.

4. Write a program that reads in two strings from a single line entered from the keyboard. Use the `next` method in the `Scanner` class. Convert the strings to type `int` using `Integer.parseInt`. Add the two values and display the sum. Enter 20 30 when your run the program.

5. Write a program that prompts for and reads in an integer number, displays `hello` that number of times, and then terminates. Sample session:

```
Enter integer
2
hello
hello
```

6. Same as Homework Exercise 5 except that the program should repeat after displaying `hello` the requested number of times. The program should stop only when the user enters a nonpositive integer. Sample session:

```
Enter integer
2
hello
hello
Enter integer
1
hello
Enter integer
0          ←—— program terminates at this point
```

7. Write a program that plays the game Nim with the user of the program. The program and the user alternate turns, picking up one, two, or three straws on each turn. The program goes first. The player to pick up the last straw loses. Your program should start by generating and displaying a random integer (which represents the number of straws) between 10 and 20 inclusive. If this number is 1 more than a multiple of 4, add 1. For example, if the random integer is 20, then start with 20 straws. But if the random integer is 17 (which is 1 more than a multiple of 4), start with 18. On a user's turn, your program should prompt for, read in, and process the user's input (which should be 1, 2, or 3—the number of straws to pick up). On the program's turn, it should determine its move by generating a random number between 1 and 3. At the end of each game, your program should display

```
Do you want to play another game?
```

It should then read in the user's yes/no response, and proceed accordingly. Use a `do-while` loop to control the repetition of games (see Lab Exercise 7). If either a user's move or the program's move is greater than the number of straws, then all the remaining straws should be picked up, resulting in a loss. For example, if there are 2 straws left, and the user's move is 3, the remaining 2 straws should be picked up, causing the user to lose.

8. Same as Homework Exercise 7 with this change in the program's strategy: If the number of straws is 1 more than a multiple of 4, it should pick up 1 straw. Otherwise, it should pick up the number of straws that leaves 1 more than a multiple of 4. For example, if the number of straws is 12, 11, or 10, your program should pick up 3, 2, or 1, respectively, leaving 9 straws (which is 1 more than 2×4).

9. Write a program that simulates the dropping of a 1-inch needle on a paper that has 2 horizontal lines two inches apart. The lower part of the needle can land anywhere between the two lines. The angle of the needle with respect to the horizontal lines can be any value between 0 and π (which is the radian equivalent of 180°). Your program

should simulate the dropping of the needle one million times. It should count how many drops resulted in the needle touching or crossing the top horizontal line. It should then divide this count *into* the number of drops and display the result. Does the result displayed by your program approximate some well-known constant?

10. What does the next method in the Scanner class return each time it is called if the input is

```
bye,      goodbye    ,    all done
```

Now try this experiment: Before calling next, execute

```
kb.delimiter(",");
```

where kb is the reference to the Scanner object. For the same keyboard input, what does next return? Repeat your experiment, but execute

```
kb.delimiter("");
```

before calling next.

CHAPTER 9

Arrays, ArrayLists, Sorting, and Searching

OBJECTIVES

- Learn how to create and use arrays
- Learn how to create loops with the `for` statement
- Learn how to access command-line arguments
- Learn some searching and sorting techniques
- Understand measures of time and space complexity

9.1 Creating an Array

An array is a structure that is a collection of memory slots all of which have the *same* type. Recall that to create an object, we use the `new` operator, which triggers the creation of the object and provides a reference to it. We can then access the object via its reference. When we create an array, we perform the same steps. For example, let's create an array that has five slots of type `double`. First, we create a reference variable q:

```
double[] q;
```

Here, we are declaring q to have type `double[]`. Read `double[]` as "double array" (the square brackets mean "array"). q is not the array—it is just the reference variable that will point to the array. Next, we create the array with the `new` operator and assign q the pointer to the array:

```
q = new double[5];
```

When we create an array with the `new` operator, we specify the associated type followed by square brackets containing the number of slots. For example, `double[5]` on the right of the preceding statement indicates that we want an array with 5 slots, each of type `double`. Alternatively, we can combine the declaration of the q variable and the creation of the array into one statement:

```
double[] q = new double[5];
```

With either approach, the structure in Fig. 9.1 results.

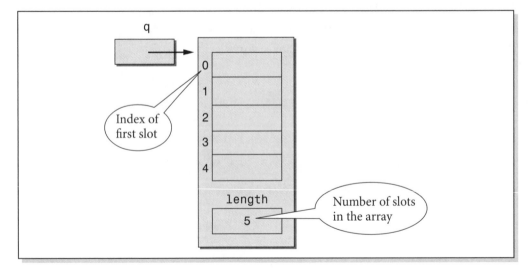

Figure 9.1

q points to a structure that contains the array itself and a `length` field. We will refer to the structure in Fig. 9.1 as the q array. By that, we mean the array structure to which q points.

The `length` field of an array contains the length (i.e., the number of slots) in the array. Once an array is created, its length is fixed. Each slot in an array has an associated number—called an **index**—that we use to designate that slot. The index of the first slot is 0, the second is 1, the third is 2, and so on. Indices are consecutive integer numbers that start from 0. *The index of the last slot in an array is one less than its length.*

Each slot in the array in Fig. 9.1 is of type `double`. Thus, each slot can hold a single `double` value. Let's assign `2.5` to the first slot in the array. We do this with

```
q[0] = 2.5;
```

The index inside square brackets here indicates which slot we want. `q[0]` is the slot of the q array that has the index 0.

We are not restricted to constants for indices. We can use any expression that yields an integer corresponding to a valid index. For example, if `i` is 2, then the following statement assigns `5.5` to `q[2]`:

```
q[i] = 5.5;        // assigns 5.5 to q[2] assuming i is 2
```

If we then execute

```
q[i + 2] = 7.7;   // assigns 7.7 to q[4] assuming i is 2
```

`7.7` is assigned to the slot whose index is given by `i + 2`. If `i` is 2, `i + 2` is 4. Thus, this statement assigns `7.7` to `q[4]`.

We access the `length` field of an array using the array's reference. For example, the following statement displays the length of the q array:

```
System.out.println(q.length);
```

`length` in an array is a field. In contrast, `length` in the `String` class is a method. Thus, we get the length of a `String` by calling its `length` method. But we get the length of an array by accessing its `length` field. For example, suppose `s` is a reference to a `String` object. Then its length is given by

```
s.length()
```

But the length of the q array is given by

```
q.length
```

Note that in the former, we use parentheses (because we are calling a method), but in the latter we do not (because we are accessing a field). Fortunately, it is not hard to remember when to use parentheses with length and when not to use them. Here is a simple mnemonic (an aid to memory): Parentheses look like strings. So to get the length of a string, use parentheses with length.

The array in Fig. 9.1 is, in effect, a collection of five double variables, q[0], q[1], q[2], q[3], and q[4]. We can use these variables the same way we use ordinary double variables: we can assign them values, use them in arithmetic expressions, we can display their values, and so on.

We can initialize an array in its declaration. If we do this, we do not use the new operator to create the array. We simply specify the initial values inside braces, each separated from the next with a comma. For example, in

```
int[] p = {10, 3, 7};     // initialization of array in declaration
```

we are specifying the initial values for an array. Because we have specified three values, an array with three slots is created. Its three slots are initialized to 10, 3, and 7. If, instead, we use

```
int[] p = new int[3];
```

we would get an array of the same size and type, but its three slots would be initialized to the default value of 0.

9.2 Why We Need Arrays

Suppose a program has three variables x1, x2, and x3. Let's display the values of these three variables using three println statements:

```
System.out.println(x1);
System.out.println(x2);
System.out.println(x3);
```

Now suppose our program has five variables. We would then need five println statements to display the values of our variables. No problem with that. But now suppose we had one million variables. We would then need one million println statements. Moreover, we would need to declare each one of those one million variables. Clearly, such a program would be unwieldy, to say the least. If, however, we use an array containing one million slots, then the code that creates the array and displays its values is quite simple.

```
 1   int[] w = new int[1000000];          // create array
 2   //
 3   // code that places values in the w array goes here
 4   //
 5   int i = 0;
 6   while (i < w.length)                  // display array
 7   {
 8       System.out.println(w[i]);         // display value in w[i]
 9       i++;                              // add 1 to i
10   }
```

Figure 9.2

Assuming we are working with numbers of type int, the code we need is given in Fig. 9.2 (we omitted the code that places values into the array).

The statement on Line 8 is executed repeatedly. The first time it is executed, i is 0. Thus, it displays w[0], the value in the first slot of the array. The second time it is executed, i is 1. Thus, Line 8 displays w[1], the value in the second slot. Each time Line 8 is executed, it displays the next value in the array. The last time Line 8 is executed i is equal to w.length - 1. This is the index of the last slot in the array. We can process all the slots in an array *with a single statement inside a loop.*

We want the loop body in Fig. 9.2 to execute for each value of i from 0 up to *but not including the length of the array.* Remember the maximum index of an array is one less than the array length because indices start from 0. Thus, if the true/false expression in the while loop were

i <= w.length

instead of

i < w.length

then the last time the loop body executed, Line 8 would attempt to display w[1000000]. But there is no such slot. The last slot is w[999999]. Thus, at this point, the program would fail.

If the exit condition in the while loop were

i < 1000000

instead of

i < w.length

the loop would execute the same number of times because w.length is equal to 1000000 for the w array in Fig. 9.2. If we use 1000000 in place of w.length, we say that we have **hard-coded** the size of the array. However, using w.length is better than using the hard-coded length for two reasons:

1. It always gives the correct length. But if we hard-code the length, we might make an error when entering the number into the program.
2. w.length does have to be adjusted if we should ever modify the size specified in the declaration of the array (for example, if we changed 1000000 to 2000000 in Line 1 in Fig 9.2).

9.3   for Loops

We typically process an array with a count-controlled loop. The loop body executes once for each slot in the array. We can easily construct a count-controlled loop using a while loop. However, an even easier way to construct a count-controlled loop is to use a for loop. In a for loop, the initialization of the counter variable, the exit condition, and the incrementation or decrementation of the counter all appear on the first line. Here is the format of a for loop:

```
for (startup action; true/false expression; update action)
    statement
```

No semicolon here

where the embedded statement can be either a simple statement or a compound statement (i.e., a sequence of statements enclosed by braces). Note that the three components inside the parentheses are separated by semicolons, but there is no semicolon after the parentheses. The startup action (the first component within parentheses) normally is used to initialize the loop counter. The update action (the third component within parentheses) normally is used to increment or decrement the loop counter.

When a for loop is executed, the startup action is executed first and only once (see Fig. 9.3). Then the exit test, the loop body, and the update action are executed repeatedly until the exit test triggers an exit. The for loop has a leading exit test—it is performed before the loop body is executed

The following for loop displays hello 10 times:

```
for (i = 1; i <= 10; i++)
    System.out.println("hello");
```

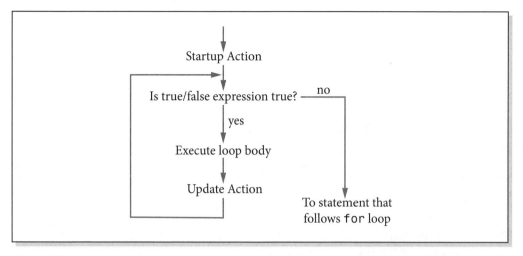

Figure 9.3

When this loop is executed, i is initialized to 1 by the startup action. After each execution of the println statement, the update action increments i. When i reaches 11, the exit condition, i <= 10 becomes false, which triggers the loop exit. Thus, the loop body is executed for the values of i running from 1 to 10.

In the preceding for loop, we are assuming that the counter variable i was previously declared. Alternatively, we can declare the counter variable in the startup action of the for loop. With this approach, the for loop becomes

```
for (int i = 1; i <= 10; i++)    // declare and init i in startup action
    System.out.println("hello");
```

Here we are both declaring and initializing the counter variable i in the startup action. When we do this, we are allowed to use the counter variable only within the for loop. The scope of the counter variable (i.e., where it can be used in a program) is limited to the for loop.

9.4 Two-Dimensional Arrays

We call the arrays we have been using so far **one-dimensional arrays** because the slots in these arrays are arranged in single-file order. In **two-dimensional arrays**, the slots are arranged in rows and columns. For example, Fig. 9.4 shows a two-dimensional array with two rows and three columns.

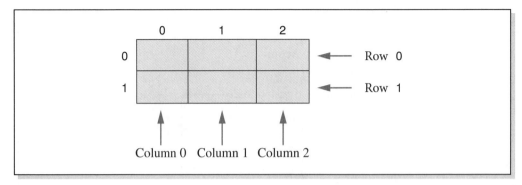

Figure 9.4

The rows and columns are numbered with indices starting from 0. The array in Fig. 9.4 is an example of a 2 × 3 array (i.e., it has two rows and three columns).

To create a two-dimensional array, we first create a reference variable. For example, to create a reference m for a two-dimensional int array, we declare m with

```
int[][] m;
```

The two sets of square brackets indicate m will point to a two-dimensional array. To create a 2 × 3 int array to which m points, we use

```
m = new int[2][3];
```

Alternatively, we can combine both statements into one:

```
int[][] m = new int[2][3];
```

To specify a particular slot, we specify its row and column indices, each in square brackets. For example, to assign −7 to the slot whose row and column indices are 1 and 2, respectively, we use

```
m[1][2] = -7;    // assign -7 to slot in row 1, column 2
```

Note that the maximum row index is one less than the number of rows. Similarly, the maximum column index is one less than the number of columns.

To process a one-dimensional array, we typically use a single for loop. To process a two-dimensional array, we typically use two for loops that are nested. For example, the following nested for loops assign 20 to each slot of m:

```
for (int row = 0; row < 2; row++)
   for (int col = 0; col < 3; col++)
      m[row][col] = 20;
```

The outer loop executes its body for `row` equal to 0 and `row` equal to 1. Its body is the inner loop. Thus, the execution of the inner loop is initiated twice. The first time it is initiated, `row` is equal to 0; the second time, `row` is equal to 1.

Each time the inner `for` loop is activated, it processes the current row (i.e., the row whose index is in the `row` variable). For example, the first time the inner `for` loop is activated, `row` is 0. Thus, the body of the inner loop is, in effect,

```
m[0][col] = 20;
```

The inner loop executes this statement three times, as `col` goes from 0 to 2. Thus, the effect is equivalent to

```
m[0][0] = 20;
m[0][1] = 20;
m[0][2] = 20;
```

These three assignment statements assign 20 to each slot in the first row. The second time the execution of the inner `for` loop is activated by the outer loop, `row` is 1. Thus, the inner loop body is, in effect,

```
m[1][col] = 20;
```

The inner loop again executes this statement three times, as `col` goes from 0 to 2. Thus, the effect is equivalent to

```
m[1][0] = 20;
m[1][1] = 20;
m[1][2] = 20;
```

Thus, the inner loop this time assigns 20 to each slot of the second row.

A two-dimensional array is actually a one-dimensional array in which each slot is, in turn, an array. For example, our 2 × 3 `m` array is actually a one-dimensional array with two slots (see Fig. 9.5a). Thus, the length of this array is 2. Accordingly, the value of `m.length` is 2.

`m[0]` designates the entire first row; `m[1]` designates the entire second row (see Fig. 9.5b). `m[0]` and `m[1]` are, in turn, references to arrays. `m[0]` is the one-dimensional array in the first row; `m[1]` is the one-dimensional array in the second row. Thus, `m[0].length` is the length of the array in the first row; `m[1].length` is the length of the array in the second row. These two lengths are both 3 for our `m` array.

When you set up nested `for` loops to process a two-dimensional array, you should avoid hard-coding the number of rows and columns. Instead, you should use the `length` fields

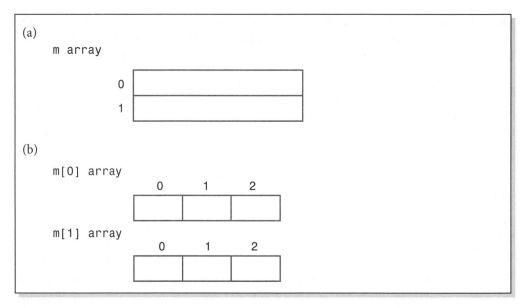

Figure 9.5

associated with the array. For our 2 × 3 m array, you should use m.length for the number of rows and m[row].length for the length of the row with index row. Using this approach to assign 20 to each slot of our array, we get the following nested loops:

```
for (int row = 0; row < m.length; row++)
    for (int col = 0; col < m[row].length; col++)
        m[row][col] = 20;
```

9.5 Passing Arrays

When we call a method, we can pass an array as an argument. When we pass an array, we actually pass only a copy of the reference to the array. The corresponding parameter should have the same type as the argument. For example, on Line 6 in Fig. 9.6, we pass the ia array and 20 to the method initArray. More precisely, we pass a copy of the reference in ia and the value 20.

The parameter v in the initArray method receives a copy of the reference in ia. Thus, v and ia point to the same array (see Fig. 9.7). But that means that the assignment per-

```
1 class ArrayExample
2 {
3     public static void main(String[] args)
4     {
5         int[] ia = new int[5]; // create ia array
6         initArray(ia, 20);       // pass value of ia and 20
7     }
8     //----------------------------------------
9     public static void initArray(int[] v, int value)
10    {
11        for (int i = 0; i < v.length; i++)
12            v[i] = value;         // initializes v array
13    }
14 }
```

Figure 9.6

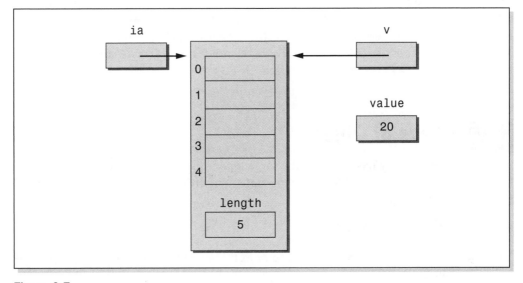

Figure 9.7

formed by Line 12 is to the ia array as well as to the v array (because ia and v point to the same array). The effect of the call of initArray in Fig. 9.6 is to initialize each slot of the ia array to 20.

```
1 public int[] returnIntArray()
2 {
3     int[] q = new int[100];
4     for (int i = 0; i < q.length; i++)
5         q[i] = 7;
6     return q;
7 }
```

Figure 9.8

9.6 Returning Arrays

Methods can return arrays. More precisely, a method can return the reference to an array. For example, in Fig. 9.8, the returnIntArray method creates an int array with 100 slots, initializes each of its slots to 7, and then returns its reference.

The return type on Line 1 is int[], which matches, as it should, the type of q, the array returned by the return statement on Line 6. Once returnIntArray returns to its caller, its local variable, q, is destroyed. However, the array to which q points is not destroyed. Thus, the caller of returnIntArray receives a reference to the array—still in existence—that returnIntArray created and initialized.

9.7 Arrays of Objects

All the slots of an array have to have the same type. This type can be either a primitive type or a class. For example, the following statement creates an array whose associated type is a class (String is a class):

```
String[] sa = new String[3];
```

Each slot can hold a reference to a String object. For example, suppose we execute the following statements,

```
sa[0] = "good";
sa[1] = "bad";
sa[2] = "ugly";
```

We then get the structure shown in Figure 9.9. To display the strings in the sa array, we can use a for loop:

```
for (int i = 0; i < sa.length; i++)
    System.out.println(sa[i]);
```

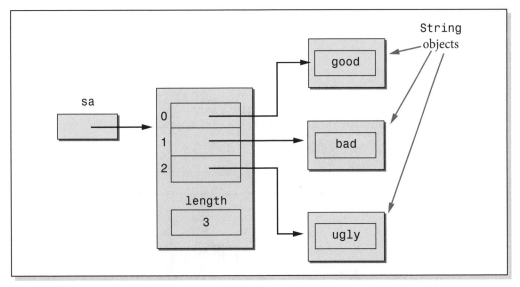

Figure 9.9

9.8 Accessing the Command-Line Arguments

Command-line arguments are arguments we specify on the command line when we invoke a program. For example, the following command line invokes the ArgsExample program in Fig. 9.10a and specifies the command-line arguments dog, 22, and cat:

```
java ArgsExample dog 22 cat
```

The command-line arguments—dog, 22, and cat in this example—are then passed to the main method of the ArgsExample program. The arguments are passed in the form of a String array. The argument-passing mechanism assigns to the args parameter of main the reference to this array. For example, if we invoke the ArgsExample program with the preceding command line, then args—the parameter in the main method of the ArgsExample program—will point to the structure shown in Fig. 9.10b.

To access the first command-line argument from main, we simply use args[0]. Similarly, to access the second and third command-line arguments, we use args[1] and args[2], respectively. To get the number of command-line arguments, we use args.length.

The ArgsExample program in Fig. 9.10a contains a for loop whose exit test uses args.length (which equals the number of command-line arguments). Thus, the body of this

```
(a)

1 class ArgsExample
2 {
3     public static void main(String[] args)
4     {
5         for (int i = 0; i < args.length; i++)
6             System.out.println(args[i]);   // access command line arg
7     }
8 }
```

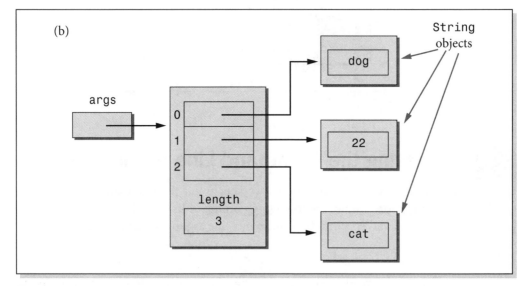

Figure 9.10

loop is executed once for each command-line argument. Each time it is executed, it displays one command-line argument. For example, if we invoke ArgsExample with

```
java ArgsExample dog 22 cat
```

it displays

```
dog
22
cat
```

If we invoke it with

```
java ArgsExample mouse
```

it displays

```
mouse
```

Each command-line argument appears in the `args` array as a `String` object. For example, the argument 22 appears as the `String` object `"22"`. Thus, if we want to perform numerical computations on a command-line argument, we have to convert it from a string to numerical form. For integer arguments, we can do this with the static method `parseInt` in the `Integer` class. For example, suppose `args[1]` is the string `"22"`. Then

```
int x;
x = Integer.parseInt(arg[1]);
```

converts a copy of the string specified by `arg[1]` to type `int` and assigns the result to `x`. `args[1]` itself is not affected. We can then perform computations with `x`. Of course, we can convert arguments to a numerical type only if they correspond to numerical values. For example, we can convert the argument `"22"` to type `int` using `parseInt`, but not the arguments `"dog"` or `"cat"`.

To convert command-line arguments that correspond to `short`, `float`, and `double` constants, use the static methods `parseShort`, `parseFloat`, and `parseDouble` in the `Short`, `Float`, and `Double` wrapper classes, respectively.

9.9 Sorting

An obscure historian has recently reported a remarkable discovery: Telephone technology was first discovered and used back in the Stone Age. Unfortunately, stone man and woman did not find telephones useful. As a result, stone man and woman did not use their telephones, and telephone technology eventually disappeared and was forgotten, only to be rediscovered by Alexander Graham Bell thousands of years later.

Why did stone man and woman not use their telephones? Apparently, the problem was with the phonebooks. No one had yet thought of the idea of sorting. So the phonebooks listed their entries in random order. Thus, to find a desired number, stone man and woman had to serially search the phonebook. That is, they had to scan the phonebook from the beginning, one entry after the next, until they found the desired number. This process took so much time that it was easier and quicker simply to walk to the cave of the party they wished to speak to. Fortunately, when the telephone was rediscovered, sorting techniques had already been discovered. The new phonebooks listed entries in alphabetical order. This order made finding a desired entry easy. As a result, telephone technology took hold and flourished.

The moral of the story is this: Sorted data is easier to use. If you are going to repeatedly access a collection of data, it makes sense to take the time and effort to sort it first. Then each time you need an item from the collection, it is easy to find.

There are many different **algorithms** (i.e., step-by-step procedures that ultimately terminate execution) for sorting data. Let's examine one that is particularly easy to code: the **selection sort**. To sort items into ascending order with a selection sort, we start by selecting the smallest element in our collection. To do this, we scan all the elements to determine the smallest. We then exchange the first element with the smallest, after which the new first element is the smallest. For example, suppose our collection is the following sequence of numbers:

7 3 2 5

We select the smallest (which is 2) and exchange it with the first element. We get

2 3 7 5

Now the 2 is where it belongs (it's the smallest, so it should be first). Next, we repeat the process, starting with the second item. We select the smallest item among the second through the last items (the smallest is 3), and exchange it with the second item (which is also 3). Because the smallest and the second items are the same, the exchange has no effect. Thus, our sequence remains

2 3 7 5

At this point, we now have the two smallest numbers, 2 and 3, where they belong. We again repeat the process, this time starting with the third item. We select the smallest item (which is 5) and exchange it with the third, to get

2 3 5 7

Each time we perform the selection and exchange process, we place the next smallest number in its proper position. Thus, after three iterations of this process, the three smallest numbers are where they belong. But this means that the last number must be the largest, and, therefore, is also where it belongs. Three iterations of our select and exchange process sort four numbers. We can generalize: To sort n numbers, we should perform the selection and exchange process $n - 1$ times. Let's call each time we perform a selection and exchange process a **pass**. We can then say that to perform a selection sort on n numbers, we have to make $n - 1$ passes.

Fig. 9.11 shows the implementation of the selection sort. In `main`, we create an array z (Line 6) and initialize it (Lines 9 and 10) with random integers. We then call `selectionSort` passing it z (Line 12).

```
1  import java.util.Random;
2  class TestSort
3  {
4     public static void main(String[] args)
5     {
6        int[] z = new int[10];
7        Random r = new Random();
8
9        for (int i = 0; i < z.length; i++)   // initialize array
10          z[i] = r.nextInt();
11
12       selectionSort(z);                    // sort array
13
14       for (int i = 0; i < z.length; i++)   // display array
15          System.out.println(z[i]);
16    }
17    //-----------------------------------
18    public static void selectionSort(int[] a)
19    {
20       for (int startIndex=0; startIndex < a.length-1; startIndex++)
21       {
22          int min = a[startIndex];   // set min to starting element
23          int indexOfMin = startIndex; // remember its index
24
25          for (int j = startIndex + 1; j < a.length; j++)
26             if (a[j] < min)                // found smaller element?
27             {
28                min = a[j];                 // rememeber its value
29                indexOfMin = j;             // remember its index
30             }
31
32          a[indexOfMin] = a[startIndex];    // switch first with min
33          a[startIndex] = min;
34       }
35    }
36 }
```

Figure 9.11

The selectionSort method consists of nested for loops. The outer loop executes one fewer times than the length of the array. Each time it executes, it activates the inner loop that performs the selection and exchange process once. The inner loop scans the array for the smallest element. Whenever it finds an element smaller than the smallest one so far, it saves the new smallest in min (Line 28) and records its index in indexOfMin (Line 29).

Thus, after the inner loop completes a pass, `min` has the smallest element and `indexOf-Min` has its index for that pass. The smallest element is then exchanged with the starting element (Lines 32 and 33).

Note that the index j for the inner loop starts at `startIndex + 1` (see Line 25), and the outer loop increments `startIndex` (see Line 20). Thus, each time the inner loop performs a pass, it starts at an index one more than on the previous pass.

9.10 Time and Space Complexity

Let's estimate how much work we have to do when we perform a selection sort. In the selection/exchange process, the exchange part requires very little work compared to the selection part. So let's simply determine how much work the selection part requires.

The first time we perform the selection process, we have to access all the elements of the array to determine the smallest. The second time we perform the selection process, we perform one fewer accesses because we start the selection process from the second element. For each succeeding selection process, we perform one fewer accesses. On the last access, we perform two accesses. Thus, for n numbers, the selection process requires a total of

```
n + (n-1) + (n-2) + ... + 2
```

accesses. A well-known formula for the sum of consecutive integers tells us the preceding expression is equal to

```
(n×(n+1)/2) − 1
```

which is equal to

```
n²/2 + n/2 − 1
```

For large n, this expression equals approximately $n^2/2$ because the $n^2/2$ term dominates the other terms. Let's use this approximation for several values of n. For 10 numbers (i.e., for n equal to 10), we have roughly $10^2/2 = 50$ accesses. For 20 numbers, we have $20^2/2 = 200$ accesses. Because of the square of n in $n^2/2$, each time we double n, $n^2/2$ increases by a factor of 4. In other words, each time we *double* the number of numbers to sort, the work required is *quadrupled*. This means that the work required grows rapidly with increasing n. As a result, using the selection sort to sort a large number of numbers requires an enormous amount of time, even on super-fast computers. Important rule: *To sort a large number of numbers, do not use the selection sort.* There are much faster (but more complex) sort algorithms available.

$n^2/2 + n/2 - 1$ is a measure of the amount of work, and, therefore, the amount of time required by the selection sort. We call this function of n the **time complexity** of the selection sort algorithm. It is a measure of the time required by the selection sort as a function of n, the number of numbers to be sorted.

Time complexities are usually specified using only the dominating term, omitting any constants and lower-order terms. When we do this, we use the phrase "of the order" to indicate that we are not specifying the precise complexity. For example, we say that the time complexity of the selection sort algorithm is "of the order n squared." We can convey the same information using **big-O notation**. For example, we can say that the complexity of the selection sort is $O(n^2)$. $O(n^2)$ means of the order n^2. Some common complexities, in order of increasing complexity, are $O(\log n)$, $O(n)$, $O(n\log(n))$, $O(n^2)$, $O(n^3)$, $O(c^n)$ where c is a constant, and $O(n!)$. $O(n!)$ algorithms are not very useful—they take too long except for very small values of n.

The space complexity of an algorithm is the measure of the amount of storage it requires as a function of n. The **space complexity** of the selection sort is n. The sort takes place in the given array. Thus, a measure of the space required is simply the size of the array to be sorted.

It is far more common for the time complexity of an algorithm to cause problems than the space complexity. That is, when you program an algorithm and run it on a computer, it is more common to require too much time than too much space.

9.11   Binary Search

Suppose we have an array q that holds numbers in ascending order, and we want to determine the index of a particular number in the array. Let's call this number x. One approach is to perform a serial search. In a **serial search**, we examine the values in the array in index order, one after another, until we find x. A much more efficient approach is the **binary search**. Suppose we want to search the q array from index i to index j using the binary search technique. We call i the **start index** and j the **end index**. We repeatedly perform the following steps until we either find x or determine that x is not in the array:

1. If i is greater than j, return –1 (a return value of –1 indicates x is not in the array).
2. Compute mid = (i + j)/2. mid is the index of the number in the middle of that portion of the q array corresponding to indices i to j.
3. If x is equal to q[mid], return mid.
4. If x is less than q[mid], set j to mid − 1 else set i to mid + 1.
   Go to Step 1.

In Step 3, we test if x is equal to q[mid]. If it is, then we are done. We return mid (which is the index of x). In Step 4, we test if x is less than q[mid]. If it is, then x can only be in that portion of the array whose indices run from i to mid − 1 (because the numbers in the array are in ascending order). So we set j (the end index) to mid − 1. If x is greater than q[mid], then x can be only in that portion of the array whose indices run from mid + 1 to j. So we set i (the start index) to mid + 1. After we have narrowed our search in Step 4 by adjusting i or j, we go back to Step 1. Each time we execute Step 4, we narrow our search. i approaches x from below; j approaches x from above. Thus, mid (the average of i and j) ultimately becomes the index of x if x is in the array. The search then ends in Step 3. If x is not in the array, then i will eventually become greater than j by the action of Step 4. This condition causes the search to end in Step 1 (a return value of −1 indicates x is not in the array).

In a serial search, each time we examine a value in the array that is not x, we eliminate only that one value from further consideration. However, in a binary search, we eliminate about half of the numbers from further consideration. For this reason a binary search is able to zero in on x much more quickly than a serial search. For an array with 1000 numbers, a serial search requires on the average about 500 probes (a **probe** is the examination of one value in the array); a binary search requires about 10 probes. The difference is even more dramatic for larger arrays. For an array with one billion numbers, the serial search requires on the average about one-half billion probes; a binary search requires only about 30 probes. The serial search does, however, have one significant advantage over the binary search: the items to be searched do not have to be sorted.

9.12 ArrayList

Suppose C is a class that has a single field whose type is int:

```
class C
{
   private int x;
   ...
}
```

There are two types associated with C. C, itself, is a type. For example, in the statement

```
C r = new C();
```

we are declaring r to have type C. Within the C class, we have a second type—int—the type of its field. Let's call this type the **base type** of the class. A class, of course, can have multiple fields of different types. However, in such cases, there is often a single data type associated with that class. This data type would then be its base type. For example, a class that uses an array to hold strings would certainly have fields of other data types (such as an int field to keep count of the current number of entries in the array). But its principal type—its base type—would be String.

The base type for the preceding C class is fixed—it is always int. Thus, whenever we create an object from the C class, we always get an instance variable x whose type is int. In Java, however, it is possible to create classes in which the types of its fields are not fixed (we will learn how to do this in Chapter 17). We call classes with this property **generic classes**.

ArrayList is a predefined generic class in the java.util package. Its base type is not fixed. An ArrayList is similar to an array. Like an array, an ArrayList object holds a collection of items, each of which can be accessed via its index. But an ArrayList object is different from an array in the following ways:

1. Its base type is not fixed.
2. Its base type must be a class. It cannot be a primitive type.
3. An ArrayList object can grow and shrink during the execution of a program. In contrast, the size of an array is fixed. Once an array is created, its size cannot change.
4. Elements of an ArrayList object are accessed via method calls—not with the square-bracket notation used by arrays.
5. ArrayList is a class in the java.util package. Thus, to use ArrayList, you should include an import statement at the beginning of your program that imports java.util.ArrayList.

When we create an ArrayList reference variable or object, we specify not only the ArrayList type but the base type we want. The base type appears within angle brackets. For example, in the following statement, we are declaring the reference variable sal to have the type ArrayList<String>:

```
ArrayList<String> sal;
```

This declaration indicates that sal is an ArrayList reference with a base type of String. The following statement creates an ArrayList<String> object and assigns its reference to sal:

```
sal = new ArrayList<String>();
```

Alternatively, we can declare the reference sal and create the object in a single statement:

```
ArrayList<String> sal = new ArrayList<String>();
```

To declare an ArrayList reference and create an ArrayList object, we do exactly what we have been doing for nongeneric classes. The only difference is that with an ArrayList the type and constructor names include the desired base type within angle brackets. Remember the base type has to be a class. Thus, the following statement is illegal:

```
ArrayList<int> ial = new ArrayList<int>();          // illegal
```

In spite of this restriction, we can store values with primitive types in an ArrayList. We simply use a wrapper class instead of a primitive type. For example, the following statement creates an ArrayList that holds integers within Integer objects:

```
ArrayList<Integer> ial = new ArrayList<Integer>(); // legal
```

Let's examine a program that illustrates some of the methods in an ArrayList (see Fig. 9.12).

On Line 6, we create an ArrayList sal whose base type is String:

```
6        ArrayList<String> sal = new ArrayList<String>();
```

The sal ArrayList—that is the ArrayList object to which sal points—initially has no slots (its size is 0). We then add two strings to the sal ArrayList by calling the add method in the sal object:

```
8        sal.add("one");              // add "one" to end of sal
9        sal.add("three");            // add "three" to end of sal
```

The add method adds the new element at the end of the current ArrayList structure. Thus, "one" goes into the first slot (because sal is initially empty). More precisely, the reference to "one" goes in the first slot (see Fig. 9.13a); the reference to "three" goes into the second slot. Each time we call add, the ArrayList "grows" to accommodate the new element. Note that the slots of the ArrayList contain references to objects—not the objects themselves.

We can also use add to insert a new element at any valid index. For example,

```
10       sal.add(1, "two");           // insert "two" at index 1
```

inserts "two" into the slot with index 1 (i.e., the second slot). Before it places "two" in this slot, it moves all the elements from index 1 and higher up one slot, freeing up the

```
 1 import java.util.ArrayList;
 2 class ArrayListExample
 3 {
 4     public static void main(String[] args)
 5     {
 6         ArrayList<String> sal = new ArrayList<String>();
 7
 8         sal.add("one");                // add "one" to end of sal
 9         sal.add("three");              // add "three" to end of sal
10         sal.add(1, "two");             // insert "two" at index 1
11         display(sal);                  // displays one two three
12
13         sal.set(1, "2.0");             // overlay slot 1 with "2.0"
14         display(sal);                  // displays one 2.0 three
15
16         System.out.println("slot 1 contains " + sal.get(1));
17
18         System.out.println("Now remove " + sal.remove(1));
19         display(sal);                  // displays one three
20
21         System.out.println("idx is " + sal.indexOf("three"));
22
23         if (sal.contains("three")) // sal obj contains three?
24             System.out.println("sal obj contains three");
25         else
26             System.out.println("sal obj does not contain three");
27
28         System.out.println("size of sal obj is " + sal.size());
29
30         if (sal.isEmpty())
31             System.out.println("sal object is empty");
32         else
33             System.out.println("sal object is not empty");
34
35         sal.clear();                   // reset sal to zero size
36     }
37     //-----------------------------------
38     public static void display(ArrayList<String> sal)
39     {
40         System.out.print("ArrayList now contains ");
41         for (int i = 0; i < sal.size(); i++)
42             System.out.print(sal.get(i) + " ");
43         System.out.println();
44     }
45 }
```

Figure 9.12

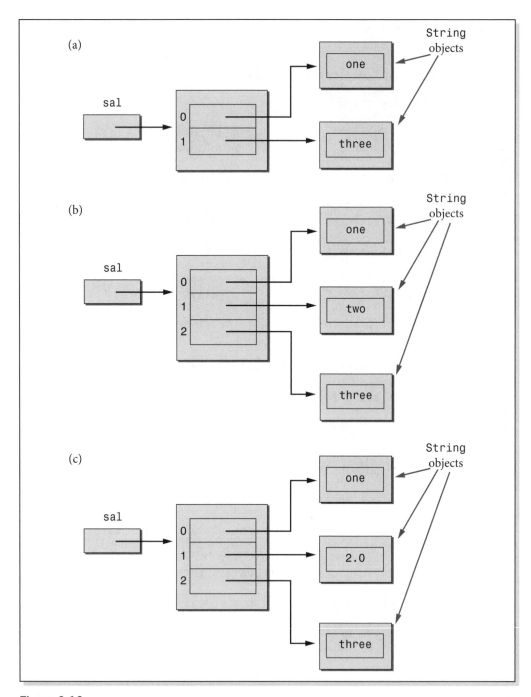

Figure 9.13

slot at index 1 for the new element. Thus, this operation also causes the ArrayList to grow (see Fig. 9.13b). The index used in a call of add can be an index of an existing slot or one more than the index of the last slot. Thus, on Line 10, we could have instead used the indices 0 (to insert at the beginning of the ArrayList) or 2 (to insert at the end of the ArrayList), but not any index greater than 2.

We can overlay any existing slot with a new element, using the set method. For example,

```
13        sal.set(1, "2.0");           // overlay slot 1 with "2.0"
```

overlays slot 1 with the reference to the string "2.0" (See Fig. 9.13c).

To retrieve an element at a specific index, we use the get method. For example, to retrieve and display the string at index 1, we use

```
16        System.out.println("slot 1 contains " + sal.get(1));
```

get does not affect the contents of the ArrayList—it simply returns a copy of the reference at the specified index.

To remove an element from an ArrayList (which causes it to "shrink"), we use the remove method. For example, to remove and display the element at index 1, we use

```
18        System.out.println("Now remove " + sal.remove(1));
```

The remove method not only removes an element, it also returns the removed element. Thus, Line 18 returns the reference to "2.0" (the element at index 1). The println statement then displays this string. Our ArrayList has now reverted back to its previous configuration shown in Fig. 9.13a. If we do not need the element we are removing at index 1, we can simply call remove with

```
sal.remove(1);
```

Like Line 18, this statement removes the element at index 1. However, it discards the reference returned by the call. It would *not*, however, make sense to call get in the same way. For example, do *not* do this:

```
sal.get(1);      // legal but serves no purpose
```

The only purpose of get is to retrieve and return an element. Thus, if we did not use the returned value, the call of get would serve no purpose.

To determine the index of an object in an ArrayList, we use indexOf. For example, the following statement returns and displays the index corresponding to "three" in the ArrayList:

```
21          System.out.println("idx is " + sal.indexOf("three"));
```

If there is no "three" element, indexOf returns −1. indexOf searches the ArrayList in order of index. Thus, if an element appears more than once, indexOf will return the index of the element with the smallest index. lastIndexOf works like indexOf, but it searches the ArrayList in reverse order. Thus, it returns the index of the matching element with the largest index.

If we only want to determine if "three" is in the ArrayList, we can call its contains method, passing it "three". For example, in the following if statement, the call of the contains method returns true if the ArrayList contains "three", and false, otherwise:

```
23          if (sal.contains("three")) // sal obj contains three?
24              System.out.println("sal obj contains three");
25          else
26              System.out.println("sal obj does not contain three");
```

To determine the number of entries in an ArrayList, we call its size method. For example, the following statement determines and displays the size of the sal ArrayList:

```
28          System.out.println("size of sal obj is " + sal.size());
```

Figure 9.14 summarizes the mechanisms for determining how big are arrays, Array-Lists, and strings. Notice they are all different.

To determine if an ArrayList is empty, we can check if its size is 0. Alternatively, we can use the isEmpty method:

```
28          if (sal.isEmpty())
29              System.out.println("sal object is empty");
30          else
31              System.out.println("sal object is not empty");
```

```
Array x          get length by accessing x.length
ArrayList x      get size by calling x.size()
String x         get length by calling x.length()
```

Figure 9.14

The clear method in an ArrayList makes its size revert to zero. For example, to clear the sal ArrayList, we use

```
35        sal.clear();              // reset sal to zero size
```

clear is useful in a program that uses a single ArrayList to hold one set of data, and then later, a second set of data. Calling clear after the processing of the first set of data has completed prepares the ArrayList to receive the second set of data.

The base type of an ArrayList cannot be a primitive type. However, this restriction is minor because we can simply use a wrapper class in place of a primitive type. Because of auto-boxing and unboxing, we can use an ArrayList almost as if it held a primitive type. For example, assume x and ial are defined as follows:

```
int i;
ArrayList<Integer> ial = new ArrayList<Integer>();
```

To add an Integer object that contains 5, we can use

```
ial.add(new Integer(5));
```

But, because of auto-boxing, we can simply pass 5 to add:

```
ial.add(5);          // 5 is auto-boxed
```

The 5 is auto-boxed (i.e., an Integer object is automatically created to hold 5). The resulting Integer object is then added to the ial. To assign x the int value in the first element of ial, we can simply use

```
i = ial.get(0);    // the Integer object at index 0 is auto-unboxed
```

The int value in the Integer object at index 0 is auto-unboxed and then assigned to i. By giving ial a base type of Integer, we can generally use it as if its base type were int.

9.13   A Milestone

The simplest of Java programs involves some advanced concepts, such as static methods, arrays, argument passing, and the void return type. So back in Chapter 1, it was impossible for you to fully understand the program in Fig. 1.2. But now you can. By covering the first nine chapters in this book, you have reached a major milestone in your study of Java: You can understand (finally!) the simple program in Chapter 1.

LABORATORY

Laboratory 9 Prep

1. Give a statement that creates an `int` array with 200 slots.

2. Give a `for` loop that initializes each slot of an `int` array `ia` to one more than its index.

3. Give the statement that creates a 5 × 10 `double` array.

4. Suppose an array contains the integers 1 to 10 in ascending order. How many probes will a binary search perform to find 3 in the array?

5. What does the program in Fig. 9.12 display?

Laboratory 9

1. Incorporate the following code in a program. Compile and run. What happens? Why?

```
int[] a;
a = new int[5];
a[5] = 10;
```

2. What is unusual about the following `for` loop (it is legal):

```
for (int i = 1, sum = 0; i < 10; i++)
   sum = sum + i;
```

You can have more than one statement in the startup or update actions in a `for` loop as long as each statement is separated from the next with a comma (the comma replaces the semicolon that normally terminates a statement).

3. Incorporate the following code in a program. Compile and run. What do the two `for` loops do?

```
int[] ia = {1, 2, 3};
for (int z, int i = 0; i < ia.length; i++)
{
   z = ia[i];
   System.out.println(z);
}
for (int z: ia)                  // enhanced for loop
   System.out.println(z);
```

The startup action in the first `for` loop declares z and i, and initializes i to 0. It then displays all the elements in the ia array. The second `for` loop is an example of an **enhanced for loop**. z in this loop is not the index used to access the array. Instead, z receives the successive values in the array. This loop is equivalent to the first loop.

4. Do enhanced for loops (see Lab Exercise 3) work for an ArrayList? Incorporate the following code in a program and run it to check your answer:

```
ArrayList<Integer> ial = new ArrayList<Integer>():
ial.add(100);
ial.add(200);
ial.add(300);
ial.add(400);

for (int z: ial)
    System.out.println(z);
```

5. When you create an array with the new operator, can you use an expression for the size? For example, is the following code legal:

```
int x = 3, y = 4;
int[] a = new int[x + y];
```

Run a test program to check your answer.

6. Try to assign a new value to the length field for an array. What happens?

7. Write a program that includes the following loop that displays the contents of the z array:

```
i = 0;
while (i < z.length)
{
    System.out.println(z[i]);
    i++;
}
```

Then replace the entire body of the loop (including the braces) with the following single statement:

```
System.out.println(z[i++]);
```

Does the loop work the same way as the original version? What would happen if the "++" operator preceded i?

8. Write a program that reads in 20 strings from the keyboard and then displays them in reverse order. Read the strings into an array. Then write a second program like the first, but use an ArrayList instead of an array.

9. In the following program, we have a nonstatic int array nsia and a static int array sia. The natural place to initialize the nonstatic array is in the constructor. However, although it is legal to initialize the static array in the constructor, you should not do so for two reasons:

LABORATORY

a) We can use a static field before creating any objects—that is, before any constructor is executed. Thus, if a constructor performs the initialization, it would be possible to use the static field before it has been initialized.

b) Each time we create an object, the static fields would be reinitialized. We want the static fields initialized only once when the class containing it is first loaded into memory.

To initialize the static array, use a **static initializer** (see Lines 6–11 that follow). It is executed only once when the class is first loaded into memory. Use it to initialize static fields when the initialization is too involved to be handled in the declaration of the static field. For example, if we have a static field x whose initial value is supposed to be 1, we can simply declare it with

```
private static int x = 1;
```

We would not need a static initializer. We could similarly declare and simultaneously initialize an array:

```
private static int[] a = {1, 2, 3, 4};
```

However, this approach is not practical if the array is large.

A static initializer has no name. It consists of the reserved world `static` followed by a block of initialization code. Run the following program. From the output generated, determine the order in which `main`, the static initializer, and the constructor are executed.

```
 1 class Initializer
 2 {
 3    private int[] nsia = new int[100];
 4    private static int[] sia = new int[100];
 5    //----------------------------------
 6    static                  // static initializer
 7    {
 8       System.out.println("In static initializer");
 9       for (int i = 0; i < sia.length; i++)
10          sia[i] = i;
11    }
12    //----------------------------------
13    public Initializer() // constructor
14    {
15       System.out.println("In constructor");
16       for (int i = 0; i < nsia.length; i++)
17          nsia[i] = i;
18    }
19 }
20 //===============================================
```

```
21 class C9e9
22 {
23    public static void main(String[] args)
24    {
25        System.out.println("Start of main");
26        Initializer r = new Initializer();
27        System.out.println("End of main");
28    }
29 }
```

10. Write a program that reads in 15 integers into a 3 × 5 array. Display the last row. Display the last column. Display the entire array with each row on a separate line.

11. Is the following code legal:

```
int[] a = new int[3];
a[0] = a[1] = a[2] = 5;
System.out.println(a.toString());
System.out.println(a);
```

Does an array have a toString method? Run a test program to check your answer. Try to decipher the output displayed.

12. Use the selection sort to sort n numbers. Determine the value of n for which the elapsed time of your sort is about 10 seconds. Double n (i.e., double the number of numbers to sort) and sort. What is the sorting time for the new value of n? Double n again and determine the sorting time. What happens to the sorting time each time you double n? Estimate how long sorting one billion numbers would take.

13. Use the selection sort to sort the numbers in the int array ia. Use calls to System.currentTimeMillis before and after the sort to determine the elapsed time:

```
long start = System.currentTimeMillis();
// do sort
long stop = System.currentTimeMillis();
```

System.currentTimeMillis returns the current time in milliseconds. Thus, to get elapsed time in seconds, divide the difference in the start and stop times by 1000.0. Then round the result to the nearest long value by calling Math.round:

```
long elapsed = Math.round((stop − start)/1000.0);
```

Determine the size of ia for which the elapsed time of the sort is about 100 seconds. Now perform the same sort using the static sort method in the Arrays class in the java.util package. Call this method with

```
Arrays.sort(ia);
```

What is the elapsed time for this sort? Is this sort significantly faster than the selection sort?

LABORATORY

14. Each row in a two-dimensional array does not have to have the same length. Arrays in which rows have differing lengths are called **ragged arrays**. The following code creates a ragged array m with three rows:

```
int[][] m = new int[3][];
m[0] = new int[3];
m[1] = new int[5];
m[2] = new int[2];
```

Write a test program in which you create a ragged array using the preceding code. Assign each slot the sum of its row and column indices. Use nested for loops. Draw a picture of the jagged array.

15. Does the `ArrayList` class have an `equals` method? For example, does the following code work as you would expect:

```
String s1 = new String("hello");
String s2 = new String("hello");
ArrayList<String> q1 = new ArrayList<String>();
ArrayList<String> q2 = new ArrayList<String>();
q1.add(s1); q1.add(s1);
q2.add(s2); q2.add(s2);
// compare two ArrayLists with equals
System.out.println(q1.equals(q2));
```

16. The `remove` method in an `ArrayList` is overloaded. One version has an `int` parameter. The second version has a reference parameter. Try out the version with a reference parameter by running the following code. When remove is passed i2 does it remove the i1 object (see the comments in the code)?

```
ArrayList<Integer> ial = new ArrayList<Integer>();
Integer i1 = new Integer(1);
Integer i2 = new Integer(1);       // construct identical object
if (i1 == i2)
    System.out.println("identical references, identical objects");
else
    System.out.println("different references, identical objects");
ial.add(i1);
ial.remove(i1);                    // remove what was just added
System.out.println(ial.size());    // should be zero
ial.add(i1);
ial.remove(i2);                    // will passing i2 remove i1?
System.out.println(ial.size());    // is it zero?
```

17. What does `indexOf` return if its argument is not in the `ArrayList`?

18. The complexity of the binary search algorithm is $O(\log_2 n)$. What is the complexity of the serial search algorithm?

Homework 9

1. Write a program that displays the sum of the command-line arguments. For example, if you enter

```
java C9h1 1 3.5 7
```

your C9h1 program will display

```
Sum = 11.5
```

Your program should work with any number of command-line arguments. (*Hint:* Use `Double.parseDouble`, which converts a string to type `double`.)

2. Write a program that prompts for and reads in 10 `int` numbers. Your program should then display every number read in that is bigger than the average of all the numbers read in. Test your program by entering the numbers 1, 2, 3, 4, 5, 6, 7, 8, 9, and 30.

3. Write a program in which you create a 5 × 10 `int` array. Using nested `for` loops, assign row 0 all zeros, row 1 all ones, and so on. Display the final contents of the array in rectangular format using a second set of nested loops.

4. Write a program that prompts for and reads in three test grades for each of five students. Your program should then display the average for each student and the average for each test. Be sure to label your output appropriately. Use a two-dimensional array. Use the following test data:

```
Student 1: 100, 100, 100
Student 2:  90,  90,  90
Student 3:  80,  80,  80
Student 4:  30,  40,  50
Student 5:   0,   1,   2
```

5. Write a program in which `main` creates two `int` arrays each with 10 slots and then initializes the first array with random integers. `main` then calls `copyArray`, passing it the two arrays. `copyArray` should copy the values from the first array to the second and then return to `main`. `main` should then display the contents of both arrays side by side.

6. Create an `ExpandableArray` class. It should have methods `add`, `get`, `set`, and `size`. These methods should work like the identically named methods in an `ArrayList`.

LABORATORY

Internally, ExpandableArray should have an int array with two slots initially. The size method should return the net number of integers added—not the number of slots in the internal array. Thus, initially size should be zero. If on a call of add the internal array is full, the add method should:

a) Create a new array with twice the number of slots as the current array.

b) Copy the contents of the original array to the new array, and thereafter use the new array (until it too is not big enough).

Write a program that uses your ExpandableArray class. It should:

a) Create an ExpandableArray object.

b) Add 1, 2, 99, 4, 6, 7, 8, 9, and 10, in that order.

c) Set 99 to 3.

d) Insert 5 after the number 4.

e) Display the current size.

f) Display the integers stored by calling get within a for loop.

7. Implement and test a **bubble sort**. To sort n numbers, make n − 1 passes. On each pass, compare every pair of adjacent numbers. If any pair is not in ascending order, switch the pair. On the first pass, start from the first element (compare the first with the second, the second with the third, and so on). On the second pass, again start from the first element but stop your compares one slot from the end of the array. In each successive pass, stop one slot before the stopping point of the previous pass. Use your bubble sort to sort 100, 23, 15, 23, 7, 23, 2, 311, 5, 8, and 3. Display the sorted numbers.

8. Modify the program in Fig. 9.11 so that is uses an ArrayList in place of an array. *Hint:* Replace Line 26 with

```
if (a.get(j).compareTo(min) < 0)
```

9. Create a Table class according to the following specifications:

Data fields: ArrayList<Integer> id, ArrayList<String> name

Constructor: public Table()
                creates the ArrayList id and name.

Methods: public void add(int i, String n)
                adds i to id, adds n to name

           public String getName(int searchID)
                returns the string in name whose id is searchID.

                If searchId is not in id, getName should return null.

Write a program that uses your `Table` class. Your program should execute the following loop:

a) Prompt for and read in an ID number (a nonnegative integer).

b) If the number is negative, exit the loop.

c) Prompt for and read in a name. Call the `add` method in a `Table` object, passing the ID number and name read in.

d) Go to Step a.

When the loop exits, execute a second loop:

e) Prompt for and read in an ID number.

f) If the number is negative, exit the loop.

g) Display the name that corresponds to the number entered. If no name corresponds to the number entered, display `INVALID NUMBER`.

h) Go to Step e.

Test your program by entering the following data: For the first loop, enter

```
151 Tom 22 Dick 16 Harriet -1
```

For the second loop, enter

```
16 151 22 55 -1
```

10. Same as Homework Exercise 1 in Chapter 8 except replace the *entire* `switch` statement in `countIt` with a *single* simple statement (not an `if` statement) that increments one of the slots of a counter array c. The c array should have five slots, each slot serving as one counter. For example, `c[0]` should count the number of 0's, `c[1]` should count the number of 1's, and so on. Design your program so that it can be modified to handle a different number of counts with almost no changes. For example, changing your program to count the occurrences of the numbers from 0 to 100 instead of from 0 to 4 should require a change of only one line of your program.

11. Create a `BinarySearch` class. It should have an `add` method that adds the integer it is passed to an internal array in the order given, and a `search` method that determines the index of the number it is passed using a binary search. Create a `BinarySearch` object. Add the following integers: 2, 44, 98, 2020, 4412, 12345, 21345, 34343, 73737, and 99999, in that order. Then call search for each of these arguments: 2, 4412, 99999, and 5000. For each call, display the value passed and the value returned.

12. Write your own `StringBuffer` class. Call it `MyStringBuffer`. Include all the `StringBuffer` methods described in Section 8.4 in your class. Use a char array whose initial

LABORATORY

size is 2 to hold the string. If on any operation the array is not big enough, a new larger array should be created to which the old array is copied. The new array should then be used. Replace `StringBuffer` in `C9h12.java` with `MyStringBuffer`. Compile and run.

13. Same as Homework Exercise 7 in Chapter 8 except use the following strategy: Create four "cups" numbered 0, 1, 2, 3, each containing the moves 1, 2, and 3. When it is the program's turn, it should select its next move randomly from the cup whose number is given by (number of straws left) % 4. If the selected cup is empty, your program should pick up one straw. When a move in a cup is selected, it should not be removed from the cup except in the following two situations:

a) If the move results in an immediate loss (i.e., if it is greater than or equal to the number of straws).

b) If the selected cup is cup number 1, and in the previous move made by the program, the selected cup was not empty. In this case, the *previous* move should be removed from the cup from which it was selected.

15. Write an `IntHasher` class according to the following specifications:

Data fields:
```
private int[] ia;
private boolean[] available;
private int entryCount;
private long probeCount;
```

Constructors: `public IntHasher()`
Creates `ia` and `available` arrays each with 1000 slots.
Initializes each slot of `available` to `true`.
Sets `entryCount` and `probeCount` to 0.

Methods: `public boolean enter(int x)`
Stores value of x in `ia[Math.abs(x)%1000]` and `false` in `available[Math.abs(x)%1000]` unless these slots are not available (as indicated by the `available` array). If the slots are not available, then `enter` should search sequentially for an available slot starting with the next slot. If the search is unsuccessful by the end of the array, the search should wrap around to the beginning of the array. If the array is full so that x cannot be stored, `enter` should return `false` to its caller. Otherwise, it should increment `entryCount` and return `true` after storing x and updating `available`.

`public int getIndex(int x)`
Returns the index at which x is stored. Increments `probeCount` on each probe—that is, each time `getIndex` accesses a slot of the

ia array. Returns -1 if x is not in the array. getIndex should use the same search sequence as enter.

```
public long getProbeCount()
```
returns probeCount.

```
public void clear()
```
Sets entryCount and probeCount to 0. Sets each slot in available to true.

Write a program that creates an IntHasher object. Your program should generate 100 random integers (call nextInt in Random without any argument), and enter each one into the IntHasher object. After all 100 integers have been entered, call getIndex for each integer previously entered (regenerate the same sequence of integers by resetting the seed of the random number generator to its original value by calling setSeed). Display entryCount, the average number of probes per integer, and the total number of probes. Call clear. Repeat the preceding procedure for 200, 300, 400, 500, 600, 700, 800, 900, and 1000 integers.

The number of integers stored divided by the array size is called the **loading factor**. As the loading factor increases, the likelihood of a **collision**—two integers having the same initial index—increases. If all the integers are loaded into the array without any collisions, then the number of probes per integer is one. But if there are collisions, then accessing some of the integers stored in the table requires a sequential search, necessitating additional probes. By keeping the loading factor low, we can keep the average number of probes to a small value. From the data generated by your program, determine the largest loading factor for which the average number of probes is small. How does the average number of probes for this loading factor compare with the number of probes for a serial search? For a binary search?

The technique of storing and retrieving data that is illustrated by this problem is called **hash coding**. Each data item has to be "hashed" to a hash code (the array index). The mathematical function that describes the hashing mechanism is called the **hash function**. For our program, the hash function is $h(x) = Math.abs(x)\%1000$.

16. Extend your IntHasher class in Homework Exercise 15 so that it keeps track of the maximum number of probes required to access any single integer in the table. Display this maximum along with the average and total number of probes. Run the program with different seeds to see how the statistics produced vary with different sets of random numbers.

17. Write a program that creates a three-dimensional array and assigns each element the sum of its three indices. Display the contents of the array by the row and column values at successive depths.

LABORATORY

18. Write a program that prompts the user for a nonnegative integer n. It should then compute and display the value of n! (n factorial). Your program should be able to compute n! for any value of n up to 100. To compute such large factorials, use an int array `factorial` to hold the successive factorials your program computes. Each slot of the `factorial` array should hold a *single* digit of a factorial. For example, 720 (6!) would be represented with the digits 0, 2, and 7 in `factorial[0]`, `factorial[1]`, and `factorial[2]`, respectively, with 0 in all the remaining slots. Suppose the `factorial` array contains k!. To compute (k+1)!

   a) Multiply each slot in `factorial` by (k+1).

   b) Propagate the carries so that each slot holds a single digit. For example, suppose after the multiplication in Step (a), 49 is in some slot. Your program should add 4 to the next higher slot and assign 9 to the slot with 49.

   Make your program as efficient as possible. For example, avoid unnecessary multiplications in Step (a). Using your program, determine the values of 0! (by definition, its value is 1), 1!, 2!, 48!, 49!, 50!, 98!, 99!, and 100! Before you run your program, can you predict how many trailing zeros are in each of these factorials?

CHAPTER 10

Inheritance: Part 1

OBJECTIVES

- Learn the advantages of inheritance
- Learn how to use inheritance
- Understand the golden rule of inheritance
- Understand the ramifications of downcasting and upcasting
- Understand the `Object` class

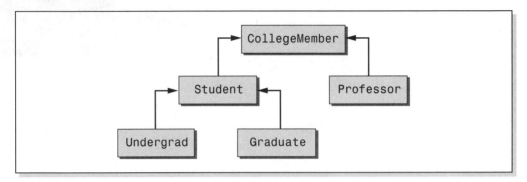

Figure 10.1

10.1 Advantages of Inheritance

Inheritance is a feature of object-oriented programming languages that allows a class to "inherit" the members of another class. It provides three significant advantages:

1. Many real-world systems form a hierarchy of categories. For example, we can view the membership of a college as such a hierarchy (see Fig. 10.1). At the top of this hierarchy is the generic category CollegeMember. Below CollegeMember, we have the Student and Professor categories. Below Student we have the Undergrad and Graduate categories. Using inheritance, we can easily model these categories and their hierarchical structure. Programs created with this approach are easier to design, implement, and modify.

2. Inheritance allows the compiled form of classes to be modified and/or extended. If a class is available that almost satisfies your requirements, you can adjust it—without any access to its source code—using inheritance to precisely meet your requirements. You then do not have to write the class from scratch. In this way, inheritance facilitates the sharing of code.

3. Inheritance eliminates the need to duplicate code. For example, suppose each class in Fig. 10.1 needs a displayName method that displays the member's name. With inheritance, we can place the displayName method in the CollegMember class only. This method is then inherited by all the classes below it. Thus, we do not have to include the displayName method in any of the classes below the CollegeMember class.

10.2 Simple Example of Inheritance

Let's start by looking at the simple example of inheritance in Fig. 10.2. The phrase "B extends A" on Line 19 in Fig. 10.2a makes B a **subclass** of A, or equivalently, it makes A a **superclass** of B. That is, class B is positioned in the class hierarchy right below class A (see Fig. 10.2b). A superclass is sometimes referred to as the **base class**, and its subclass as the **derived class**.

(a)

```
 1 class A                      // This is the superclass
 2 {
 3    private int x = 1;
 4    //----------------------------------
 5    public int xGet()
 6    {
 7       return x;
 8    }
 9    //----------------------------------
10    public String toString()
11    {
12       return("x = " + x);
13    }
14 }
15 /*================================================
16   B is a subclass of A.  B inherits x, xGet, and toString from A.
17   toString defined in B overrides toString inherited from A.
18 */
19 class B extends A // "B extends A" makes B a subclass of A
20 {
21    int y = 7;
22    //----------------------------------
23    public int yGet()
24    {
25       return y;
26    }
27    //----------------------------------
28    public String toString() // overrides toString from A
29    {
30       return "x = " + xGet() + " y = " + y;
31    }
32 }
33 //================================================
34 class Inheritance1
35 {
36    public static void main(String[] args)
37    {
38       A a = new A();                        // create A object
39       System.out.println(a.xGet());      // get and display x
40       System.out.println(a.toString()); // displays x = 1
41
```

Figure 10.2   (continues)

```
42          B b = new B();                      // create B object
43          System.out.println(b.yGet());       // get and display y
44          System.out.println(b.xGet());       // get and display x
45          System.out.println(b.toString());   // displays x = 1 y = 7
46       }
47 }
```

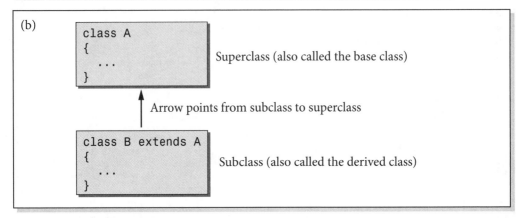

Figure 10.2   (continued)

The B class has a y field, a yGet method, and a toString method. However, because it is a subclass of A, it also inherits all the members of the A class. Thus, it also has an inherited x field and inherited methods xGet and toString. x is private. Thus, the methods of B cannot directly access x, even though B is a subclass of A. However, B has indirect access of x through the public method xGet it inherits from A.

When we create an object from the A class with

```
38          A a = new A();                      // create A object
```

a will point to an object that has an x instance variable, the xGet method, and the toString method—the three members of A (see Fig. 10.3a). However, when we create an object from the B class with

```
42          B b = new B();                      // create B object
```

b will point to an object that has all the members of A as well as B (see Fig. 10.3b).

We, of course, can invoke the xGet and toString methods in the A object with

```
39          System.out.println(a.xGet());       // get and display x
40          System.out.println(a.toString());   // displays x = 1
```

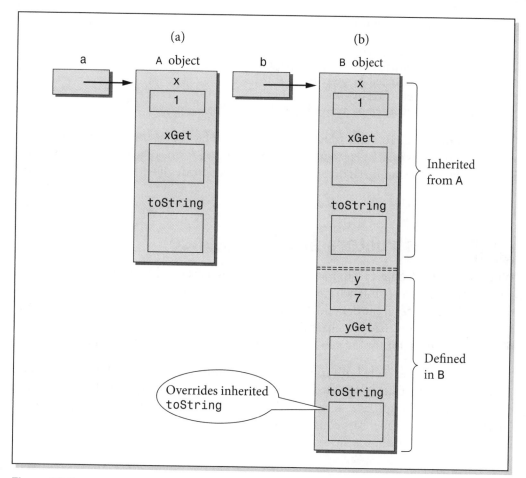

Figure 10.3

We can similarly invoke the yGet method in the B object with

43   System.out.println(b.yGet());   // get and display y

We can also invoke the inherited xGet method in the B object with

44   System.out.println(b.xGet());   // get and display x

The B object has two toString methods—one defined in B and one inherited from A. The toString defined in B **overrides** the inherited one. That is, a call of toString in a B object will execute the toString defined in the B class rather than the inherited toString. Thus, the call of toString on Line 45 executes the toString defined in B:

45   System.out.println(b.toString()); // displays x = 1 y = 7

When executed, the program in Fig. 10.2 displays

```
1                       (returned by xGet in A)
x = 1                   (returned by toString in A)
7                       (returned by yGet in B)
1                       (returned by inherited xGet)
x = 1 y = 7             (returned by toString defined in B)
```

The program in Fig. 10.2 illustrates how inheritance facilitates the sharing of code. By making B a subclass of A, B gets to use the public items in A, one of which—toString—is inappropriate for B. But that's no problem. B simply overrides it with a toString method of its own.

10.3 Constructors and Inheritance

When we create an object from a subclass, we have to execute the constructor for the superclass as well as the constructor for the subclass. We need to execute both constructors to properly initialize all the data fields in the object of the subclass. Execution of the constructor for the superclass initializes the data fields that the subclass inherits. The execution of the constructor for the subclass initializes the data fields defined in the subclass.

Exactly how do we execute both constructors? It is quite simple for the following reason: Every subclass constructor *necessarily* calls a constructor in its superclass. Thus, by calling the constructor of a subclass, we automatically trigger the execution of both the subclass constructor and the superclass constructor. For example, suppose B is a subclass of A, and we create an object from B with

```
B b = new B();
```

Here we are calling the B constructor. The B constructor, in turn, calls the A constructor. The B constructor initializes the data fields defined in B; the A constructor initializes data fields inherited from A. The result is that all the fields in the B object are properly initialized.

But what if a subclass constructor does not call a constructor in its superclass? This cannot happen. If we do not include an explicit call of a superclass constructor at the beginning of a subclass constructor, the compiler will insert one in the code it generates. Moreover, if we do not supply any constructors for a class, the compiler will insert one—a **default constructor**—in the code it generates whose only operation is to call the superclass constructor. Thus, we are guaranteed that

1. Every class has at least one constructor.
2. Every subclass constructor calls a constructor in its superclass.

Let's now look at the example in Fig. 10.4 that illustrates these concepts.

```
 1 class A
 2 {
 3     private int x;
 4     //---------------------------------
 5     public A()
 6     {
 7         x = 1;
 8     }
 9     //---------------------------------
10     public void xDisplay()
11     {
12         System.out.println("x = " + x);
13     }
14 }
15 //================================================
16 class B extends A
17 {
18     private int y;
19     //---------------------------------
20     public B()
21     {
22         y = 2;                    super();
23     }                             inserted here
24     //---------------------------------
25     public B(int yy)
26     {
27         super();          // explicit call of superclass constructor
28         y = yy;
29     }
30     //---------------------------------
31     public void xyDisplay()
32     {
33         xDisplay();       // call inherited method
34         System.out.println("y = " + y);
35     }
36 }
37 //================================================
38 class C extends B
39 {                                    Default constructor
40     private int z = 4;               inserted here
41     //---------------------------------
42     public void xyzDisplay()
```

Figure 10.4 (continues)

```
43     {
44         xyDisplay();
45         System.out.println("z = " + z);
46     }
47 }
48 //================================================
49 class Inheritance2
50 {
51     public static void main(String[] args)
52     {
53         B b = new B();
54         b.xyDisplay();      // displays x = 1 y = 2
55         b = new B(3);
56         b.xyDisplay();      // displays x = 1 y = 3
57         C c = new C();
58         c.xyzDisplay();     // displays x = 1 y = 2 z = 4
59     }
60 }
```

Figure 10.4   (continued)

A constructor should not call a superclass constructor by name. Instead, it should call it with the reserved word super. For example, the B constructor that starts on Line 25 explicitly calls the A constructor with

```
27         super();        // call constructor of superclass
```

not with

```
A();                       // illegal
```

The B constructor that starts on Line 20 does not explicitly call its superclass constructor. Thus, the compiler inserts a call of the superclass constructor in the bytecode it generates. That is, it generates bytecode as if

```
super();
```

were at the beginning of the B constructor.

The class C has no constructor. Thus, the compiler inserts a default constructor in the bytecode it generates. That is, it generates bytecode as if the C class had the following constructor:

```
public C()      // default constructor
{
    super();
}
```

When we construct a C object with

```
57          C c = new C();
```

the default C constructor calls the B constructor on Line 20, which in turn calls the A constructor on Line 5. The A constructor initializes x to 1 and returns to the B constructor. The B constructor then initializes y to 2 and returns to the C constructor, where z is already initialized to 4 by the statement that declares it (see Line 40). The instance variables in C (x, y, and z) are all initialized: x by the A constructor, y by the B constructor, and z by the statement that declares it.

The default constructor that the compiler inserts contains a call of super that has *no arguments*. Thus, there should be a constructor in the superclass that has *no parameters*. Otherwise, a compile-time error results. For example, suppose the A class in Fig. 10.4 had only one constructor, and this constructor had a single parameter. Then the B constructor that starts on Line 20 would generate a compile-time error: the zero-argument call of super the compiler inserts would have no compatible constructor in A to call.

10.4   A Toolbox and a Toolbox with a Cheese Sandwich

In this section, we start to examine some of the nuances of inheritance in Java. On your first reading, you may find this material confusing. However, if you keep in mind the **golden rule of inheritance** (we will explain what it means shortly), you should be able to master this material quickly:

A reference can point "across" or "up" but not "down."

Suppose you have a toolbox with tools and another toolbox with tools and a cheese sandwich. A toolbox with a cheese sandwich is, of course, a toolbox. It is just a special kind of toolbox: it has not only tools but also a cheese sandwich. However, a toolbox is not necessarily a toolbox with a cheese sandwich because not all toolboxes have cheese sandwiches. We can say that there is an "**is a**" relationship between a toolbox with a cheese sandwich and a tool box. That is, it is always true that a toolbox with a cheese sandwich "is a" toolbox. But the converse relationship is not true. That is, it is not always true that a toolbox "is a" toolbox with a cheese sandwich.

A toolbox and a toolbox with a cheese sandwich are analogous to a class and a subclass. Suppose B is a subclass of A. Through inheritance, a B object has everything an A object has. Thus, it is always true that a B object is an A object. But not all A objects are B objects. If we execute

```
A a = new A();
B b = new B();
```

then the object to which b points is a B object. Through inheritance, it has everything an A object is required to have. Thus, this object is also an A object. However, the object to which a points is an A object but not a B object. It does not have the fields and methods defined in the B class. The A object is like a toolbox; the B object is like a toolbox with a cheese sandwich. As a toolbox with a cheese sandwich "is a" toolbox, a B object "is a" A object. The subclass B has an "is a" relationship with its superclass A.

An A reference variable is allowed to point to A objects only. But if B is a subclass of A, then a B object *is also an* A *object.* Thus, an A reference variable can also point to a B object. For example, consider the following code:

```
A a;
B b = new B();   // B is a subclass of A
a = b;           // legal because a B object is also an A object
```

We are creating a B object here. We assign its reference to b. We then assign b to a. So both a and b point to the same object (see Fig. 10.5).

Because A is higher than B in the class hierarchy (A is a superclass of B), we can think of a in Fig. 10.5 as pointing "down" because it is pointing to an object whose type is lower than its own in the class hierarchy. b, on the other hand, is pointing "across" because it is pointing to an object of its own type.

Is it legal for b, a type B reference variable, to point across to a B object? Yes, it is because a B reference variable is supposed to point to B objects. Is it legal for a, a type A reference variable, to point down to a B object? Yes it is because an A reference variable

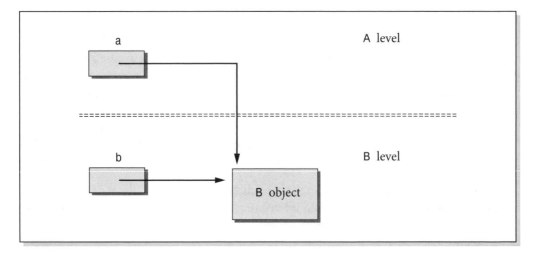

Figure 10.5

is supposed to point to A objects, and a B object is also an A object. However, it is *not* legal for a B reference variable to point "up" to a regular A object (i.e., an A object that is not also a B object) because it can point to B objects only. For example, consider the following code:

```
B b;                // B is a subclass of A
A a = new A();
b = a;              // illegal because b would point "up"
```

b is a B reference variable so it can point to B objects only. Thus, it is illegal to assign a (which is pointing to an A object that is not also a B object) to b (see Fig. 10.6).

If we were to do this assignment, then b would point up to an A object. If we compile the preceding code, we will get a compile-time error on the statement that assigns a to b. If we replace the offending statement with

```
b = (B)a;           // compiles ok but still illegal
```

we will eliminate the compile-time error. However, we will then get a run-time error on this statement. Thus, with or without a cast, it is illegal for a reference to point up.

Finally, let's consider the following code:

```
A a;
B b1, b2;           // B is a subclass of A
b1 = new B();
a = b1;             // okay because a is pointing "down"
```

Here we are creating a B object to which both a and b1 point (see Fig. 10.7).

Now suppose we attempt to assign a to b2 with

```
b2 = a;
```

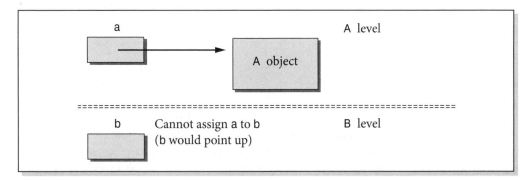

Figure 10.6

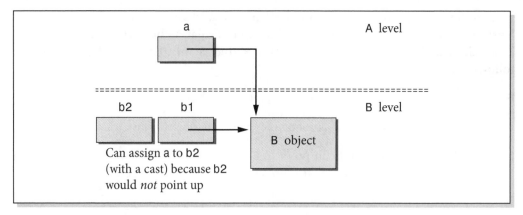

Figure 10.7

This statement causes a compile-time error because the compiler assumes a points to a regular A object (because a has type A). Remember that compile-time precedes run-time. Thus, the compiler does not know what will be in a at run-time. It assumes a is pointing to a regular A object, in which case this statement would have the effect of making b2 point up. If, however, we assign a to b2 using

```
b2 = (B)a;    // legal because a is pointing down
```

the cast prevents the compile-time error. Moreover, because a points to a B object in this example, the assignment is legal at run-time, after which both a and b2 will both point to the same B object. a will point down; b2 will point across.

10.5 Downcasting and Upcasting

Suppose B is a subclass of A, b is type B, a is type A, and a is initialized with

```
a = new A();
```

In the statement

```
B b = (B)a;
```

we are **downcasting** a. That is, we are changing the type of reference to one that is lower in the class hierarchy. The value of the reference does not change—just the type. In our example, the reference obtained from a is type A. The cast produces a type B reference, which is lower in the class hierarchy. Because the reference obtained from a is cast to a type B reference, the compiler allows the assignment to b. However, as we saw in the preceding section, a type B reference cannot point up to a type A object. Thus, this particular downcast fails at run-time because it attempts to create a type B reference that points up to a regular A object.

A downcast does not necessarily produce a run-time error. For example, in the following sequence, the downcast succeeds:

```
A a
B b1, b2;
b1 = new B();
a = b1;
b2 = (B)a;        // this downcast is legal
```

Here, a is pointing down to a type B object (see Fig. 10.7). Thus, the downcast does not produce a type B reference that points up to a regular A object. Instead, it produces a type B reference that points across to a B object.

To avoid run-time errors when downcasting, we can use the instanceof operator to test if the downcast is legal. The instanceof operator returns true if its left operand points to an object whose type is the same as its right operand, and false otherwise. For example, suppose a is as shown in Fig. 10.6 (a is pointing to a regular A object). Then if we execute

```
B b;
if (a instanceof B)
    b = (B)a;
```

the instanceof operator will return false because a does not point to a B object. Thus, the downcast will not be performed. If, however, a is as shown in Fig. 10.7, then the instanceof operator will return true, and the downcast will be successfully performed.

We can also use the instanceof operator to determine which of several possible downcasts to perform. For example, suppose C is also a subclass of A, and a is pointing down to either a B object or a C object. We can use the instanceof operator to determine which downcast to perform:

```
B b;
C c;
if (a instanceof B)
    b = (B)a;
else
if (a instanceof C)
    c = (C)a;
```

Let's now examine some of the ramifications of downcasting. Consider the program in Fig. 10.8. Line 33 assigns b (a reference to a B object) to a (a type A reference).

```
 1 class A
 2 {
 3     public void f()
 4     {
 5         System.out.println("f in A");
 6     }
 7     //-------------------------------------
 8     public void g()
 9     {
10         System.out.println("g in A");
11     }
12 }
13 //=================================================
14 class B extends A
15 {
16     public void g()
17     {
18         System.out.println("g in B");
19     }
20     //-------------------------------------
21     public void h()
22     {
23         System.out.println("h in B");
24     }
25 }
26 //=================================================
27 class Inheritance3
28 {
29     public static void main(String[] args)
30     {
31         A a;
32         B b = new B();
33         a = b;                 // upcast--a now points down to B object
34         a.f();                 // displays "f in A"
35         a.g();                 // displays "g in B"
36         a.h();                 // illegal: compile-time error
37         ((B)a).h();            // displays "h in B"
38         b.h();                 // displays "h in B"
39     }
40 }
```

Figure 10.8

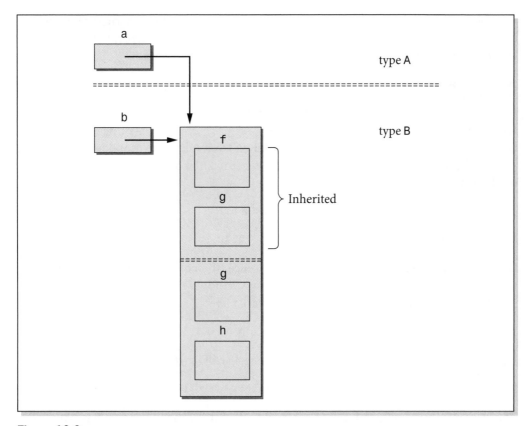

Figure 10.9

As a result, a points down. The object to which a points contains the f and g methods that it inherits from class A, and the g and h methods defined in the B class (see Fig.10.9)

Line 34 then calls the f method in this object via the a reference:

```
34        a.f();              // displays "f in A"
```

This statement works as expected. Similarly, the call of g on Line 35 works as expected:

```
35        a.g();              // displays "g in B"
```

It invokes the g method defined in B (this g method overrides the inherited g). However, if we attempt to call h in the same way, we will get a compile-time error. For example, the statement on Line 36 is illegal:

```
36        a.h();              // illegal: compile-time error
```

It is illegal *even though the object to which* a *points has an* h *method.* The compiler flags this statement because it assumes a is pointing to a regular A object. It assumes this because a is a type A reference variable. Objects instantiated from A have an f and a g method but no h method. Thus, as far as the compiler is concerned, the object to which a points does not have an h method.

To call h via the a reference, we must downcast a to B:

```
37        ((B)a).h();         // displays "h in B"
```

Because the downcast produces a type B reference, the compiler assumes the object to which the downcast reference points has an h method. We can also call h via b without any downcast because b is a type B reference variable:

```
38        b.h();              // displays "h in B"
```

Now consider the assignment statement on Line 33 of Fig. 10.8:

```
33        a = b;              // a now points down to B object
```

The reference obtained from b has type B. But when it is assigned to a, it has type A. Because A is higher in the class hierarchy, we call this change in type **upcasting**. Upcasting is always legal because it results in a reference that points down. Moreover, it does not require a cast. However, as we have just seen in Fig. 10.8, *the upcast reference does not provide access to a method defined at the lower level unless the method overrides a method from the higher level.* If there is no override, then the upcast reference has to be downcast before it can be used in a call of the method at the lower level.

Downcasts require casts, and even then do not always work. They can produce run-time errors. The downcast on Line 37 works only because the reference in a was previously upcast on Line 33. Because of the upcast, the downcast on Line 37 does not produce a reference that points up. This observation gives us the following rule: *A reference can be downcast only if it was previously upcast.*

As we have seen, if we upcast a reference (as on Line 33 in Fig. 10.8), we may have to subsequently downcast it (as on Line 37 in Fig. 10.8). Why then would we ever want to upcast? We will answer this question in Chapter 16 when we discuss generic programming.

10.6 Object Class

Whenever we define a class without specifying a superclass using extends, the compiler translates the class as if we used extends Object. For example, the compiler translates a class of the form

```
class A
{
    ...
}
```

as if it were written this way:

```
class A extends Object
{
    ...
}
```

In the examples of inheritance we have seen so far in this chapter, B is a subclass of A. Because A in all of these examples does not use the extends reserved word, all these A classes are, by default, subclasses of Object. Thus, we have the class structure shown in Fig. 10.10.

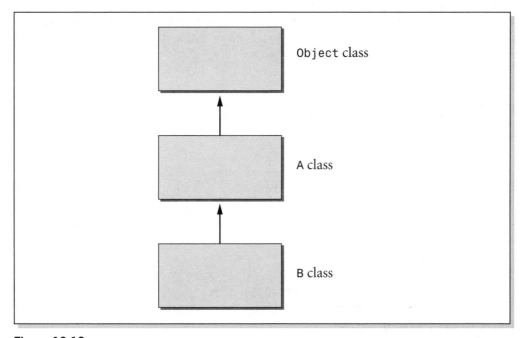

Object class

A class

B class

Figure 10.10

A inherits what is in Object, and B inherits what is in A (which includes everything in Object). From this example, we can make the following generalization: *Every class inherits what is in the* Object *class*—either directly (like A in the preceding example) or indirectly (like B in the preceding example).

Because B inherits what is in A, a B object is also an A object. Thus, it is legal for a type A reference to point down to a B object. Similarly, because B inherits what is in Object, a B object is also an Object object (i.e., an object whose type is Object). Thus, it is legal for a reference of type Object to point down to a B object.

Now let's consider the general case: Because every class inherits what is in Object, every object is an instance of the Object class. Thus it is legal for a type Object reference to point down to an object of *any* class. In other words, an Object reference is a universal pointer. That is, it can point to any object, regardless of its type. For example, if we define obj with

```
Object obj;
```

then obj can point to an object of any type. obj could never violate the rule that a reference must never point up because there are no objects higher in the hierarchy than obj.

The Object class has several methods, two of which are toString and equals. Thus, through inheritance, every class necessarily has these two methods. For example, consider the program in Fig. 10.11. Class A appears to have no methods. But it has, in fact, a toString method and an equals method, both of which it inherits from the Object class. B, in turn, inherits these methods from A.

```
 1 class A            // inherits toString and equals from Object
 2 {
 3    private int x = 1;
 4 }
 5 //================================================
 6 class B extends A // inherits toString and equals from A
 7 {
 8    private int y = 2;
 9 }
10 //================================================
11 class Inheritance4
12 {
13    public static void main(String[] args)
```

Figure 10.11   (continues)

```
14    {
15        A a1, a2;
16        a1 = new A();
17        a2 = new A();
18        System.out.println(a1.toString());  // displays A@3e25a5
19        System.out.println(a1.equals(a2));  // displays false
20
21        B b1, b2;
22        b1 = new B();
23        b2 = new B();
24        System.out.println(b1.toString());  // displays B@19821f
25        System.out.println(b1.equals(b2));  // displays false
26    }
27 }
```

Figure 10.11   (continued)

Line 18 in Fig. 10.11 calls the toString method in the a1 object:

```
18        System.out.println(a1.toString());  // displays A@3e25a5
```

This statement displays the string that toString returns. Since the a object contains an instance variable x with the value 1, we would probably want toString to return the string "x = 1". Instead, it returns "A@3e25a5", a string consisting of the class name of the a object followed by a strange code. Similarly, the call of toString on line 24,

```
24        System.out.println(b1.toString());  // displays B@19821f
```

returns "B@19821f", the class name of the b object followed by another strange code. The problem here is that the toString method we inherit from Object does not know anything about the A or B classes. Thus, it cannot possibly know how to display the data in the A and B objects. To fix this problem, we should include in the A and B classes their own toString methods tailored specifically to these classes.

We have the same problem with the inherited equals method that we have with the inherited toString method. The equals method in Object does not know anything about the A and B classes so it does not know how to compare objects of these classes. The inherited equals method simply compares the two references of the objects—not the objects themselves. Thus, the statement

```
19        System.out.println(a1.equals(a2));  // displays false
```

is equivalent to

```
System.out.println(a1 == a2);
```

Because a1 and a2 in Fig. 10.11 are not pointing to the same object, a1.equals(a2) necessarily returns false. A correct equals method for class A would return true because the objects to which a1 and a2 point are identical.

Let's add toString methods to the A and B classes in Fig. 10.11 (we will learn how to write the equals methods for these classes in the next chapter). We get the program in Fig. 10.12.

```
 1 class A              // inherits toString and equals from Object
 2 {
 3    protected int x = 1;   // protected access allows B to access x
 4    //--------------------------------
 5    public String toString()
 6    {
 7       return "x = " + x;
 8    }
 9 }
10 //================================================
11 class B extends A
12 {
13    private int y = 2;
14    //--------------------------------
15    public String toString()
16    {
17       return "x = " + x + " y = " + y;
18    }
19 }
20 //================================================
21 class Inheritance5
22 {
23    public static void main(String[] args)
24    {
25       A a;
26       a = new A();
27       System.out.println(a.toString()); // displays x = 1
28
29       B b;
30       b = new B();
31       System.out.println(b.toString()); // displays x = 1 y = 2
32    }
33 }
```

Figure 10.12

The `toString` method in class A returns a string that gives the value of x. Specifically, it returns "x = 1". The `toString` method in class B returns a string that gives the value of the inherited x and the value of y. Specifically, it returns "x = 1 y = 2".

The `toString` method in B directly accesses x in class A:

```
17        return "x = " + x + " y = " + y;
```

direct access of x

This access of x is from outside the class A. Thus, for this access of x to be legal, x in class A must not be private. But we do not want to make x public because that would allow too much access to x. Instead, we make x **protected** by declaring it with

```
3    protected int x = 1;       // protected access allows B to access x
```

Protected access allows greater access than private but less than public. Specifically, it allows access from the class itself, from any subclass, and from any class in the same package. Thus, by making x protected, we make the access on Line 17 of x from the class B legal.

Instead of accessing x directly from the `toString` method in B, the `toString` method in B can call the `toString` method in A (see Fig. 10.13). This call returns the value of x already in string form. This string can then be concatenated with the string for y. Unfortunately, there is a problem with this approach. The B object has three `toString` methods: one defined in `Object`, one defined in A, and one defined in B. The one defined in the B class overrides the two inherited ones. Thus, if we call `toString` from within the B class, we will call the one defined in B, not the one defined in A. The solution to our problem is simple: qualify the call of `toString` with `super`. This qualifier indicates that the method to be called is defined in the superclass of the class containing the call. Line 17 in Fig.10.13 shows this approach:

```
17        return super.toString() + " y = " + y; // call A toString
```

The call to `super.toString` calls the `toString` method in class A. It returns "x = 1". This string is then concatenated to the string "y = " and the value of y (which is 2). Thus, the string "x = 1 y = 2" is returned by this statement.

```
 1 class A          // inherits toString and equals from Object
 2 {
 3    private int x = 1;
 4    //----------------------------------
 5    public String toString()
 6    {
 7       return "x = " + x;
 8    }
 9 }
10 //================================================
11 class B extends A
12 {
13    private int y = 2;
14    //----------------------------------
15    public String toString()
16    {
17       return super.toString() + " y = " + y;// call A toString
18    }
19 }
20 //================================================
21 class Inheritance6
22 {
23    public static void main(String[] args)
24    {
25       A a;
26       a = new A();
27       System.out.println(a.toString()); // displays x = 1
28
29       B b;
30       b = new B();
31       System.out.println(b.toString()); // displays x = 1 y = 2
32    }
33 }
```

Figure 10.13

Note that x in Fig. 10.13 is private rather than protected. Because the toString method in B accesses x indirectly through the toString method in the A class, x can be private.

To call a method defined in a superclass from a subclass, you normally do not have to use the super qualifier. You need this qualifier *only if the subclass has a method that overrides the method in the superclass you want to call.*

A third approach for accessing x in the class A is to use a public accessor method—a method that returns the value of x. Fig. 10.14 shows this approach.

```
 1 class A          // inherits toString and equals from Object
 2 {
 3    private int x = 1;  // x can be private
 4    //-----------------------------------
 5    public String toString()
 6    {
 7       return "x = " + x;
 8    }
 9    //-----------------------------------
10    public int xGet()         // accessor method
11    {
12       return x;
13    }
14 }
15 //================================================
16 class B extends A
17 {
18    private int y = 2;
19    //-----------------------------------
20    public String toString()
21    {
22       return  "x = " + xGet() + " y = " + y;  // use accessor
23    }
24 }
25 //================================================
26 class Inheritance7
27 {
28    public static void main(String[] args)
29    {
30       A a;
31       a = new A();
32       System.out.println(a.toString()); // displays x = 1
33
34       B b;
35       b = new B();
36       System.out.println(b.toString()); // displays x = 1 y = 2
37
38    }
39 }
```

Figure 10.14

We use the accessor method xGet on Line 22 to access x:

```
22          return  "x = " + xGet() + " y = " + y;  // use accessor
```

It returns the value of x (which is 1). Thus, this return statement returns the string "x = 1 y = 2". We are not accessing x directly. We are accessing it indirectly through the public method xGet. Thus, x can be private.

10.7 Why Are toString and equals in the Object Class?

You may be wondering why the toString and equals methods are in Object. The versions of these methods in Object do not provide the functions we typically need. Why, then, are they included in the Object class? To answer this question, consider the following scenario (see Fig. 10.15):

a is a reference of type A. Class A does not define its own toString method. B is a subclass of A. B defines its own toString method. a is pointing down to a B object.

The B object has two toString methods: one inherited from Object and one defined in B.

Suppose we now execute

```
System.out.println(a.toString());
```

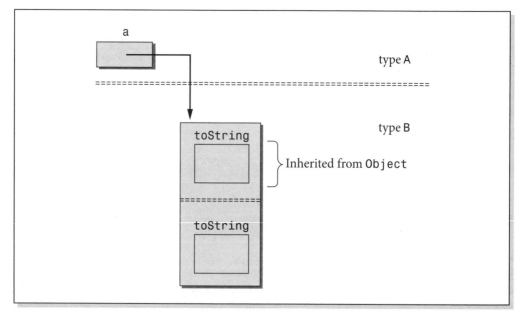

Figure 10.15

Which toString method is called by this statement? The toString method defined in B overrides the toString inherited from Object. Thus, this statement calls the toString method defined in B. This is the toString method we want. a is pointing to a type B object, so we, of course, want the toString method defined in the B class to be invoked.

But suppose Object did not have its own toString method. Then the statement

```
System.out.println(a.toString());
```

would be illegal. a is type A so the compiler would assume a is pointing to a regular A object. But if A does not have a toString method, the compiler would conclude that a points to an object that does not have a toString method. As we know, Object does, in fact, have a toString method. Thus, every class has at least this toString method. So the compiler will never assume an object does not have a toString method. We can, therefore, always call the toString method in an object via any reference pointing to that object, regardless of its type.

We have exactly the same situation with the equals method in Object. It does not provide a function we need. However, like toString, it serves an important purpose: it allows the equals method in an object to be called via any reference pointing to that object.

10.8   Access Specifiers

public, private, and protected specify the accessibility of the members of a class. For this reason, we call them **access specifiers** (or **access modifiers**). public means an item's access is unrestricted. private means an item is accessible from only the class in which the item appears. protected means an item is accessible only from its own class, any subclass, and any class in the same package. If an item in a class has no access specifier, then by default it gets **package access**—that is, it is accessible only from its own class and from classes in the same package. Thus, package access is more restrictive than protected access. public is the least restrictive (no restrictions at all). private is the most restrictive. In the following class, the four fields are in the order of increasing access. w has the least access; z, the most. Because x does not have an access specifier, it defaults to package access.

```
class Specifiers
{
    private int w;     // private access
    int x;             // package access
    protected int y;   // protected (i.e., package + subclass) access
    public int z;      // public access
    ...
}
```

We can attach an access specifier to a class itself. For example, to give class C public access, we use

```
public class C        // public access
{
    ...
}
```

If we define a class without an access specifier, it by default gets package access. **Inner classes** are classes inside classes (we will discuss inner classes in Chapter 15). Inner classes can have private, package, protected, or public access. However, classes that are not inner classes can have only public or package access.

One of the requirements of the Java compiler is that public classes must be in files whose base names match the class names. For example, a public class C must be in a file named C.java. Thus, you cannot have more than one public class in a file. For this reason, we have given all our classes the default access (i.e., package access). Package access allows us to have just one file for each program in the textbook. This approach makes it easier to work with the sample programs in this textbook. However, in general, you should make your classes public to give them maximum accessibility.

When the compiler translates a program in one file that contains multiple classes, it creates a class file for each class. The file name of the source program does not affect the names of the class files that the compiler creates. The names of the class files depend only on the names of the classes in the file. For example, suppose the X.java file contains classes A, B, and C, all of which have package access. Then the command

```
javac X.java
```

would produce the class files A.class, B.class, and C.class.

Laboratory 10 Prep

1. What happens if you delete the first B constructor in C10p1.java (a copy of Inheritance2 in Fig. 10.4)? Will the program compile without error?

2. Suppose B is a subclass of A. Suppose A has a public method f with no parameters that displays hello. Suppose B has a public method f with one int parameter that displays the value of its parameter. Thus B has two f methods, one of which is inherited. Which f methods are called when the following code is executed:

```
B b = new B();
b.f();
b.f(5);

A a;
a = b;
a.f();
```

Why is the inherited f not overridden by the f defined in B? Is the following call legal:

```
a.f(5);
```

3. Suppose B is a subclass of A. Is an A object also a B object?

4. What does the default constructor do?

5. Why can the toString method be called via any non-null reference?

Laboratory 10

1. Run a test program to confirm that Object has a hashCode method that takes no arguments and returns an int. Because Object has a hashCode method as well as an equals and a toString method, *every* class inherits these three methods. Classes can, of course, override the methods inherited from Object. hashCode is a method that can be used for hash coding (see Homework Exercise 15 in Chapter 9).

2. What is returned by the two calls of hashCode in the following code:

```
Integer i= new Integer(12345);
System.out.println(i.hashCode());
Double d = new Double(123.45);
System.out.println(d.hashCode());
```

3. Create a class `Cub` that does not define a `hashCode` method or a `toString` method. Execute the following code:

```
Cub c = new Cub();
int i = c.hashCode();
System.out.println(Integer.toHexString(i));
System.out.println(c.toString());
```

The call of the preceding `toHexString` method converts the integer in `i` to hex (i.e., base 16). In hex, the symbols A, B, C, D, E, and F have values equal to the decimal numbers 10, 11, 12, 13, 14, and 15, respectively. Where do the `hashCode` and `toString` methods called in the preceding code come from? How is the string returned by the `toString` method constructed?

4. What is wrong with the following program? Compile it to check your answer. Modify the program so that it works.

```
class Ale
{
    protected int x = 1;
    public Ale(int x)
    {
        this.x = x;
    }
}
//===================================================
class Bud extends Ale
{
    private int y = 2;
    public void display()
    {
        System.out.println("x = " + x + " y = " + y);
    }
}
//===================================================
class C10e4
{
    public static void main(String[] args)
    {
        Bud b = new Bud();
        b.display();
    }
}
```

5. What is displayed by the following program? Run it to check your answer. What can you conclude about the order in which constructors are executed?

```
class Ate
{
    public Ate()
    {
        System.out.println("Ate constructor");
    }
}
//===================================================
class My extends Ate
{
    public My()
    {
        System.out.println("My  constructor");
    }
}
//===================================================
class Pie extends My
{
    public Pie()
    {
        System.out.println("Pie constructor");
    }
}
//===================================================
class C10e5
{
    public static void main(String[] args)
    {
        Pie c = new Pie();
    }
}
```

6. Create a class Asp and a subclass Bee. Asp should have a public int field x whose initial value is 1, and a public method f that displays "in Asp". Bee should have a public int field x whose initial value is 2, and a public method f that displays "in Bee". Thus, a Bee object has two f methods and two x instance variables. Which x variables are accessed and which f methods are called in the following sequence:

```
Asp a = new Bee();                     // a points "down" to Bee object
a.f();                                 // Which f() is executed?
System.out.println(a.x);               // Which x is displayed?
Bee b = (Bee)a;                        // b points "across" to Bee object
b.f();                                 // Which f is executed?
System.out.println(b.x);               // Which x is displayed?
((Bee)a).f();                          // Which f() is executed?
System.out.println(((Bee)a).x);        // Which x is displayed?
```

LABORATORY

The method executed depends on the *type of the object*—not the type of the reference. Because both a and b point to a Bee object, all the calls of f in the preceding code call the f method defined in the Bee class. However, the instance variable accessed depends on the *type of the reference*—not on the type of the object. x defined in Bee does *not* override the inherited x. Instead, the x defined in Bee **shadows** the inherited x.

7. Create a Coy class that contains a private int x, a constructor that initializes x to 5, and a method f that displays x. It does not contain its own toString or equals methods. Then execute in main

```
Coy r, s;
r = new Coy();
s = new Coy();

if (r == s)
   System.out.println("equal");
else
   System.out.println("not equal");
```

What happens? Why? Then execute

```
if (r.equals(s))
   System.out.println("equal");
else
   System.out.println("not equal");
```

Where is this equals method coming from? What happens? Why? Then execute

```
System.out.println(r.toString());
System.out.println(s.toString());
```

What happens? Why? Where is the toString method coming from?

8. Write a program that has three classes: Ark, Boa, and C10e8. Boa is a subclass of Ark. Ark has a public method f that displays hello. Boa has a public method f that first calls the f method in Ark and then displays bye. Both f methods have no parameters. C10e8 contains main. main should execute

```
Ark a = new Ark();
a.f();
Boa b = new Boa();
b.f();
a = b;
a.f();
```

Before you run your program, predict what it will display.

9. Create three classes: Ash, Bow, and Cup. Cup is a subclass of Bow; Bow is a subclass of Ash. Ash should have a private int x field; Bow should have a private int y field;

Cup should have a `private int z` field. Each class should have a constructor with one parameter that provides the initial value for the data field defined in that class. The Cup constructor should pass 2 to the Bow constructor. The Bow constructor should pass 1 to the Ash constructor. Each class should have its own public `display` method. The `display` method in Ash should display x. The `display` method in Bow should display x and y. It should access x using a `public` accessor method `xGet` in Ash. The `display` method in Cup should display x, y, and z. It should access x and y using public accessor methods `xGet` in Ash and `yGet` in Bow. Create a C10e9 class with a main method that executes

```
Ash a = new Ash(10)
a.display();
Bow b = new Bow(20);
b.display()
Cup c = new Cup (30);
c.display();
```

10. Recall from Fig. 8.13 that `println` is an overloaded method. The implementation of the version that has a parameter of type `Object` is

```
public void println(Object obj)
{
    println(obj.toString());
}
```

Knowing the implementation of this `println` method, you should be able to predict how changing the argument on Line 31 in C10e10.java (a copy of Inheritance5.java in Fig. 10.12) to b will affect the output displayed. Check your answer by running C10e10.java with and without the indicated change.

The `obj` parameter in the preceding `println` method can be passed the reference to any type of object because a reference of type `Object` is a "universal" pointer. Why is it safe for this `println` method to call the `toString` method in the `obj` object? Does every object have a `toString` method? What other methods can be called safely?

11. Run the following code (it is in C10e11.java). From the output displayed, you will see that the `remove` method works differently depending on the base type of the ArrayList. Why?

```
import java.util.ArrayList;
class Strange
{
    int x = 3;
}
class C10e11
```

LABORATORY

```
{
    public static void main(String[] args)
    {
        ArrayList<Integer> ial = new ArrayList<Integer>();
        Integer i1 = new Integer(1);
        Integer i2 = new Integer(1);     // construct identical object
        if (i1 == i2)
            System.out.println("i1 == i2 is true");
        else
            System.out.println("i1 == i2 is false");
        ial.add(i1);
        ial.remove(i1);                   // remove what was just added
        System.out.println(ial.size());  // should be zero
        ial.add(i1);
        ial.remove(i2);                   // will passing i2 remove i1?
        System.out.println(ial.size());  // is it zero?

        ArrayList<Strange> ral = new ArrayList<Strange>();
        Strange r1 = new Strange();
        Strange r2 = new Strange();       // construct identical object
        if (r1 == r2)
            System.out.println("r1 == r2 is true");
        else
            System.out.println("r1 == r2 is false");
        ral.add(r1);
        ral.remove(r1);                   // remove what was just added
        System.out.println(ral.size());  // should be zero
        ral.add(r1);
        ral.remove(r2);                   // will passing r2 remove r1?
        System.out.println(ral.size());  // is it zero?
    }
}
```

12. javadoc is a program that comes with the Java compiler and interpreter. It automatically creates a documentation file on any *public* class. It extracts out information on the public members in a public class and creates a file with this information that is viewable with a web browser. If the class includes javadoc **comments** (comments that start with "/**" and end with "*/" that appear immediately before the public members), these comments will also be included in the file created. javadoc comments can include **tags** that provide specific information on a public member. For example, the @param tag provides information on parameters; the @return tag provides information on the value returned by a method. For example, in the following class, the @param provides information on the parameters of the constructor; @return provides information on the return value of the toString method.

```
/** This class models a rational number (a number
    that can be represented as the ratio of two integers).
*/
public class RationalNumber     // class must be public for javadoc
{
   private int numerator, denominator;
   /**
      @param n numerator of rational number
      @param d denominator of rational number
   */
   public RationalNumber(int n, int d)
   {}
   /** adds the rational number r to this rational number */
   public RationalNumber add(RationalNumber r)
   {}
   /** multiplies the rational number r to this rational number */
   public RationalNumber multiply(RationalNumber r)
   {}
   /** reduces this rational number to lowest terms */
   public void reduce()
   {}
   /**
      @return a string with rational number in
      "numerator/denominator" form
   */
   public String toString()
   {}
}
```

Run javadoc on the RationalNumber.java file by entering

javadoc RationalNumber.java

With a web browser, view the file created and compare with RationalNumber.java.

Homework 10

1. Create three public classes (they must be in separate files because they are public) : CollegeMember, Student, and Professor. Student and Professor are subclasses of CollegeMember. CollegeMember has a String name field and a String telNumber field. Its constructor has two parameters that provide the initial values for the name and telNumber fields. CollegeMember also has accessor methods getName and getTelNumber that return name and telNumber, respectively. Student has an int year field (1 = first year, 2 = second year, 3 = third year, 4 = fourth year). Its

LABORATORY

constructor has three parameters: name, year, and telNumber that provide initial values for the name, year, and telNumber fields. It also has an accessor method getYear that returns year. Professor has an int rank field (1 = assistant, 2 = associate, 3 = full). Its constructor has three parameters: name, rank, and telNumber that provide initial values for the name, rank, and telNumber fields. It also has an accessor method getRank that returns rank. Create a C10h1 class with a main method that executes

```
Student s = new Student("Bert", 2, "555-5555");
System.out.println("name = " + s.getName());
System.out.println("year = " + s.getYear());
System.out.println("telephone = " + s.getTelNumber());
Professor p = new Professor("Jane", 1, "555-9999");
System.out.println("name = " + p.getName());
System.out.println("rank = " + p.getRank());
System.out.println("telephone = " + p.getTelNumber());
```

Include javadoc comments in your class files. Use javadoc to create documentation files (see Lab Exercise 12).

2. Same as Homework Exercise 1 except use only two classes: Student and Professor, neither of which is a subclass of the other or of CollegeMember. Student should have a name, year, and telNumber fields, and accessor methods for each of these fields. Its constructor should have three parameters: name, year, and telNumber. Professor should have a name, rank, and telNumber fields, and accessor methods for each of these fields. Its constructor should have three parameters: name, rank, and telNumber. Compare your program with your program from Homework Exercise 1. Which is better?

3. Same as Homework Exercise 1 except add a String address field to the CollegeMember class. Change the constructor of CollegeMember so that it also has an address parameter. CollegeMember should also have an accessor method getAddress that returns address. In main, execute the following code:

```
Student s = new Student("Bert", 2, "555-5555", "5 Bouton");
System.out.println("name = " + s.getName());
System.out.println("year = " + s.getYear());
System.out.println("telephone = " + s.getTelNumber());
System.out.println("address = " + s.getAddress());
Professor p = new Professor("Jane", 1, "555-9999", "3 Oak St.");
System.out.println("name = " + p.getName());
System.out.println("rank = " + p.getRank());
System.out.println("telephone = " + p.getTelNumber());
System.out.println("address = " + p.getAddress());
```

4. Same as Homework Exercise 2 except add a String address field to the Student and Professor classes. Modify their constructors accordingly. Add an accessor method

getAddress to both classes. In main, execute the code shown in Homework Exercise 3. Which modification—the modification in Problem 3 or the modification in this problem—is easier to implement?

5. An **enumeration** creates a new type and associates constants with that type. For example, the following enumeration creates the type ProfRank with constants Assistant, Associate, and Full:

```
enum ProfRank {Assistant, Associate, Full}
```

We can then declare a variable of type ProfRank and assign it any of the constants listed. For example:

```
ProfRank rank;
rank = ProfRank.Associate;
```

Do Homework Exercise 1 using enumerations rather than integer codes for the student year and professor rank.

6. Write a program that displays in decimal the codes used to represent the space, the digits, the uppercase letters, and the lowercase letters. (*Hint:* Use charAt on a string that contains the characters whose codes you want to display.)

7. Determine the hash code (see Lab Exercises 1, 2, and 3 in this chapter and Homework Exercise 15 in Chapter 9) returned by the hashCode method in a String object that contains AB. Repeat for BA. Are the hash codes different? Because the two strings are not the same, they ideally should hash to different hash codes. Suppose the hashCode method computed the hash code simply by summing the individual codes of each letter in the string. Then the hash codes for AB and BA would be the same. Simply summing the component data in an object to compute a hash code is a poor technique for hash coding. The hash code should *depend on the position of the component data in an object as well as the data itself*, in which case rearrangements of data would likely produce different hash codes.

8. Same as Homework Exercise 7 but for a class with two integer variables. Use the hashCode method inherited from Object. Is the hash code returned dependent on the position of the data as well as the data itself? That is, is the hash code returned when the two variables have the values 1 and 2 the same when the two variables have their values switched?

9. The equals and toString methods in Object do not perform functions you would likely need in a program. Why then are they in Object? The hashCode method is in Object. Does this hashCode method perform a function you might need in a program? Why is hashCode in Object?

10. Same as Homework Exercise 4 in Chapter 6 but include `javadoc` comments (see Lab Exercise 12).

11. The `Object` class has a `clone` method that duplicates objects. Thus, through inheritance, all objects have a `clone` method. If r is a reference to an object, then `r.clone()` returns a reference to a duplicate of the r object. Experiment with `clone` to determine if it creates a shallow or deep copy.

Inheritance: Part 2

11.1   Overriding Versus Overloading

It is important to distinguish between *overriding* a method and *overloading* a method. Let's consider the example in Fig. 11.1.

```
 1 class A
 2 {
 3    public void f()
 4    {
 5        System.out.println("f in A");
 6    }
 9    //--------------------------------
 7    public void g()
 8    {
 9        System.out.println("g in A");
10    }
11 }
12 //=============================================
13 class B extends A
14 {
15    public void f()
16    {
17        System.out.println("f in B");
18    }
19    //--------------------------------
20    public void g(int x)
21    {
22        System.out.println("g in B");
23    }
24 }
25 //=============================================
26 class OverrideOverload
27 {
28    public static void main(String[] args)
29    {
30        B b;
31        b = new B();
32        b.f();           // displays f in B
33        b.g();           // displays g in A
34        b.g(5);          // displays g in B
35    }
36 }
```

Figure 11.1

An object constructed from the B class will contain the f and g methods that are defined in B. It will also contain the f and g methods that it inherits from the A class. The two f methods have the same **signature**. That is, they have the same name, and their parameter lists agree in the number, type, and order of the parameters.

A method in a class overrides an inherited method only when the signatures of the two methods are the same. Because the f defined in B in Fig. 11.1 and the f inherited from A have the same signature, the former overrides the latter in a B object. Both are present in a B object, but the overriding method—the f method defined in B—has priority. Thus, when we call f via b on Line 32, we execute the f method defined in B, not the inherited f.

Now let's consider the two g methods in an object constructed from the class B. They do not have the same signature. The g method defined in B has one int parameter; the g method inherited from A has no parameters. The two g methods have different signatures. We call this situation method overloading. With overloading, one method does not have priority over another. The method called *depends on the argument list in the call.* For example, on Line 33 in Fig. 11.1, we call g with

```
33       b.g();          // displays g in A
```

Here, we are calling the inherited g because the void argument list in this call matches the void parameter list of the inherited g. On Line 34, we call g with

```
34       b.g(5);         // displays g in B
```

Here, we are calling the g defined in B because the argument list in this call (a single int) matches the parameter list in the g defined in B.

11.2 Calling a Constructor with this

We have already learned that a constructor in a class can explicitly call a constructor in its superclass. Such a call does not use the constructor's name. Instead, it uses super. For example, consider the following constructor for a class B:

```
public B()
{
   super(1);        // call constructor of superclass
   y = 2;
}
```

```
 1 class ThisExample
 2 {
 3    private int x, y, z;
 4    //-----------------------------------
 5    public ThisExample()
 6    {
 7       this(2, 3, 4);  // calls the second constructor
 8    }
 9    //-----------------------------------
10    public ThisExample(int x, int y, int z)
11    {
12       this.x = x;      // assign parameters to instance variables
13       this.y = y;
14       this.z = z;
15    }
16 }
```

Figure 11.2

Here the statement

```
super(1);
```

calls a constructor of the superclass, passing it 1.

A constructor can also call a constructor in its own class. In this case, it uses the reserved word this. For example, in Fig. 11.2, the first A constructor calls the second A constructor with

```
7        this(2, 3, 4);    // calls the second constructor
```

The two constructors are overloaded. Thus, because this call passes three int arguments, the corresponding constructor—the one with three int parameters on Line 10—is called.

Fig. 11.2 shows two distinct uses of this. On Line 7, we use this to call a constructor from a constructor in the same class. On Lines 12, 13, and 14, we qualify the instance variables with this to distinguish them from the identically named parameters.

11.3 Writing an equals Method

Consider the class A in Fig. 11.3. It has its own toString and equals methods.

```
 1 class EqualsExample
 2 {
 3     private int x;
 4     //---------------------------------
 5     public EqualsExample(int xx)
 6     {
 7         x = xx;
 8     }
 9     //---------------------------------
10     public String toString()
11     {
12         return "x = " + x;
13     }
14     //---------------------------------
15     public boolean equals(EqualsExample r)
16     {
17         return x == r.x;
18     }
19 }
```

Figure 11.3

If we execute the following code that uses this class,

```
EqualsExample e1 = new EqualsExample(3);
System.out.println(e1.toString());
```

we would then execute the toString method in the EqualsExample class, which overrides the toString method inherited from Object. This code displays

```
x = 3
```

If we also execute

```
EqualsExample e2 = new EqualsExample(3);
System.out.println(e1.equals(e2));
```

we would see

```
true
```

on the display because the e1 and e2 objects are equal. That is, they have the same type and the data they contain (i.e., their x values) are equal.

When we call the equals method with

```
e1.equals(e2)
```

we execute the equals method in the e1 object. Thus, the x on the left of Line 17 in Fig. 11.3 is the x in the e1 object. r.x on the right of Line 17 is the x in the object to which r points. But r is the parameter that receives the argument e2. Thus, r.x is the x in the e2 object. Thus, Line 17 compares the x data in the e1 and e2 objects.

Now let's examine the preceding call of equals at a more technical level. It passes e1 and e2 to the this and r parameters, respectively, in the equals method (see Fig. 11.4).

Consider what happens when we then execute Line 17 within the equals method in the e1 object:

```
17          return x == r.x;
```

The x on the left is an unqualified access of an instance variable. Thus, the compiler translates it as if it were written as this.x (see Section 6.4). For this call, this points to e1. Thus, the x on the left of Line 17 is the x in the e1 object. r is the parameter in the equals method. For this call, r receives the pointer in e2. Thus, r.x is the x in the e2 object. The return statement here compares these two values of x. If they are equal, it returns true. Otherwise, it returns false. This is precisely the action we want equals to perform. However, the implementation of the equals method in Fig. 11.3 is not quite correct. Before we see why, let's examine the equals method in the Object class.

The equals method in the Object class is given in Fig. 11.5. Note that the parameter has type Object. Thus, it is a universal pointer. That is, it can be passed a reference to an object of any class.

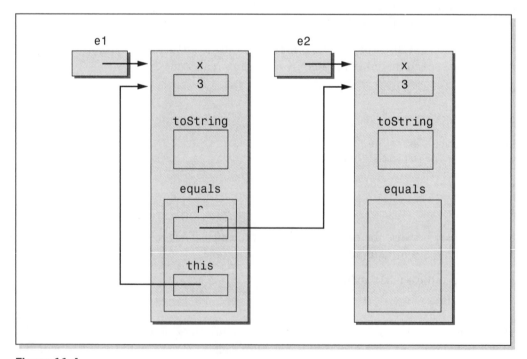

Figure 11.4

Because Object is at the top of the class hierarchy, its equals method is inherited by every class. Now suppose we execute the following code:

```
C c1 = new C();
C c2 = new C();
```

where C is a class whose only equals method is the one inherited from Object. Assume the c1 and c2 objects are identical. If we then execute

```
if (c1.equals(c2))
   ...
```

the equals method inherited from Object is called (because C does not have its own equals method). We would expect the call of equals here to return true because the c1 and c2 objects are identical. But it, in fact, returns false. Let's see why. In this call, both c1 and c2 are passed to the equals method. c1 is passed to the this parameter in the equals method; c2 is passed to the r parameter (see Fig. 11.6).

```
public boolean equals (Object r)
{
    if (r == null) return false;
    return this == r;
}
```
} equals method in
   the Object class

Figure 11.5

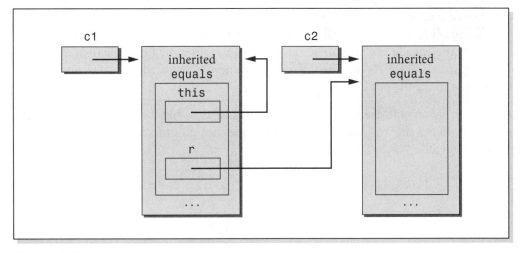

Figure 11.6

Thus, the statement in the inherited `equals` method,

```
return this == r;
```

simply compares the reference in `this` (which is also in c1) with the reference in r (which is also in c2). c1 and c2 are different (although the objects to which they point are identical). Thus, the preceding return statement returns `false`. The `equals` method in `Object` *compares references—not the objects to which those references point.*

Now let's return to the `equals` method in the `EqualsExample` class in Fig. 11.3. An `Equal-sExample` object has two `equals` methods: one defined in the `EqualsExample` class and one inherited from the `Object` class. The parameters for these two methods are different. Thus, the `equals` method in the `EqualsExample` class *does not override* the inherited `equals` method. Instead, the `equals` methods are overloaded. The argument in the call of `equals` determines which `equals` method is called. If the argument is type `Equals-Example` or a subclass of `EqualsExample`, then the `equals` defined in `EqualsExample` is called (because its parameter is type `EqualsExample`). If the parameter is any other type of reference, the inherited `equals` is called (remember, its parameter is universal because it has type `Object`). Suppose, for example, e1 and e2 point to identical `EqualsExample` objects. Consider what happens when the following code is executed:

```
Object obj = e2;
if (e1.equals(obj))
    ...
```

Because the type of `obj` (which is `Object`) is compatible with the parameter in the `equals` method inherited from the `Object` class but not with the parameter in the `equals` method defined in `EqualsExample`, the inherited `equals` method is called. As we just observed, it compares references rather than the objects to which the references point. Thus, here it compares the e1 reference and obj reference. e1 and obj are not equal because they point to different objects. Thus, this call *incorrectly* returns `false`. To fix this problem, we need to modify the `equals` method in Fig. 11.3 so that it, rather than the inherited `equals`, is called regardless of the type of the reference argument it is passed. We never want to use the `equals` in the `Object` class.

Another problem with the `equals` method in Fig. 11.3 is that it does not handle a `null` argument. Recall that `null` is a reference that does not point to any object. Suppose we call `equals` with

```
e1.equals(null)
```

This call should return false because we do not have equality (e1 points to an object but null does not point to anything). Instead, this call triggers a run-time error. null is compatible with any reference parameter (i.e., it is legal to assign it to any reference variable). Thus, it is compatible with the parameter r in the equals method in the EqualsExample class. This means that this call will invoke the equals method defined in the EqualsExample class. null is received by the r parameter in this method. But because r is null, it cannot be used to access any fields. As a result, the use of r.x in Line 17 of the equals method in Fig. 11.3 triggers a run-time error.

The correct equals method for the class EqualsExample in Fig. 11.3 appears in Fig. 11.7.

Notice the parameter r is now type Object, making it compatible with any reference it is passed. Moreover, this equals method overrides the equals method in the Object class. Line 3 handles a null argument. getClass is a method inherited from Object. When getClass is called, it is passed a reference to an object. It returns the class of that object. The call of getClass on the left of Line 4 is translated as if it were qualified with this. Thus, this call passes this to getClass. It returns the class of the object to which this points. The second call of getClass returns the class of the object to which r points. If we call equals with

e1.equals(e2)

e1 is passed to this; e2 is passed to r. Thus, the first call of getClass returns the class of the e1 object; the second call returns the class of the e2 object. If these two classes are not the same, then the two objects cannot be equal. In this case, false is returned immediately. The x on the left of Line 5 is translated as if it were qualified with this. Because e1 is passed to this, this x accesses the x in the e1 object. The x on the right on Line 5 accesses the x in the r object (which is also the e2 object). The cast of r to type EqualsExample is required. Without it, we would get a compile-time error. r has the type Object. Thus, the compiler would assume r is pointing to an object that does not have an x field.

```
1 public boolean equals(Object r)
2 {
3    if (r == null) return false;
4    if (getClass() != r.getClass()) return false;
5    return x == ((EqualsExample)r).x;
6 }
```

Figure 11.7

11.4 Late Binding

When the call of f on line 10 in Fig. 11.8 is translated by the compiler, the compiler generates machine code that calls the machine code corresponding to the f method that is defined on Lines 3–6.

Thus, it is at compile-time that this call is associated with a specific sequence of bytecode instructions it is to invoke. The making of this association is called a **binding**.

Under some circumstances, binding occurs at run-time rather than at compile-time. We call run-time binding **late binding** because it occurs late (i.e., after compile-time) or **dynamic binding** because it occurs during run-time ("dynamic" here means "during run-time").

In late binding, the binding for a method call does not occur until run-time when the call occurs. The first part of the calling mechanism does the binding—that is, it determines which sequence of machine instructions to call.

Why would we ever want to use late binding? One obvious disadvantage of late binding is that it makes your program run longer. A call with late binding increases run-time because it has to perform the binding (i.e., determine which code sequence to call) as well as invoke the method. There are, however, situations in which it is impossible to determine the method to call at compile-time. In these situations, late binding is a necessity. Let's look at an example of late binding in Fig. 11.9.

On Line 22, a is assigned a pointer to a type A object:

```
22        a = new A();
```

```
 1 class Binding1
 2 {
 3    public static void f()
 4    {
 5        System.out.println("hello");
 6    }
 7    //------------------------------------
 8    public static void main(String[] args)
 9    {
10        f();      // compile-time binding
11    }
12 }
```

Figure 11.8

```
 1 class A
 2 {
 3    public void f()
 4    {
 5        System.out.println("f in A");
 6    }
 7 }
 8 //==================================================
 9 class B extends A
10 {
11    public void f()
12    {
13        System.out.println("f in B");
14    }
15 }
16 //==================================================
17 class Binding2
18 {
19    public static void main(String[] args)
20    {
21        A a;
22        a = new A();
23        a.f();          // displays f in A
24
25        B b;
26        b  = new B();
27        a = b;          // a points "down" to B object
28        a.f();          // displays f in B
29    }
30 }
```

Figure 11.9

Thus, the call

```
23       a.f();          // displays f in A
```

calls the f method defined in the A class.

An object constructed from the B class has two f methods: one defined in the B class and one inherited from the A class. The f method defined in B overrides the inherited f method. Thus, if f is called via a reference that is pointing to a B object, the f method defined in B is called. This is precisely what happens on Line 28 (a at this point in the execution is pointing to a B object):

```
28       a.f();          // displays f in B
```

Note that Lines 23 and 28 are identical but they call different methods. The binding of these calls depend on what a is pointing to: If a is pointing to an A object, then the binding should be to the f method in A. If, however, a is pointing to a B object, then the binding should be to the f method in B. The contents of a are determined at run-time. Thus, the binding *has to be delayed* until run-time. You might argue that by reading the program, you can always determine what the contents of a reference variable will be at run-time, and theoretically at least, compile-time binding should always be possible. But this conclusion is incorrect. To see why, consider the code in Fig. 11.10. Assume A and B are the classes in Fig. 11.9.

When i is even (i.e., whenever i%2 == 0 is true), a2 is assigned a1 (which points to an A object). When i is odd, a2 is assigned b1 (which points to a B object). Thus, for even i,

```
12        a2.f();
```

should call the f method in A. But for odd i, it should call the f method in B. Any compile-time binding would necessarily be wrong. If the binding were to the f in A, then the wrong method would be called when i is odd; if the binding were to the f in B, then the wrong method would be called when i is even. Because the correct binding changes with each iteration of the loop, the binding clearly has to change each time the call is executed. Thus, the binding here *must* occur at run-time, not at compile-time.

Polymorphism is a feature of the Java language. It means a single construct can have more than one meaning depending on how it is used. One example of polymorphism is the "+" operator. It means addition or concatenation, depending on the types of its operands. Another example of polymorphism is late binding. Because of late binding, the call a2.f() on Line 12 in Fig. 11.10 has more than one meaning: It can call the f method in the B class or the f method in the A class, depending on the object to which a2 points.

```
 1 A a1, a2;
 2 a1 = new A ();
 3 B b;
 4 b = new B();
 5
 6 for (int i = 0; i < 100; i++)
 7 {
 8        if (i % 2 == 0)
 9            a2 = a1;    // execute if i is even
10        else
11            a2 = b;     // execute if i is odd
12        a2.f();
13 }
```

Figure 11.10

11.5 Final Methods and Classes

A **final method** is a method that cannot be overridden in a subclass. A **final class** is a class that cannot be extended. That is, it cannot have any subclasses. Thus, all the methods in a final class are automatically final. To mark a method final, place the reserved word final in its header (see Line 16 of Fig. 11.11). Similarly, to mark a class final, place final in its header (see Line 1 of Fig. 11.11).

The A class in Fig. 11.11 is final. Thus, Line 9, which attempts to extend A, is illegal. The C class (Lines 14–20) is not final, although its only method f is final. Thus, the D class

```
 1 final class A
 2 {
 3    public void f()
 4    {
 5        System.out.println("hello");
 6    }
 7 }
 8 //================================================
 9 class B extends A          // illegal because class A is final
10 {
11    ...
12 }
13 //================================================
14 class C
15 {
16    public final void f()
17    {
18        System.out.println("hello");
19    }
20 }
21 //================================================
22 class D extends C          // legal because class C is not final
23 {
24    public void g()
25    {
26        System.out.println("bye");
27    }
28    public void f()          // illegal because f is final in class C
29    {
30        System.out.println("bye");
31    }
32 }
```

Figure 11.11

can extend C (see Line 22). However, it cannot override the f method from C because f is final. Thus, the definition of f on Lines 28–31 is illegal.

Inheritance allows a user of a class to change its functionality (by overriding its methods). A class designer who does not want to provide this flexibility can simply mark methods and classes final so that the inheritance mechanism is restricted. Another reason for making methods and classes final is to decrease run-time (see Lab Exercise 9).

Laboratory 11 Prep

1. Write a constructor for the class Fox that calls the constructor of the superclass of Fox, passing it 5.

2. Write a constructor for the class Chicken that initializes the x instance variable with the parameter x.

3. Write a constructor for the class Owl that calls another constructor in Owl, passing it 7.

4. Why does a call with late binding take more time at run-time than a comparable call with compile-time binding?

5. If you define an equals method for a class, why should its parameter be type Object?

Laboratory 11

1. What is unusual about the classes below? Is there anything wrong with them? Does the f in B override the f in A? Compile test programs to check your answers.

```
class Ave
{
   public void f()
   {
      System.out.println("hello");
   }
}
//=================================================
class Bye extends Ave
{
   public int f()
   {
      return 5;
   }
}
```

Write test programs similar to the preceding to determine the answers to the following questions: Can a public int f() method override a protected int f() method? Can a protected int f() method override a public int f() method?

2. What does the following program display? (*Hint:* Late binding is in effect.) Run the program to check your answer.

```
1 class Arc
2 {
3    void f()
```

LABORATORY

```
 4    {
 5        System.out.println("f in Arc");
 6    }
 7    //-------------------------------------
 8    void g()
 9    {
10        f();
11    }
12 }
13 //===================================================
14 class Bam extends Arc
15 {
16    void f()
17    {
18        System.out.println("f in Bam");
19    }
20 }
21 //===================================================
22 class C11e2
23 {
24    public static void main(String[] args)
25    {
26        Arc a = new Arc ();
27        Bam b = new Bam ();
28        a.g();
29        b.g();
30    }
31 }
```

3. Create a class Any and a subclass Bod. Both Any and Bod should have public f methods with identical signatures. Both Any and Bod should have a public int field x but with different initial values. Thus, a Bod object has two f methods and two x instance variables. What happens when you execute in main the following code:

```
Any a;
a = new Bod();              // a points down
a.f();                      // which f() is executed?
System.out.println(a.x);    // which x is displayed?
```

When does the binding in the call of f occur? When does the binding of x occur (i.e., when is the identifier associated with a storage location)?

4. What will be displayed by the following program? Run the program to check your answer.

```
class Cut
{
    public void f(String s)
```

```
      {
         System.out.println("String parameter");
      }
      //-----------------------------------
      public void f(Object o)
      {
         System.out.println("Object parameter");
      }
   }
   //==================================================
   class C11e4
   {
      public static void main(String[] args)
      {
         Cut a = new Cut();
         String s = "hello";
         a.f(s);
         Integer i = 1;
         a.f(i);
      }
   }
```

5. Can a private method be overridden? Compile a test program to check your answer.

6. Can a private instance variable be shadowed? Run a test program to check your answer.

7. finalize is a method in Object that is inherited by the C class in the following program. It is executed when the memory in use by an object is reclaimed by the garbage collector. System.gc activates the garbage collector. What happens when the following program is executed?

```
class Can
{
   int x = 1;
   protected void finalize() throws Throwable
   {
      super.finalize();
      System.out.println("in finalize");
   }
}
//========================================================
class C11e7
{
   public static void main(String[] args)
   {
      Can c = new Can ();
      c = null;            // object is now subject to reclamation
```

```
        System.out.println("Calling garbage collector");
        System.gc();
    }
}
```

8. Create a class in which you include the following method:

```
public Class getClass()
{
    System.out.println("hello");
}
```

What happens when you compile the class? Explain.

9. If f is not final, when does binding occur for the call

```
r.f();
```

If f is final in class Gum, r has type Gum, and r points to a class Gum object, when does binding occur? If f is final in class Gum, r has type Gum, and r points down to a class Drop object, when does binding occur? What is the advantage of marking methods final?

10. Is String a final class? Compile a test program to check your answer.

11. Is it legal for a constructor to first execute some code and then call another constructor of the same class? For example, is the constructor below legal?

```
public Cry()
{
    System.out.println("hello");
    this(5);            // does this statement have to be first?
}
```

Compile a test program to check your answer.

12. Will the compiler insert a call of the superclass constructor in a constructor if the constructor calls another constructor of the same class on its first line? For example, suppose Bat is a subclass of Att. Does the compiler insert a call of the Att constructor at the beginning of the following Bat constructor?

```
public Bat()
{
    // Does the compiler insert a call of an Att constructor here?
    this(7);
}
```

If it does, would that not mean that the Att constructor would be called twice (once by each Bat constructor)? Run a test program to check your answer.

13. Incorporate the following code in a program and execute it:

```
String s1 = new String("hello");
String s2 = new String("hello");
ArrayList<String> q1 = new ArrayList<String>();
q1.add(s1);
int index = q1.indexOf(s2);
System.out.println(index);
```

s1 and s2 are distinct but identical objects. What does indexOf return in the preceding code? Does it find a match for s2? What can you conclude about the operation of indexOf? Specifically, does it compare the references or does it compare the objects to which those references point? Now repeat with

```
Cold h1 = new Cold();
Cold h2 = new Cold();
ArrayList<Cold> q2 = new ArrayList<Cold>();
q2.add(h1);
index = q2.indexOf(h2);
System.out.println(index);
```

where Cold is defined as

```
class Cold
{
    private int x = 3;
}
```

Why do the two preceding cases give different results?

Homework 11

1. Modify the following program by adding an equals method to the Dude class. Test your equals method to make sure it is working correctly.

```
class Dude
{
    private int[] ia;
    //-----------------------------------
    public Dude()
    {
        ia = new int[10];
    }
    //-----------------------------------
    public void set(int index, int value)
    {
        ia[index] = value;
    }
}
```

LABORATORY

```
//====================================================
class C11h1
{
    public static void main(String[] args)
    {
        Dude d1 = new Dude();
        Dude d2 = new Dude();
        System.out.println(d1.equals(d2)); // should display true
        d1.set(9, 100);
        System.out.println(d1.equals(d2)); // should display false
    }
}
```

2. Same as Homework Exercise 1 except add a copy constructor.

3. Write a class that has three int fields: x, y, and z. This class should have four constructors: one with no parameters, one with one parameter, one with two parameters, and one with three parameters. The constructor with three parameters should set x, y, and z to the values of its parameters. The one with two parameters should set x and y to the values of its parameters, and set z to 30. The one with one parameter should set x to the value of its parameter, and y and z to 40 and 50, respectively. The one with no parameters should set x, y, and z to 60, 70, and 80 respectively. Each constructor, except for the one with three parameters, should contain exactly one statement (not three statements on one line). Include a display method in your class that displays the values of x, y, and z. Write a program that invokes each constructor and displays the resulting values of x, y, and z.

4. Write a program with classes M1, M2, and C11h4 defined as follows:

   M1:   M1 has a private instance variable m2 whose type is M2. The constructor for M1 creates an M2 object and assigns its reference to m2.

   M2:   M2 has a private instance variable m1 whose type is M1. The constructor for M2 creates an M1 object and assigns its reference to m1.

   C11h4: C11h4 contains main. main creates an M1 object and assigns its reference to r1 whose type is M1. main also creates an M2 object and assigns its reference to r2 whose type is M2.

   What is wrong with this program?

5. Here is a possible fix for the problem with the program in Homework Exercise 4:

   Delete the constructor in M1. Thus, M1 will have only the default constructor inserted by the compiler. To the M1 class, add a static variable m1 of type M and a static method getReference. M1.getReference checks if m1 is null. If m1 is null, M1.getReference calls the constructor for M1, assigning the reference returned to m1, and it calls

M2.getReference, assigning the reference returned to m2. M1.getReference terminates by returning m1. Make the parallel changes to M2. Change the body of main to

```
M1 r1 = M1.getReference();
M2 r2 = M2.getReference();
```

Draw a diagram that shows r1, r2, the objects created. In your diagram, show to
what objects r1, r2, m1, and m2 point. Does the proposed fix work?

6. Here is another possible fix for the problem with the program in Homework
   Exercise 4:

   The constructor for M1 should call the constructor for M2, passing it this. It should
   assign the reference returned to m2. Add a public accessor method getm2 to M1 that
   returns the value of m2. The constructor for M2 should assign the parameter it is
   passed to m1. Change the body of main to

   ```
   M1 r1 = M1();
   M2 r2 = r1.getm2;
   ```

   Does the proposed fix work?

7. Write a copy constructor for the following class:

   ```
   import java.util.Random;
   class Rue
   {
       private Random r;
       //-----------------------------------
       public Rue()
       {
           r = new Random();
       }
   }
   ```

   Test your copy constructor. Does it create a copy that behaves exactly like the original? Is a Random object immutable?

8. Create classes Aye, Boo, and X. Boo is a subclass of Aye. X is unrelated to Aye and Boo.
   Suppose the following statements are executed:

   ```
   Aye a1 = new Aye();
   Aye a2 = new Aye();
   Boo b = new Boo();
   X x = new X();
   ```

   Which of the following expressions are then true:

   ```
   b instanceOf Boo
   b instanceOf Aye
   ```

LABORATORY

```
b instanceOf X
a1.getClass() == a2.getClass()
a1.getClass() == b.getClass()
a1.getClass() == x.getClass()
```

Run a test program to check your answers. Based on the results, describe how the `instanceOf` operator works. How does it differ from the `getClass` method?

9. Create two classes `Art` and `Bag`. `Bag` is a subclass of `Art`. Both contain an instance method named `shell` with no parameters whose body is empty. `main` should execute:

```
Art a = new Bag();
for (long i = 1; i < N; i++)
  a.shell();
```

Adjust the value of `N` so total execution is roughly 5 seconds. Write and run a second program in which `main` executes

```
for (long i = 1; i < N; i++)
   shell();
```

where `shell` is a static method with an empty body. Use the same value for `N` as in the first program. How does the execution time compare with that of the first program? Is there a noticeable difference? If so, explain why.

10. Suppose an OO program has objects with a high degree of **coupling**. Coupling results when one object accesses the data in another object. Some coupling is generally necessary. But too much coupling is bad. It makes objects interdependent, which, in turn, makes, modification or reuse more difficult. Suggest a way to reduce coupling. Specifically, suppose object A accesses the data in object B. How can this interaction be modified to reduce coupling?

11. Suppose B is a subclass of A. Which of these overloadings are legal? Which are illegal?

```
public int f()     // in superclass
protected int f() // in subclass (less access)

protected int f() // in superclass
public int f()     // in subclass (more access)

public A f()       // in superclass
public B f()       // in subclass (return type is subclass)

public B f()       // in superclass
public A f()       // in subclass (return type is superclass)
```

Sample Exam 2 (Chapters 6–11)

Each question is worth 20%

Name _____

1. Write a Java program that prompts for integers. If you enter an integer in the range 11–27 inclusive, your program should terminate. Otherwise, your program should output the square of the number entered, and then repeat. The output of your program should look like the output in the following sample session:

```
Enter integer
3
3 squared = 9
Enter integer
-5
-5 squared = 25
Enter integer
-1
-1 squared = 1
Enter integer
11         ◄──── program terminates at this point
```

2. Write a method (just a method—not a complete program) that is passed two `int` arrays. Your method should copy the numbers in the second array to corresponding slots in the first array. If the first array is smaller than the second, copy only enough numbers from the second array to fill up the first array.

3. Write a complete Java program that simulates the tossing of two dice. Your program should determine empirically the probability of getting a 7 or 11 on one toss.

4. Write a complete Java program in which you have three classes: `Test`, `Parent`, and `Child`. `Child` is a subclass of `Parent`.

   `Test` contains the `main` method with the following code:

   ```
   Child c = new Child();
   c.display();
   ```

   `Parent` contains

   ```
   private int x
   ```

   ```
   public Parent(int xx)
   ```
   Initializes x to xx.

   ```
   public void display()
   ```
   Displays the value of x.

LABORATORY

Child contains

```
        private int y;

        public Child()
                Calls the other Child constructor passing it 5 and 7.

        public Child(int xx, int yy)
                Calls the Parent constructor, passing it xx.
                Initializes y to yy.

        public void display()
                Displays the value of x and y.
```

5. a) When the following program is run, what is displayed? Explain your answer briefly.

```
class See
{
    public static int x = 10;
    //----------------------------------
    public See()
    {
        x++;
    }
}
//==================================================
class TestSee
{
    public static void main(String[] args)
    {
        See z = new See();
        for (int i = 1; i <= 100; i++)
            z = new See();
        System.out.println(See.x);
    }
}
```

b) Write a copy constructor for the following class. Be as efficient as possible. (*Hint:* Integer is an immutable class.)

```
import java.util.Random;
class Saw
{
    private int x;
    private Integer p;
    //----------------------------------
    public Saw()
```

```
    {
        Random r = new Random();
        x = r.nextInt();
        p = new Integer(r.nextInt());
    }
}
```

CHAPTER 12

Exception Handling

OBJECTIVES

- Understand error processing
- Learn how to create and throw exceptions
- Learn how to catch exceptions
- Learn how to use the throws clause
- Learn how to create exception classes

12.1 Error Processing: What to Do and Where to Do It

Two questions to ask about the error processing performed by a program are

1. What does the program do when a run-time error is detected?
2. Where does the program handle errors?

There are three possible answers to the first question (What does the program do?):

1. The program does nothing in which case the error will typically force the program to terminate.
2. The program executes statements that display an error message and then terminates.
3. The program recovers from the error and continues executing.

There are two possible answers to the second question (Where does the program do it?):

1. The program handles errors where they occur. The advantage of this approach is that it is usually easier to handle errors where they occur rather than elsewhere.
2. The program handles the error in a method that is higher in the chain of method calls. For example, suppose main calls f, and f, in turn, calls g. In this case, we have the following chain of method calls:

main ⟶ f ⟶ g

If an error occurs during the execution of g, the program could handle the error higher up in the chain of method calls—for example, in f or main. The advantage of this approach is that we can have a single error handler high in the call chain that handles the errors for all the methods below it.

There is no single best approach to error handling. The beauty of Java is that its error handling capabilities are flexible. We can easily implement whichever approach best satisfies our requirements.

12.2 Exceptions

Exceptions are unusual conditions that occur during the execution of a program. They usually are errors. Exceptions are represented by objects. For example, dividing by zero (an illegal operation) causes an ArithmeticException object to be "thrown." The thrown object propagates up the call chain unless the exception is "caught" (i.e., handled). Catching an exception stops its propagation up the call chain.

When an exception object is thrown in a method, it can be caught in that method. If it is not caught, then it propagates to the next method higher in the call chain. For example, in the program in Fig. 12.1, an ArithmeticException is thrown in method g on Line 21 because it divides by 0. This exception propagates up the chain of method calls—to f and then to main. Because the exception is not caught at any point as it propagates up the call chain, it ultimately causes the program to terminate.

Because of the exception thrown on Line 21, the statements that would normally be executed after Line 21 (Lines 22, 14, and 7) are not executed. The program displays only

```
Start of main
Start of f
Start of g
```

This output is produced by the statements executed before the exception occurs (Lines 5, 12, and 19).

```
 1 class TestException1
 2 {
 3    public static void main (String[] args)
 4    {
 5       System.out.println("Start of main");
 6       f();
 7       System.out.println("End of main");   // not executed
 8    }
 9    //----------------------------------
10    public static void f()
11    {
12       System.out.println("Start of f");
13       g();
14       System.out.println("End of f");      // not executed
15    }
16    //----------------------------------
17    public static void g()
18    {
19       System.out.println("Start of g");
20       int x;
21       x = 5/0;                             // Exception thrown
22       System.out.println("End of g");      // not executed
23    }
24 }
```

Figure 12.1

Because the exception in Fig. 12.1 is not caught, it forces the program to terminate. The error message displayed is

```
Exception in thread "main" java.lang.ArithmeticException: / by zero
        at TestException1.g(TestException1.java:21)
        at TestException1.f(TestException1.java:13)
        at TestException1.main(TestException1.java:6)
```

The first line of this message displays the type of the exception and the reason for the error. `java.lang.ArithmeticException` is the fully qualified name of the exception. "`/ by zero`" is short for "divide by zero." The next three lines display the call chain starting from the location where the error occurred (Line 21 in g) to where g was called from (Line 13 in f) to where f was called from (Line 6 in main).

Exceptions can be caught, in which case they do not propagate further. Exceptions are caught with `catch` blocks. `catch` blocks are always preceded by a `try` block. A `catch` block is called only if an error occurs within the preceding `try` block. Let's look at the example in Fig. 12.2.

Because an `ArithmeticException` is thrown during the execution of Line 23 in the `try` block on Lines 21 to 24, the `catch` block that follows the `try` block is called (i.e., execution jumps to the `catch` block). When the `catch` block is called, the reference to the thrown exception is passed to the parameter of the `catch` block parameter (e in this example—see Line 25).

The `catch` block in Fig. 12.2 displays the error message embedded in the thrown exception with

```
28                System.out.println(e.getMessage());
```

The method `getMessage` in the thrown exception returns the message embedded in the exception. Line 28 displays

```
/ by zero
```

After the `catch` block is executed, execution then proceeds normally with the code that follows the `catch` block unless the `catch` block contains a statement that terminates execution. Thus, in Fig. 12.2, after the `catch` block executes, execution proceeds with Line 30. g then returns to Line 14 in f. After Line 14 is executed, f returns to Line 7 in main. The output displayed is

```
Start of main
Start of f
Start of g
```

```
 1 class TestException2
 2 {
 3    public static void main (String[] args)
 4    {
 5       System.out.println("Start of main");
 6       f();
 7       System.out.println("End of main");   // Executed
 8    }
 9    //----------------------------------
10    public static void f()
11    {
12       System.out.println("Start of f");
13       g();
14       System.out.println("End of f");      // Executed
15    }
16    //----------------------------------
17    public static void g()
18    {
19       System.out.println("Start of g");
20       int x;
21       try
22       {
23          x = 5/0;                          // Exception thrown
24       }
25       catch (ArithmeticException e)
26       {
27          System.out.println("In catch block");
28          System.out.println(e.getMessage());
29       }
30       System.out.println("End of g");      // Executed
31    }
32 }
```

Figure 12.2

```
In catch block
/ by zero
End of g
End of f
End of main
```

The ArithmeticException class is in the java.lang package. Thus, to use Arith-meticException in our program, we do not need to import it or use its fully qualified name.

The type of the parameter in a catch block determines the type of exception that the catch block will catch. For example, the catch block in Fig. 12.2 catches only exceptions of type ArithmeticException or its subclasses because the type of its parameter is ArithmeticException.

In the program in Fig. 12.3, we catch the exception in main. As the exception propagates from g to f to main, no statements in the program are executed. However, once the exception is caught in main, execution then proceeds normally in main.

```java
 1 class TestException3
 2 {
 3    public static void main (String[] args)
 4    {
 5       System.out.println("Start of main");
 6       try
 7       {
 8          f();
 9       }
10       catch (ArithmeticException e)
11       {
12          System.out.println(e.getMessage());
13       }
14       System.out.println("End of main");  // Executed
15    }
16    //---------------------------------
17    public static void f()
18    {
19       System.out.println("Start of f");
20       g();
21       System.out.println("End of f");     // Not executed
22    }
23    //---------------------------------
24    public static void g()
25    {
26       System.out.println("Start of g");
27       int x;
28       x = 5/0;                            // Exception thrown
29       System.out.println("End of g");     // Not executed
30    }
31 }
```

Figure 12.3

The output displayed by the program in Fig. 12.3 is

```
Start of main
Start of f
Start of g
/ by zero
End of main
```

Note that the exception prevented the completion of the g and f methods. However, main completed normally because the exception was caught in main.

12.3 Creating and Throwing Exceptions

A Java program will automatically detect and throw exceptions for many types of errors. For example, as we saw in Fig. 12.1, a division by 0 is automatically detected. However, some types of errors are not automatically detected. For example, suppose a program reads in a test grade using the nextInt method in a Scanner object. Suppose grades must be greater than or equal to 0. Then it is an error if the user enters a negative number. However, the program cannot automatically detect this error because it is perfectly legitimate for the nextInt method to read in negative integers. Thus, if we want an exception thrown if this error occurs, we must include code in our program that tests for the error and explicitly throws an exception if the error occurs.

Before we throw an exception, we have to create it. To do this, we use the new operator together with a call of a constructor for the exception we want. For example, RuntimeException is a predefined class we can use for any run-time error. To create a RuntimeException object with the embedded error message "Invalid grade", we use

```
RuntimeException r;
r = new RunTimeException("Invalid grade");
```

We can then throw this object with

```
throw r;
```

A simpler approach is to use only one statement to both create the exception object and throw it:

```
throw new RunTimeException("Invalid grade");
```

We then do not need the reference r.

The program in Fig. 12.4 illustrates the technique of creating and throwing an exception.

Line 19 uses an if statement to test if an error has occurred. If it has, a RuntimeExcep-tion is thrown, which propagates to main. The exception is not caught in main, so it causes the program to terminate. Here are two sample runs for this program. In the first, the exception does not occur; in the second, it occurs and is not caught.

```
java TestException4
Enter grade
3
grade = 3

java TestException4
Enter grade
-1
Exception in thread "main" java.lang.RuntimeException: Invalid grade
     at TestException4.getGrade(TestException4.java: 20)
     at TestException4.main(TestException4.java: 6)
```

```
 1 import java.util.Scanner;
 2 class TestException4
 3 {
 4    public static void main(String[] args)
 5    {
 6        int grade = getGrade();
 7        System.out.println("grade = " + grade);
 8    }
 9    //-----------------------------------
10    public static int getGrade()
11    {
12        Scanner kb = new Scanner(System.in);
13
14        System.out.println("Enter grade");
15        int grade = kb.nextInt();
16
17        // the throw statement throws the exception that the new
18        // operator creates
19        if (grade < 0)
20            throw new RuntimeException("Invalid grade");
21
22        return grade;
23    }
24 }
```

Figure 12.4

Because RuntimeException is in the java.lang package, we do not need to import it or use its fully qualified name.

12.4 throws Clause

We use the reserved word throw in a Java program to throw an exception. Distinct from throw is the reserved word throws. We use throws to indicate that a method might possibly propagate an exception of the indicated type to its caller. For example, suppose we define the method f with

```
public static void f() throws IOException
{
   ...
}
```

IOException, like ArithmeticException, is an exception class. It is thrown when an error occurs during an input/output operation. The clause throws IOException after the parentheses in the header of the preceding f method indicates that it is possible for an IOException to propagate from f to its caller.

Java has many exception classes. Every exception class is either **checked** or **unchecked**. If a checked exception can propagate from a method to its caller, the method *must* so indicate with a throws clause. For unchecked exceptions, however, there is no such requirement.

IOException is a checked exception. Thus, if it is possible for an IOException to propagate from a method to its caller, the method must indicate this with a throws clause. All the subclasses of IOException are also checked.

An ArithmeticException is an unchecked exception. Thus, in Figs. 12.1, 12.2, and 12.3, we did not have to use the throws clause in the main, f, and g methods. RuntimeException and its subclasses (which include ArithmeticException) are also unchecked. Thus, we did not have to use the throws clause in the getGrade method in Fig. 12.4.

The IOException class is in the java.io package. Thus, to use IOException in a program, we must either import it or use its fully qualified name.

12.5 Creating Your Own Exception Classes

Suppose a program can detect several types of errors. For each of these errors, it could throw a RuntimeException. But if it did this, the program would not be able to use different catch blocks to catch the different types of errors (because they all throw the same type of exception). What we need here is a unique exception class for each type of error. Each error can then throw its own unique exception. We can then use a different catch block for each type of error. The program in Fig. 12.5 illustrates this technique. In it, we define two new exception classes: TooSmallException and TooLargeException. These classes must be subclasses of the Exception class. For this program, the number entered should be between 100 and 200. A number less than 100 triggers a TooSmallException; a number greater than 200 triggers a TooLargeException.

```
 1  import java.util.Scanner;
 2  class TooSmallException extends Exception
 3  {
 4      public TooSmallException()
 5      {
 6          super("Number too small");
 7      }
 8      //-----------------------------------
 9      public TooSmallException(String msg)
10      {
11          super(msg);
12      }
13  }
14  //================================================
15  class TooLargeException extends Exception
16  {
17      public TooLargeException()
18      {
19          super("Number too large");
20      }
21      //-----------------------------------
22      public TooLargeException(String msg)
23      {
24          super(msg);
25      }
26  }
27  //================================================
28  class TestException5
```

Figure 12.5 (continues)

```
29 {
30      public static void main(String[] args)
31      {
32          Scanner kb = new Scanner(System.in);
33          System.out.println("Enter number");
34          int x = kb.nextInt();
35          try
36          {
37              if (x < 100)
38                  throw new TooSmallException();
39              if (x > 200)
40                  throw new TooLargeException(x + " is too large");
41          }
42          catch (TooSmallException e)
43          {
44              System.out.println(e.getMessage());
45              System.out.println("Next time enter larger number");
46          }
47          catch (TooLargeException e)
48          {
49              System.out.println(e.getMessage());
50              System.out.println("Next time enter smaller number");
51          }
52      }
53 }
```

Figure 12.5   (continued)

On Lines 2–13, we define a TooSmallException class by extending the Exception class. This class has two constructors: one calls the Exception constructor, passing it a default message:

```
6       super("Number too small");
```

The other constructor calls the Exception constructor passing the message it was passed when called:

```
11      super(msg);
```

The message passed to the Exception constructor is embedded in the exception object that is created and is available via the getMessage method in the Exception class. For example, Line 38 creates and throws a TooSmallException with

```
38              throw new TooSmallException();
```

Here, the constructor on Line 4 is called. This constructor passes the default message, "Number too small", to the Exception constructor. Line 40 creates and throws a Too-LargeException with

```
40                    throw new TooLargeException(x + " is too large");
```

In this case, the constructor on Line 22 is called. This constructor passes to the Exception constructor the message it itself is passed (the argument on Line 40).

The program in Fig. 12.5 uses two catch blocks to distinguish between the two types of errors. The first catch block—with a parameter whose type is TooSmallException—catches exceptions of that type only. The second catch block—with parameter TooLargeException—catches exceptions of that type only. The program uses different catch blocks to distinguish between different types of errors.

Here are two sample sessions with the program in Fig. 12.5:

```
Enter number
2
Number too small
Next time enter larger number

Enter number
500
500 is too large
Next time enter smaller number
```

Laboratory 12 Prep

1. If an exception is not caught, what happens?

2. Write a `catch` block that catches `RuntimeException`. The `catch` block should display the message embedded in the exception it catches.

3. Write a statement that creates and throws a `RuntimeException` whose error message is `"Don't worry."`

4. What is the difference between a checked and an unchecked exception?

5. Write an exception class named `InvalidNumber`. Its constructor should call its superclass, passing it the message `"Invalid Number."`

Laboratory 12

1. What is the effect of the following statement:

```
System.exit(1);
```

Include it in a program and see what happens when it is executed. By convention, any nonzero argument used in a call of `exit` indicates an abnormal termination. A zero argument indicates a normal termination.

2. Add `throws ArithmeticException` clauses to the methods in `C12e2.java` (a copy of `TestException1` in Fig. 12.1). Do these unnecessary clauses cause compile-time errors? Now replace the `throws ArithmeticException` clauses with `throws IOException` clauses. Also import `java.io.IOException`. Do these incorrect `throws` clauses cause compile-time errors?

3. Write a program that includes the following method and an `import` statement for `java.io.IOException`.

```java
public static void f()
{
    throws new IOException("hello");
}
```

What problem occurs during compile time? Fix the problem.

4. Repeat Lab Exercise 3, but use `RuntimeException` in place of `IOException`. You do not need to import `RuntimeException`. What happens at compile time? Why is the result different from the result in Lab Exercise 3?

LABORATORY

5. Replace the f method in C12e5.java (a copy of TestException1 in Fig. 12.1) with

```java
public static void f()
{
   try
   {
      System.out.println("Start of f");
      g();
      System.out.println("End of f");
   }
   catch (ArithmeticException e)
   {
      System.out.println("In catch block");
      System.out.println(e.getMessage());
   }
   finally
   {
      System.out.println("In finally block");
   }
}
```

Determine what happens for each of the following three cases. For which of these cases is the finally block executed?

a) No exception is thrown in the try block.

b) An exception is thrown and caught by the catch block.

c) The exception is thrown but not caught (which happens if the thrown exception does not match the type of exception specified in the catch block). To try out this case, change the type of the parameter e in the preceding code to IOException. Import java.io.IOException.

6. Change the statement on Line 28 in Fig. 12.2 to

```java
System.out.println(e);
```

Is the output displayed by the program different? What method provides the string that is displayed?

7. When you create a new RuntimeException, can you call its constructor without using any arguments? Run a test program to check your answer.

8. What kind of exception occurs when the following program is executed?

```java
class NullPointer
{
   public void f()
   {
      System.out.println("hello");
   }
}
```

```
//==================================================
class C12e8
{
    public static void main(String[] args)
    {
        NullPointer r;
        r = null;
        r.f();
    }
}
```

9. Write a program in which main calls a method that uses a too large index when accessing an array. Let the exception propagate until it terminates the program. What kind of exception occurs? Now include a catch block for this type of exception in main. Your catch block should display a meaningful error message in addition to the message embedded in the exception. It should then terminate the program immediately (see Lab Exercise 1).

10. RuntimeException is a superclass of both ArithmeticException and NullPointer-Exception. Will a catch block whose parameter has type RuntimeException catch both ArithmeticException and NullPointerException exceptions? Run a test program to check your answer.

11. Given the following code, what would happen if an ArithmeticException occurred in the try block? A NullPointerException? A RuntimeException? (*Hint:* ArithmeticException, NullPointerException, and RuntimeException are all subclasses of Exception.) Would it make sense to reverse the order of the two catch blocks? Run a test program to check your answers.

```
try
{
    ...
}
catch(Exception e)
{
    ...
}
catch(NullPointerException e)
{
    ...
}
```

12. Write a program that prompts for and reads in a string. It should throw a NoEException (a class you define) if the string has no occurrences of the letter E (either upper- or lower-case). Test your program.

Homework 12

1. Write a program in which main calls a nonstatic method f. f should prompt the user for and read in an integer from the keyboard. If the integer is negative, f should construct and throw an IOException (you can do this even though an I/O error has not actually occurred). If the integer is positive, f should construct and throw a NullPointerException. If the integer is zero, f should construct and throw an ArithmeticException. main should catch the three types of exceptions with separate catch blocks. It should then display one of the following messages according to the type of exception it catches, after which the program should terminate:

```
IOException caught
NullPointerException caught
ArithmeticException caught
```

2. Write a program in which main prompts for and reads in a double constant and then displays the square of the constant. If the user does not enter a double constant, your program should reprompt the user for a valid input. Your program should use the prompt and error messages illustrated by the following sample session:

```
Enter non-negative double constant
hello
Not a double constant.  Re-enter
goodbye
Not a double constant.  Re-enter
4
Square of 4 = 16.0      ←—— program terminates at this point
```

Do not use hasNextDouble to determine if the input is valid. Instead, catch the exception that nextDouble throws if the input is invalid.

3. Write a program that adds and displays the sum of the command-line arguments. If no command-line arguments are given, your program should display

```
Error: no command line arguments
```

and then terminate execution. If any line argument is not a valid number, your program should display

```
Error: invalid command line argument
```

and then terminate execution.

4. Write a class named IntCompute. It should contain an add, a subtract, a multiply, a divide, and a remainder method. Each of the methods should perform the operation implied by its name on its two parameters and return the result. However, if the result is out of the range of type int, then it should throw an Overflow excep-

tion. Define the Overflow class appropriately. Write a program that uses your Int-Compute class. Your program should call all the methods in IntCompute, both with arguments that do not cause overflow and with arguments that do.

5. Create a class named CandyBars that throws a TooManyCandyBars exception if the creation of more than the allowed limit of CandyBars objects is attempted. Write a program that tests your CandyBars class.

6. Write a class named Print. It should contain a print and a println method that work like System.out.print and System.out.println. However, the methods in Print should throw a TooManyLines exception if the total number of lines displayed exceeds 25. Define the TooManyLines class appropriately. Write a program that tests your Print class.

CHAPTER 13

File Processing

OBJECTIVES

- Learn the difference between text and binary files
- Learn how to read from and write to a text file
- Learn how to handle IOException
- Learn how to read from and write to a binary file
- Understand the exception hierarchy

13.1 Reading from a Text File

In Chapter 1, we learned how to write to the display screen using the println method. In Chapter 4, we learned how to read from the keyboard. In this chapter will learn how to read and write files. A **text file** is a file that contains a sequence of binary codes, each corresponding to some character. When we view a text file with a text editor, we see the corresponding character displayed for each code.

Before we can read from a text file, we, of course, have to create the file. One way we can create a text file is to use a text editor. We simply enter the character data (not the binary codes) into the file via the keyboard in the same way we create a file that contains a Java program.

Suppose we have created a text file named t1.txt (see Fig. 13.1). The extension txt in the file name is not required. We can use any extension or no extension for a text file. However, it is useful to use the txt extension because it identifies the file as a text file.

To read the data in t1.txt, we use a Scanner object that is associated with t1.txt. Recall that to read from the keyboard, we used a Scanner object created with

```
Scanner kb = new Scanner(System.in);
```

By passing System.in (which is a reference to an object that represents the keyboard) to the constructor for Scanner, we get a Scanner object that reads from the keyboard. Similarly, to read from the file t1.txt, we have to pass to the constructor for Scanner an object that represents this file. To create the object that represents t1.txt, we use

```
File tf = new File("t1.txt");
```

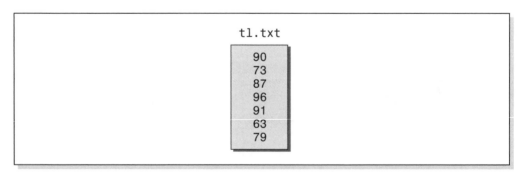

Figure 13.1

Here, we are passing the name of the file to the constructor for the File class. We get back an object that represents that file. We can then use this File object to create the Scanner object we need:

```
Scanner inFile = new Scanner(tf);
```

Alternatively, we can create the File object and pass it to the Scanner object all in one statement:

```
Scanner inFile = new Scanner(new File("t1.txt"));
```

We then do not need the File reference variable tf.

The parameter we pass to the File constructor does not have to be a string constant. It can also be a reference variable that points to a string. For example, in the following code, the file name that the user enters on the keyboard is read into a String object referenced by fileName. fileName is then passed to the File constructor.

```
// Create Scanner object that reads from the keyboard
Scanner kb = new Scanner(System.in);

// Prompt user for file name
System.out.println("Enter file name");

// Read file name from keyboard
String fileName = kb.next();

// Create Scanner object for file
Scanner inFile = new Scannner(new File(fileName));
```

Once we have a Scanner object associated with the file t1.txt, we can use it in the same way we use a Scanner object for the keyboard. The hasNextInt, hasNextDouble, has-Next, and hasNextLine methods all go false when the end of the file is reached during the reading process. We can use these methods in the exit condition for the loop that processes the file. For example, a loop to display all the integers in the t1.txt file is

```
while (inFile.hasNextInt())    // any numbers left?
{
    x = inFile.nextInt();      // read number
    System.out.println(x);     // display number
}
```

As long as hasNextInt returns true (which means there are numbers in the file to be processed), the loop continues to execute. When we reach the end of the file, hasNextInt goes false, and we exit the loop.

Whenever a program finishes inputting from a file, it should close the file. Closing an input file releases the resources your computer is using to read from the file. To close a file, call the `close` method in the `Scanner` object. For example, if `inFile` is the `Scanner` object you are using to read from a file, close the file with

```
inFile.close();
```

The `File` class, as well as most other classes associated with I/O, is in the `java.io` package. One exception is the `Scanner` class, which is in `java.util`.

13.2 Writing to a Text File

To write to a text file, we create a `PrintWriter` object associated with the file to which we want to write. A `PrintWriter` object has the same collection of `println` and `print` methods that `System.out` has. To write to a file, we simply call the `println` and `print` methods in the `PrintWriter` object for that file. For example, suppose we want a program that creates a text file named `numbers.txt` that contains the integers 1 to 100, each on a separate line. First, we create a `PrintWriter` object associated with the file `numbers.txt`:

```
PrintWriter outFile = new PrintWriter("numbers.txt");
```

We can then call the `println` method in the `outFile` object. This methods writes to the `numbers.txt` file. For example, to write the numbers 1 to 100 to `numbers.txt`, we can use

```
for (int i = 1; i <= 100; i++)
   outFile.println(i);
```

The statement

```
outFile.println(i);
```

calls the `println` method in the `outFile PrintWriter` object. This method writes the value of `i` to the associated file.

When a program is finished writing to a file, it should close it by calling the `close` method in the `PrintWriter` object. For example, to close the file represented by `outFile`, it should execute

```
outFile.close();
```

When you write to a file, the data you write may be **buffered** (i.e., temporarily stored) in main memory. When you explicitly `close` a file by calling the close method, any buffered data is written to the file before it is closed. If you do not explicitly close a file, the file will automatically be closed when the program terminates. However, in this case, buffered data may not be written to the file before it is closed, in which case that data is lost. Thus, *it is essential to close output files* by calling `close`.

13.3 Handling IOException

It is possible that an `IOException` may occur during the creation of a `File` object. Because `IOException` is a checked exception, you must either indicate that the method creating the `File` object may throw an `IOException` object, or you must catch the exception. For example, suppose the `f` method creates a `File` object. Then you can use the `throws` clause on `f`:

```
public void f() throws IOException
{



                                          indicates f may
                                          throw an IOException


    Scanner inFile = new Scanner(new File("t1.txt"));
    ...
}
```

Alternatively, you can catch the `IOException` in `f`:

```
public void f()
{
    Scanner inFile = null;        // need null to keep compiler happy
    try
    {
        inFile = new Scanner(new File("t1.txt"));
    }
    catch (IOException e)
    {
        ...
    }
    ...
}
```

Be sure to declare `inFile` before the `try` block. If, instead, you declare it inside the `try` block, it will be local to the `try` block, in which case you will be able to use it only within the `try` block. You must also initialize `inFile` when you declare it. If you do not, the compiler will complain. To understand why, consider the `f` method in Fig. 13.2.

An `IOException` may occur when Line 8 is executed. For example, an `IOException` would occur if the `t1.txt` file does not exist. If this happens, the assignment statement on Line 8 is not completed. Thus, `inFile` has no value. Then after the `catch` block is executed, Line 15 would attempt to use `inFile`. But `inFile` is undefined because it was never assigned a reference. The compiler detects this potential problem and generates a compile-time error.

Suppose we add the following statement to the end of the catch block in Fig. 13.2:

```
System.exit(1);
```

This statement terminates program execution immediately. With this statement included in the `catch` block, we can reach Line 15 only if the assignment to `inFile` is successful on Line 8. Nevertheless, the compiler will still complain about Line 15. To fix this problem, we replace Line 4 with

```
Scanner inFile = null;
```

The compiler will then not flag Line 15. Note that the `f` method in Fig. 13.2 still has a logic error if we do not insert a call of `System.exit` into the catch block. Without the call of `System.exit`, Line 15 can be reached without a valid reference in `inFile`. The compiler does not detect this error, but it is, nevertheless, a serious bug.

```
 1 public void f()
 2 {
 3    int x;
 4    Scanner inFile;              // inFile not initialized
 5
 6    try
 7    {
 8        inFile = new Scanner(new File("t1.txt"));
 9    }
10    catch (IOException e)
11    {
12        System.out.println("File may not exist");
13    }
14    // following code is executed even if line 8 fails
15    x = inFile.nextInt();       // inFile may be undefined here
16 }
```

Figure 13.2

The two programs in Fig. 13.3 copy t1.txt to t2.txt. The program in Fig. 13.3a uses a catch block; the program in Fig. 13.3b does not. Instead, it uses the throws clause in the method header (see Line 5). Thus, if an IOException occurs, it propagates up the call chain, and ultimately causes the program to terminate.

When a PrintWriter object is created, an IOException can occur. Thus, in Fig. 13.3, we handle the construction of a PrintWriter object the same way we handle the construction of a File object. Specifically, in Fig. 13.3a, we create the File and PrintWriter objects within a try block; in Fig. 13.3b, we use a throws clause to indicate an IOException can propagate from main.

(a)

```
 1 import java.util.Scanner;
 2 import java.io.*;    // for IOException, File, and PrintWriter
 3 class IOExample1
 4 {
 5    public static void main(String[] args)
 6    {
 7       Scanner inFile = null;
 8       PrintWriter outFile = null;
 9
10       try
11       {
12          inFile = new Scanner(new File("t1.txt"));
13          outFile = new PrintWriter("t2.txt");
14       }
15       catch (IOException e)
16       {
17          System.out.println(e.getMessage()); // display error
18          System.exit(1);                     // terminate program
19       }
20
21       String s;
22       while (inFile.hasNextLine())
23       {
24          s = inFile.nextLine();    // read one line
25          outFile.println(s);       // write this line
26       }
27
28       inFile.close();             // close files
29       outFile.close();
30    }
31 }
```

Figure 13.3 (continues)

(b)

```
1 import java.util.Scanner;
2 import java.io.*;                    // java.io has IOException
3 class IOExample2
4 {
5     public static void main(String[] args) throws IOException
6     {
7         Scanner inFile = new Scanner(new File("t1.txt"));
8         PrintWriter outFile = new PrintWriter("t2.txt");
9
10        String s;
11        while (inFile.hasNextLine())
12        {
13            s = inFile.nextLine();      // read one line
14            outFile.println(s);         // write this line
15        }
16
17        inFile.close();                 // close files
18        outFile.close();
19    }
20 }
```

Figure 13.3   (continued)

Once the programs in Fig. 13.3 close the output files they create, we can examine the files they create using any text editor.

13.4   Binary Files

A text file holds text—that is, a sequence of characters, each represented by a binary code. When you view a text file with a text editor, the characters represented by the codes—not the codes themselves—are displayed on the screen. A **binary file**, on the other hand, contains the raw binary representation of data. For example, suppose we execute

x = 20;

where x has type int. x then contains 20. More precisely, it contains the 32-bit binary number equal to decimal 20 (see Fig. 13.4a).

If we write x to a text file, the binary number in x is converted to decimal. Then the code for each digit in this decimal number is written to the file (see Fig. 13.4b). The code that

```
(a) Binary number equal to decimal 20:

00000000000000000000000000010100

(b)

code for '2'

   │
   ▼
- - - - - - - -
0011001000110000
        - - - - - - - -
            ▲
            │
        code for '0'
```

Figure 13.4

represents the character '2' is 00110010; the code that represents the character '0' is 00110000. If, on the other hand, we write x to a binary file, then the raw binary number in x (Fig. 13.4a) is written *as is* to the file.

Fig. 13.5 illustrates the writing to both a text file and a binary file.

```
 1 import java.io.*;
 2 import java.util.Scanner;
 3 class TextandBinOutExample
 4 {
 5     public static void main(String[] args) throws IOException
 6     {
 7         PrintWriter textOut = new PrintWriter("t3.txt");
 8         int x = 20;
 9         textOut.println(x);        // output text
10         textOut.close();
11
12         DataOutputStream binOut = new DataOutputStream(
13                                   new FileOutputStream("b1.bin"));
14         binOut.writeInt(x);        // output binary
15         binOut.close();
16     }
17 }
```

Figure 13.5

To write to a text file t3.txt, we first create a PrintWriter object with

```
7          PrintWriter textOut = new PrintWriter("t3.txt");
```

We then write x with

```
9          textOut.println(x);
```

To create and write to a binary file b1.bin, we follow the same general steps. However, we have to use different classes and methods. To create a binary file, we create a DataOut-putStream object with

```
12         DataOutputStream binOut = new DataOutputStream(
13                          new FileOutputStream("b1.bin"));
```

We pass to the DataOutputStream constructor a FileOutputStream object that represents the output file. We then write x by calling the writeInt method in the DataOut-putStream object:

```
14         binOut.writeInt(x);
```

We need the throws clause on Line 5 because Line 7 (where we create a PrinterWriter object) and Line 13 (where we create a FileOutputStream object) can throw an IOException.

The extension on a binary file name does not have to be bin. In addition to bin, there are a variety of extensions in use for binary files such as exe, class, zip, jpg, and mp3.

Fig. 13.6 illustrates reading from a binary file whose name is specified on the command line. For example, if we invoke the program with

```
java BinInExample b1.bin
```

the program reads from b1.bin.

To read from the file whose name is given by args[0], we create a DataInputStream object:

```
9          DataInputStream binIn =
10              new DataInputStream(new FileInputStream(args[0]));
```

Recall that args[0] accesses the first argument specified on the command line (see Section 9.8). To read one number from the file, we call the readInt method:

```
16              x = binIn.readInt();
```

The program in Fig. 13.6 reads and displays all the numbers in the input file. It does this with a while loop that contains Line 16. At the end of the file, Line 16 throws an EOF-

```
1  import java.io.*;
2  import java.util.Scanner;
3  class BinInExample
4  {
5      public static void main(String[] args) throws IOException
6      {
7          int x;
8
9          DataInputStream binIn =
10             new DataInputStream(new FileInputStream(args[0]));
11
12         try
13         {
14             while (true)
15             {
16                 x = binIn.readInt();
17                 System.out.println(x);
18             }
19         }
20         catch (EOFException e)
21         {
22             binIn.close();
23         }
24     }
25 }
```

Figure 13.6

`Exception` because at that point there is no more data to read. The `catch` block on Lines 20–23 then closes the file.

Lines 10 and 22 in Fig. 13.6 can throw an `IOException`. Because these lines are not in a `try` block, the exceptions they can throw are not caught. For this reason, we need a `throws` clause in the header of `main` (see Line 5), even though `main` contains a `catch` block.

Binary files are more time efficient than text files because they do not require the conversion that text files require. For example, when we write the value in an `int` variable to a text file, the binary number in the variable has to be converted to decimal. But writing it to a binary file requires no conversion. The number is written, *as is*, to the file. Because binary files contain raw binary data, they are not viewable with a standard text editor (try viewing the `b1.bin` file created by the program in Fig. 13.5 with a text editor).

Fig. 13.7 lists the various methods available in the `DataInputStream` and `DataOutput-Stream` classes that we can use for binary I/O.

```
DataInputStream

    byte readByte(byte b)
    short readShort(short s)
    int readInt(int i)
    long readLong(long l)
    float readFloat(float f)
    double readDouble(double d)
    char readChar(int c)
    boolean readBoolean(boolean b)
    String readUTF(String s)
    void close()

DataOutputStream

    void writeByte(byte b)
    void writeShort(short s)
    void writeInt(int i)
    void writeLong(long l)
    void writeFloat(float f)
    void writeDouble(double d)
    void writeChar(int c)
    void writeBoolean(boolean b)
    void writeUTF(String s)
    void close()
```

Figure 13.7

13.5 Exception Hierarchy

Fig. 13.8 shows the hierarchy among the exception classes you are likely to encounter.

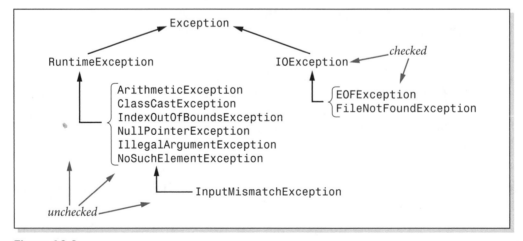

Figure 13.8

Laboratory 13 Prep

1. What is the difference between a text file and a binary file?

2. Why is it essential to close an output file?

3. Assume `inFile` points to a `Scanner` object for a text file that contains integers only. Write code that counts and displays the number of integers in the file.

4. Why should a `Scanner` reference variable not be declared within a `try` block?

5. Write the statement that creates a `PrintWriter` object associated with the file `x.txt`.

Laboratory 13

1. Write a program that writes the integers 1 to 10,000 to a text file. Do not close the file. Run the program. Check the output file created with a text editor. Were all 10,000 integers written to the output file?

2. Using a text editor, create the following file, formatted as shown, or use the `lab13.txt` file provided:

```
        lab13.txt
┌──────────────────────────┐
│  1   2            4       │
│        7                  │
│ 14   17                   │
│                           │
│    20 30 40               │
└──────────────────────────┘
```

Write a program that copies `lab13.txt` to a file named `C13e2.txt`. `C13e2.txt` should have one number per line.

3. Write a program that reads in the numbers in `lab13.txt` (see Lab Exercise 2) and computes and displays their average.

4. Write a program that reads in the numbers in `lab13.txt` and displays them in reverse order.

5. If you run a program that outputs to a file that already exists, what happens? Runtime error? New data appended to the back end of the old file? New data replaces the old file? Run a test program to check your answer.

6. Run a program that attempts to read from a file that does not exist. What happens?

7. Create a program that includes `C13e7.java` (a copy of f in Fig. 13.2). What message does the compiler generate?

LABORATORY

8. Write a program in which you try to read a text file immediately after you close it. What happens? What if after closing it, you again create a Scanner object to read it. Can you use this new Scanner object to read the file from its beginning? Run a test program to check your answer.

9. Run the program in C13e9.java (a copy TextandBinOutExample in Fig. 13.5) several al times. Then examine the text file t3.txt with a text editor. What can you conclude happens each time you run the program? Is the data appended to the end of the file if it already exists, or is a new file created? What about the binary file b1.bin? Is data appended or is a new file created? Run the program in Fig. 13.6 (BinInExample) to check your b1.bin file. Now change Line 13 in C13e9.java to

```
new FileOutputStream("b1.bin", true));
```

Run the modified program several times. What is the effect of passing true to the constructor for FileOutputStream?

10. The PrintWriter class has a printf method as well as the println and print methods. printf allows you to easily format output. The first argument is always a string. printf outputs this string. However, before it outputs it, it replaces any conversion codes in the string with values obtained from the other arguments. Conversion codes start with "%". For example, when the following printf statement is executed, the first conversion code is replaced with the value of i; the second conversion code is replaced by the value of j.

```
int i = 10;
int j = 20;
System.out.printf("i = %d        j = %d%n", i, j);
```

The string that results is then displayed:

```
i = 10        j = 20
```

"%n" in the preceding printf statement is not a conversion code—it represents the end-of-line marker. The conversion code to use in a call of printf depends on the type of the value to be converted. Use "%d" for integers, "%f" for float and double values, "%c" for char values, "%b" for boolean values, and "%s" for strings. Run the following program. From the output it generates, determine how each printf statement works.

```
class C13e10
{
    public static void main(String[] args)
    {
        int i = 1, j = 2; double x = 1.23456789;
        System.out.printf("%d%d%f%n", i, j, x);
```

```
            System.out.printf("%d    %d    %f%n", i, j, x);
            System.out.printf("%9d%9d%9f%n", i, j, x);   // 9 field width
            System.out.printf("%-5d%-5d%n", i, j);
            System.out.printf("%f%n", x);
            System.out.printf("%5.1f%n", x);
            System.out.printf("%10.5f%n", x);
    }
}
```

Homework 13

1. Write a program that reads a text file containing integers, determines the average, and then outputs to a file every number in the input file greater than the average. Test your program with the input file lab13.txt (see Lab Exercise 2). Write to an output file named C13h1.txt.

2. Write a program that reads in two text files both containing an unspecified number of integers. The numbers in each file are in ascending order. Your program should merge the numbers in the two files into a single sequence of numbers in ascending order. Output this sequence to the file C13h2.txt. Test your program with lab13.txt (see Lab Exercise 2) as one of the input files. Use a second input file that contains the numbers 5, 8, 15, and 30 in that order. Run your program a second time in which both input files are lab13.txt.

3. Write a program that determines and displays the number of lines in the file whose name you specify on the command line. Test your program with lab13.txt (see Lab Exercise 2). Sample run:

```
java C13h3 lab13.txt
5 lines in lab13.txt
```

4. Write a program that determines and displays the number of bytes in the file specified on the command line. Your program should work for both binary and text files. Test your program on the t3.txt and b1.bin files that the program in Fig. 13.5 creates. Sample runs:

```
java C13h4 t3.txt
4 bytes in t3.txt

java C13h4 b1.bin
4 bytes in b1.bin
```

5. Write a program that reads a text file and outputs its contents with all sequences of two or more spaces replaced by a single space. Output to the C13h5.txt file. Test your program on the lab13.txt file (see Lab Exercise 2).

LABORATORY

6. Write a program that reads in a text file and displays its average "word" length. Treat any sequence of consecutive non-whitespace bounded by whitespace, the beginning of the file, or the end of the file as a word.

7. Write a program that reads a binary file and outputs its contents as a text file. Output each bit in the binary file with a '0' or "1" character in the text file. That is, represent the bit 0 with the character '0', and represent the bit 1 with the character '1'. The text file should display characters in groups of eight, with eight groups per line, separating successive groups on a line by one space. Test your program with the b1.bin file created by the program in Fig. 13.5.

8. Write a program that determines if the two files whose names are specified on the command line are identical. Your program should work for both text and binary files.

9. Write a program that reads in two text files whose names are specified on the command line and outputs a text file that contains the contents of the first input file followed by the contents of the second input file. Test your program with two files, one containing the numbers 1 to 5, each on a separate line, the other containing the numbers 6 to 20, each on a separate line.

Recursive Methods

14.1 You Already Understand Recursive Methods

A **recursive method** is a method that calls itself. What happens when a method calls itself is no different from what happens when a method calls a method other than itself. So you really have nothing new to learn to understand recursive methods.

Let's review what happens when a method calls another method. The same sequence of events also happens when a method calls itself:

1. The parameters, if any, for the called method are created.
2. The values of the arguments, if any, in the call are automatically assigned to their corresponding parameters in the called method.
3. Local variables, if any, are created.
4. The body of the called method is executed.
5. Local variables and parameters created in Steps 1 and 3 are destroyed.
6. The called method returns to its caller.

14.2 Stepping Through a Recursive Method

Let's step through the execution of the recursive method r1 in Fig. 14.1. Note that on Line 15, r1 calls itself.

```
 1 class Recursion1
 2 {
 3    public static void main(String[] args)
 4    {
 5       r1(2);
 6    }
 7 //-----------------------------------
 8    public static void r1(int x)
 9    {
10       if (x == 0)
11          System.out.println("bottom");
12       else
13       {
14          System.out.println("down");
15          r1(x - 1);                        // recursive call
16          System.out.println("up");
17       }
18    }
19 }
```

Figure 14.1

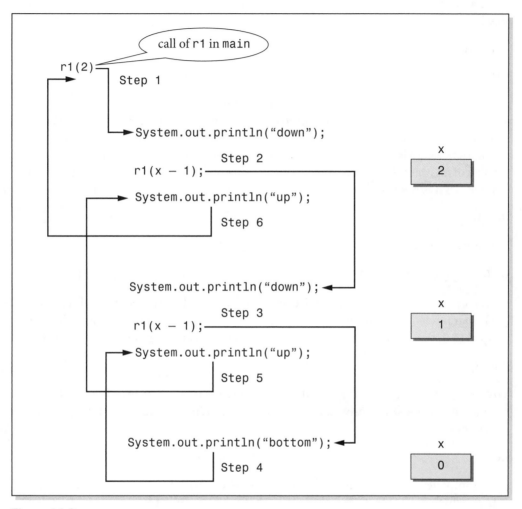

Figure 14.2

Fig. 14.2 shows the execution of r1 in six steps:

Step 1

main calls r1, passing it 2. The parameter x in r1 is created. This x receives 2. Because x is not equal to 0, execution proceeds to the else part of the if-else statement. down is displayed.

Step 2

The recursive call

```
15              r1(x - 1);                      // recursive call
```

is executed. Because x is 2, the value of the argument in this call is 1. The parameter x (a second x) is created. This x receives the value 1. Because this x is not equal to 0, execution proceeds to the else part of the if-else statement. down is displayed. You may ask, why is a second x created? The reason is simple: when you pass the value of an argument in a method call, a parameter is *always* created to receive that value. That is how all method calls—recursive and nonrecursive—work.

Step 3

The recursive call

```
15              r1(x - 1);                      // recursive call
```

is executed. Because x (the second x) is 1, the value of the argument in this call is 0. The parameter x (a third x) is created. This x receives the value 0. Because this x is equal to 0, the if part of the if-else statement is executed. bottom is displayed.

Step 4

r1 completes. The current x (the third x) is destroyed. r1 returns to the point from which it was most recently called, where the x in effect is the second x. up is displayed.

Step 5

r1 completes. The current x (the second x) is destroyed. r1 returns to the point from which it was most recently called, where the x in effect is the first x. up is displayed.

Step 6

r1 completes. The current x (the first x) is destroyed. r1 returns to main.

You can think of the execution of the r1 method in Fig. 14.1 as consisting of three phases: down, bottom, and up. First, as the recursive calls takes place, we recurse "down." In this phase, the x parameters are created. Next, when r1 does not call itself (this occurs when we execute the if part of the if-else statement), we hit "bottom." Finally, we recurse back "up" as the execution of each call of r1 completes. In this phase, the x parameter at each level is destroyed as control returns to the next level up. During the down phase, down is displayed twice; during the bottom phase, bottom is displayed once; during the up phase, up is displayed twice. Thus, the net effect of the program is to display

```
down
down
bottom
up
up
```

Note that as we recurse down, we repeatedly execute the statement that *precedes* the recursive call (Line 14 in Fig. 14.1). As we recurse back up, we repeatedly execute the statement that *follows* the recursive call (Line 16 in Fig. 14.1).

If there are no statements following the recursive call, then the up phase does nothing other than repeated returns. For example, if we delete Line 16 in Fig. 14.1 (this is the line that follows the recursive call), the program displays

```
down
down
bottom
```

If we delete the statements that precede the recursive call, then the down phase does nothing other than repeated recursive calls. For example, if we delete Line 14 in Fig. 14.1 (this is the line that precedes the recursive call) but include Line 16, the program displays

```
bottom
up
up
```

An Easy Way to Determine What a Recursive Method Does

To determine what a recursive method does, we can always step through its execution as we did in Fig. 14.2. However, an easier way is to work from the bottom case backward to the original call. For example, in Fig. 14.1, the x parameters assume the values 2, 1, and 0, in that order. The value 0 corresponds to the bottom case (i.e., when a recursive call does not occur). To determine what r1 displays, we work backward from 0 to 1 to 2. First, determine what r1 does when it is passed 0. This is easy because the bottom case does not involve a recursive call. A quick look at Fig. 14.1 tells us it displays

bottom $\Big\}$ what r1 displays when it is passed 0

Next, we determine what r1 displays when we pass it 1. For this case, r1 executes

```
System.out.println("down");
r1(x - 1);
System.out.println("up");
```

Because x is 1, the recursive call in the preceding code passes the value of 0. But we already know what r1 does when it is passed 0: it displays bottom. Thus, the preceding code for the x equals 1 case displays

down
bottom $\Big\}$ What r1 displays when it is passed 1
up

Similarly, for the x equals 2 case, r1 executes

```
System.out.println("down");
r1(x - 1);
System.out.println("up");
```

For this case, the recursive call passes 1. But we already know what r1 does when it is passed 1—namely, it displays

down
bottom
up

Thus, for the preceding code for the x equals 2 case displays

down
down
bottom $\Big\}$ what r1 displays when it is passed 2
up
up

By working backward starting from the bottom, it is easy to determine what is displayed at each level because we know what is displayed at the previous level.

Let's use our "backward from the bottom" technique to determine what is displayed by the program in Fig. 14.3.

```
 1 class Recursion2
 2 {
 3    public static void main(String[] args)
 4    {
 5       r2(5);
 6       System.out.println();       // go to next line
 7    }
 8    //---------------------------------
 9    public static void r2(int x)
10    {
11       if (x == 0)
12          System.out.print("E");
13       else
14       if (x == 1)
15       {
16          System.out.print("A");
17          r2(6);                    // parameter value jumps up to 6
18          System.out.print("B");
19       }
20       else
21       {
22
23          System.out.print("C");
24          r2(x - 2);
25          System.out.print("D");
26
27       }
28    }
29 }
```

Figure 14.3

First, let's determine the sequence of values the x parameters assume as the method r2 executes. The first call of r2 passes 5 to x (see Line 5). With this value, we recurse on Line 24:

24   r2(x - 2);

Because x is 5, the value of the argument in the recursive call on Line 24 is 3. Thus, when we re-enter r2, x is 3. When x is 3, we again recurse on Line 24, causing the next x value to be 1. However, when we re-enter r2 with 1, we recurse on Line 17 with

17   r2(6);

x	r2 displays
0	E
2	CED
4	CCEDD
6	CCCEDDD
1	ACCCEDDDB
3	CACCCEDDDBD
5	CCACCCEDDDBDD

Figure 14.4

which causes the next x value to jump up to 6. From there, we recurse down to 4, then to 2, and finally to 0 where we hit bottom. Thus, the sequence of x values is

5 ⟶ 3 ⟶ 1 ⟶ 6 ⟶ 4 ⟶ 2 ⟶ 0

To determine what is displayed, we start from 0 and work backward in the preceding sequence until we reach 5. When x is 0, r2 displays E. When x is 2, Lines 23–25 are executed:

```
23          System.out.print("C");
24          r2(x - 2);
25          System.out.print("D");
```

The value of the argument on Line 24 when x is 2 is 0. We just determined that r2 displays E when r2 is passed 0. Thus, when x is 2, r2 displays CED. Continuing this approach, we can easily determine what r2 displays for parameter values back to 5 (see Fig. 14.4).

14.4 Performing a Subtask Using a Recursive Call

When writing a recursive method, you can use a recursive call to perform a subtask that is almost as "big" as the task you have to perform. The recursive call does most of the work (by performing the subtask). Thus, in addition to the recursive call, you have very little code to write to perform the original task. For example, consider the numbersToOne method in Fig. 14.5.

The numbersToOne method displays all the integers from the value of the argument it is passed down to 1. main calls numbersToOne, passing it 10. numbersToOne then displays the numbers from 10 down to 1, each on a separate line.

```
 1 class Recursion3
 2 {
 3     public static void main(String[] args)
 4     {
 5         numbersToOne(10);
 6     }
 7     //----------------------------------
 8     public static void numbersToOne(int n)
 9     {
10         if (n > 0)
11         {
12             System.out.println(n);
13             numbersToOne(n - 1);
14         }
15     }
16 }
```

Figure 14.5

If you look at the code inside numbersToOne, you can see it does very little. It displays the number in the parameter n with

12   System.out.println(n);

The next statement,

13   numbersToOne(n - 1);

recursively calls numbersToOne, passing it the value of n − 1. What does this call do? Remember that numbersToOne displays all the integers from the value of the argument down to 1. The argument on Line 13 is n − 1. Thus, this call displays the integers from n − 1 down to 1. *The recursive call is doing most of the work.* Line 12 displays only the first number. The recursive call displays all the remaining numbers down to 1.

Because we can use a recursive call to do most of a task, writing recursive methods is easy. By using a recursive call to do most of a task, there is not much coding required to complete the task. It is so easy to program tasks with recursive methods, it seems too good to be true.

Here is another way to view what happens when we execute the program in Fig. 14.5: main calls numbersToOne, passing 10 to the parameter n. The recursion causes numbers-ToOne to be repeatedly re-entered with n equal to 9, 8, ..., 0. The n equals 0 case is the bottom case. For this case, numbersToOne simply returns. For n equal to 10, 9, 8, ..., 1, however, Line 12 displays the current value in n. Thus, it is Line 12 that is *really doing all the work* by virtue of the recursion.

Let's write another recursive method that uses a recursive call to perform a subtask. The recursive method in this example returns the reverse of the string it is passed. For example, if it is passed `"ABCDEF"`, the recursive method returns `"FEDCBA"`.

Let's call the **tail** of a non-null string that part of the string that remains when its first character is removed. One way of reversing a string is to remove its first character, reverse the tail of the original string, and then attach the first character to the end of the reversed tail. For example, consider the string `"ABCDEF"`. We first remove the first character:

`"A"`   `"BCDEF"`

We then reverse the tail `"BCDEF"` to get

`"A"`   `"FEDCB"`

We then append the first character to the end of the reversed tail to get

`"FEDCBA"`

It is easy to implement this approach with a recursive method. We can use a recursive call to perform a subtask: namely, reversing the tail. Thus, in addition to the recursive call, the recursive method simply has to strip off the first character and attach it to the end of the reversed string.

To isolate the first character in a string from the tail of a string, we can use the `substring` method in the `String` class. For example, suppose s is a `String` reference that points to `"ABCDEF"`. Then

`s.substring(0,1)`

returns `"A"`, the first character of the s string, and

`s.substring(1, 6)`

returns `"BCDEF"`, the tail of the string. Recall that `substring` returns the string that includes the characters whose indices run from the first parameter up to *but not including the second parameter*. Thus,

`s.substring(1, 6)`

returns the substring that includes the characters with indices 1, 2, 3, 4, and 5. 5 is the index of the last character in the s string. Thus, this call of `substring` provides the complete tail of the substring. Equivalently, we can use `s.length()` in place of 6:

`s.substring(1, s.length())`

The `length` method returns 6, the length of the string. If we hardcode 6 in the call of `substring`, then the call returns the tail only if the string has length 6. If, however, we use `s.length()` for the second argument, then the call of `substring` returns the tail of the s string regardless of its length. We need this generality in our recursive method because on the successive recursive calls, the strings that are passed are progressively shorter. 6 is the correct second argument only for the first call.

Now we are ready to code our recursive method, reverse, that reverses a string. The reverse of a string whose length is 0 or 1 is just the given string. Thus, if we pass reverse a string s whose length is 0 or 1, reverse should simply return it:

```
if (s.length() <= 1)
    return s;
```

Otherwise, we return the following string:

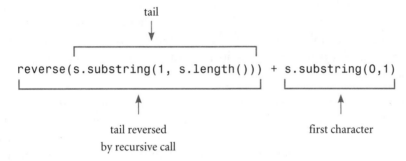

This complicated expression represents the string consisting of the tail of s reversed by the recursive call concatenated to the first character of s. The complete implementation of the reverse method is in Fig. 14.6

```
 1 class Recursion4
 2 {
 3    public static void main(String[] args)
 4    {
 5        System.out.println(reverse(""));        // null string
 6        System.out.println(reverse("A"));       // 1-char string
 7        System.out.println(reverse("ABCDEF"));  // multi-char
 8    }
 9    //-----------------------------------
10    public static String reverse(String s)
11    {
12        if (s.length() <= 1)
13            return s;
14        return reverse(s.substring(1, s.length())) + s.substring(0, 1);
15    }
16 }
```

Figure 14.6

14.5 **Loops Versus Recursion**

Loops in a program cause statements to be executed repeatedly. Recursion also causes statements—the method itself—to be executed repeatedly. Thus, it is no surprise that we can usually use a loop in place of recursion and vice versa. For example, we can implement the body of numbersToOne in Fig. 14.4 with a simple for loop:

```
for (int i = n; i >= 1; i--)
   System.out.println(i);
```

Which is better, loops or recursion? Recursion has the inefficiency associated with repeated method calls. By its very nature, a recursive method is called repeatedly to perform a task. Each time it is called, parameters have to be created and values assigned to them. This takes time and memory space. If, on the other hand, we use a loop, we call its method only once. Thus, only a single set of parameters is created and assigned values. If a recursive method recurses many times, its run time and memory space requirements can be significantly larger than an equivalent method that uses a loop.

The loop approach is more efficient than recursion in both time and space. However, there are some tasks for which a solution is much easier to implement with recursion than with a loop. A good rule to follow is to *use recursion whenever it yields a significantly simpler implementation than a loop.* If, on the other hand, the loop approach is just as simple or nearly as simple, then use it because it is more efficient.

Recursion itself is a repetitive process. Thus, the recursive methods do not need explicit loops, such as a while loop or a for loop. But they do need an if statement to determine when the recursion process should stop. Remember this rule: *When you write a recursive method, use an if statement.*

Laboratory 14 Prep

1. What is wrong with the following recursive method:

```java
public static void rp1(int x)
{
    System.out.println(x);
    rp1(x - 1);
}
```

2. What is displayed when the following method is passed 5:

```java
public static void rp2(int x)
{
    if (x == -1)
    {
        System.out.println("A");
        rp2(6);
    }
    else
    if (x == 3)
        System.out.println("E");
    else
    {
        System.out.println("B");
        rp2(x - 3);
        System.out.println("C");
    }
    System.out.println("D");
}
```

3. What does the following method do:

```java
public static int rp3(int x, int y)
{
    if (y == 0)
        return x;
    return rp3(x, y-1) + 1;
}
```

4. What does the following method do:

```java
public static void rp4(int x)
{
    if (x == 0)
        return 0;
    return x + rp4(x-1);
}
```

5. When should you use recursion rather than a loop?

LABORATORY

Laboratory 14

1. Write a program equivalent to C14e1.java (a copy of Recursion3 in Fig. 14.5), but implement numbersToOne using a while loop instead of recursion.

2. The following method returns the *i*th number in the **Fibonacci sequence**: 1, 1, 2, 3, 5, 8, 13, ... Each number after the first two is the sum of the two preceding numbers. fib(0) returns 1; fib(1) returns 1; fib(2) returns 2, fib(3) returns 3, fib(4) returns 5, fib(5) returns 8, and so on.

```java
public static long fib(long i)
{
   if (i < 2)
      return 1;
   return fib(i - 1) + fib(i - 2);
}
```

Each time you call this method and pass it a value greater than or equal to 2, it calls itself twice because it has two recursive calls (fib(i - 1) and fib(i - 2)). As a result, the total number of calls can become excessive, making this method extraordinarily inefficient. Write a program that includes this method. Your program should prompt for and read in an integer. It should then call fib passing it the integer read. For what integer passed is the program's run time 10 seconds? Double the integer passed and rerun your program. Does the run time also double? Again double the integer passed and rerun. What is the relation between the integer passed and run time?

3. Implement the fib method in Lab Exercise 2 using a loop instead of recursion. Perform the same type of timing measurements that you performed in Lab Exercise 2. Is the loop implementation more efficient?

4. Rewrite the reverse method in Fig. 14.6. Reverse a string by placing its last character at the beginning of the reverse of the substring that contains the entire string except for its last character. Test your program.

5. Rewrite the reverse method in Fig. 14.6. Use the reverse method in the String-Buffer class.

6. Write a method that does multiplication on nonnegative integers using recursion. Test your method by using it to compute the product of 0 and 0, the product of 0 and 5, the product of 5 and 0, and the product of 5 and 10. *Hint:*

```
a×b = a×(b - 1) + a    for b > 0
a×b = 0                for b = 0
```

7. Write a recursive method that returns the number of occurrences of 'A' in the string it is passed. Test your method with the following strings: "", "A", "B", "BCA", "ABC", and "ABACAD".

8. Write a recursive method that returns the maximum integer in the array it is passed. Test your method by passing it a 20-slot int array initialized with random integers. Generate integers with nextInt() in the Random class. Use the seed 1 when you construct the Random object.

9. A recursive method does not have to first recurse down and then up. It can first recurse up and then down. Write a recursive method that returns the sums of the integers from 1 to n when passed n. Your method should first recurse up, hit the top when the parameter is equal to the largest integer to be summed, and then recurse down. (*Hint:* Your method should have two parameters.)

10. Write a method that implements **Ackermann's function**:

```
Ack(x, y) = y + 1              when x = 0
Ack(x, y) = Ack(x-1,1)         when x > 0 and y = 0
Ack(x, y) = A(x-1, A(x,y-1))   when x > 0 and y > 0
```

Use type long. Write a program that displays the value of Ack(n, n) for n = 0, 1, 2, ... For what value of n is the value of Ack(n, n) too large for type long? Ackermann's function is famous because Ack(n, n) grows so rapidly with increasing n.

11. Write a recursive method that determines if the first string it is passed is a substring of the second string it is passed. Test your method with the following pairs: " " and " ", " " and "A", "C" and "ABC", "ABC" and "ABC", "mine" and "determines", "minee" and "determines".

Homework 14

1. Write two methods, one recursive, one using a loop, that compute n! *Hint:*

```
n! = n×(n - 1)!   for n > 0
n! = 1            for n = 0
```

2. Write a program that reads in a file and outputs it to another file. The output file created should be identical to the input file but with its lines in reverse order. Use recursion. Obtain the names of the input and output files from the command line. For the input file, use a file that contains the integers 1 to 10, each on a separate line.

3. Write a program that prompts for and reads in a string. Your program should call a recursive method stringLength, passing it the string. stringLength should return the length of the string. Implement stringLength using recursion. Do *not* use the length method in the string object. Test your program with the strings " " (the null string), "A", and "ABCDEF".

LABORATORY

4. Write a program in which main prompts for and reads in a nonnegative int constant into an int variable. main should then call a recursive method reverseInt, passing it the int value read in. reverseInt should return to main the int value obtained by reversing the digits of the number it is passed. For example, if reverseInt is passed 123, it should return (not display) the value 321. main should then display the value returned. Test your program with 0, 1, 12, and 123. (*Hint:* Divide by 10 to strip off the rightmost digit. To isolate the rightmost digit, divide by 10 and take the remainder (use the "%" operator). reverseInt should not convert the int value it is passed to a string.)

5. Write a method that is passed a string consisting of digits. Your method should return the sum of the digits. For example, if the string is "135", your method should return the int value 9. If the null string is passed to your method, your method should return 0. Use recursion. Test your method by passing it "", "0", "00", and "03405". The parameter type of your method should be String—not int.

6. Write a program in which main prompts for and reads in nonnegative integers into an array. The user signals the end of the data by entering a negative number (which should not be entered into the array). main should then display the numbers in the array and call a sort method, passing it the array. Your sort method should sort the array *using a recursive implementation of the selection sort* (see Section 9.9). When your sort method returns to main, main should again display the numbers (now sorted) in the array.

7. Do Homework Exercise 11 from Chapter 9 but implement the binary search method recursively.

8. Write a program that uses recursion to display all the solutions to the **eight queens problem**. A solution is a board configuration with eight queens only, each not attacking any other queen (i.e., each queen should not be in the same row, same column, or same diagonal as another queen). Here is the basic structure of a recursive method that solves this problem:

```
public static void queens (int[] board, int row)
{
    if (row == 9)
        display board
    else
        for (int col = 1, column <= 8; col++)
        {
            Attempt queen placement on square (row, col)
            If successful
                queens(board, row + 1);
        }
}
```

main should call this method passing it an empty board (an 8 × 8 array) and 1 (the initial row number). (*Hint:* A queen on square (r1, c1) and a queen on square (r2, c2) are attacking each other if any of the following conditions are true: r1 = r2 (same row), c1 = c2 (same column), r1 + c1 = r2 + c2 (same positive slope diagonal) or r1 − c1 = r2 − c2 (same negative slope diagonal).)

9. Write a recursive method that performs a merge sort on the array of integers it is passed. A **merge sort** divides the numbers to be sorted into two halves, sorts each half, and then merges them. Test your method by sorting 20 random integers. Each time the number of numbers to be sorted is doubled, how is the sort time affected? The merge sort is an example of a **divide and conquer** algorithm. Divide and conquer algorithms break up a problem into smaller and easier subproblems. These subproblems are, in turn, broken up into even smaller and easier subproblems. This process continues until we are left with subproblems all of which are very small and trivially easy to solve. In a merge sort, the problem of sorting n items is broken up into two sorts, each of n/2 items. Each of these sorts of n/2 items is, in turn, broken up into two sorts, each of n/4 items. This process continues until we are left with sorts all of which are of one item only—a trivial problem, indeed (we don't have to do anything to sort one item).

CHAPTER 15

Linked Data Structures

OBJECTIVES

- Understand the advantages of linked lists
- Learn how to create and process linked lists
- Learn how to use an inner class
- Learn how to create a linked list class
- Learn how to use recursion to process a linked list

15.1 Advantages of Linked Lists

Once an array is created, its size is fixed. If, during the execution of a program, an array is not big enough, we cannot make it "grow." To avoid this problem, we should always use arrays that are sufficiently big that they will always be big enough. For example, if an array is to hold test grades for the 50 students in a class, we can use an array with 100 slots. Then it is unlikely that the array would ever be too small. Unfortunately, this approach wastes space. Most class sizes will probably be significantly less than 100, in which case many slots in our array will be unused, and, therefore, represent wasted space. We, of course, can always use an ArrayList in place of an array. An ArrayList grows as we add more elements to it. Thus, we do not have the upper limit on its size that we have with an array. Actually, an ArrayList grows in spurts. It only grows if we add an element when it is full. It then grows a number of new slots, only one of which is used for the new element. The ArrayList then does not have to grow again until all the remaining new slots become occupied. The problem with an ArrayList is that the growing process is inefficient. It takes an appreciable amount of time for an ArrayList to grow. Thus, although an ArrayList does not have a fixed size limitation that arrays have, it is less efficient if it has to grow repeatedly.

An alternative to an array and an ArrayList is a linked list. A **linked list** is a structure consisting of nodes linked together in serial fashion with pointers. A linked list can grow during run time. Thus, it never has to be bigger than necessary. If, for example, class size is 50, a linked list can grow to precisely that size. There is no wasted space.

15.2 Working with Linked Lists

Figure 15.1 shows a linked list whose size is 3.

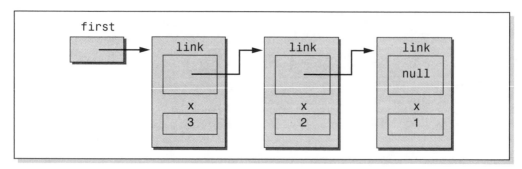

Figure 15.1

It consists of three nodes, each containing a `link` field and an x field. The `link` field of each node, except for the last, points to the next node in the list. The `link` field of the last node contains the `null` pointer. `first` is a reference variable that points to the first node on the list. The x fields in the nodes contain the data. Each node in Fig. 15.1 has just a single data field. However, this is not a requirement—nodes can have multiple data fields. Moreover, these data fields can have any type.

Each node in the linked list in Fig. 15.1 is an object constructed from the following `Node` class:

```
private class Node
{
    private Node link;
    private int x;
}
```

We will explain shortly why the access specifier on this class is `private`.

Suppose we have the list in Fig. 15.1, and we execute the following code:

```
Node p = first;
```

Then p will also point to the first node on the list (see Fig. 15.2a). Consider what happens if we now execute

```
p = p.link;
```

This is a *very* important statement. Please be sure to understand how it works. The right side of this assignment statement accesses the `link` field of the node pointed to by p.

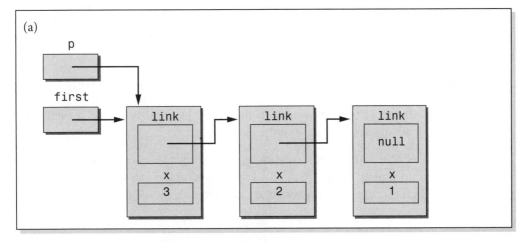

Figure 15.2 (continues)

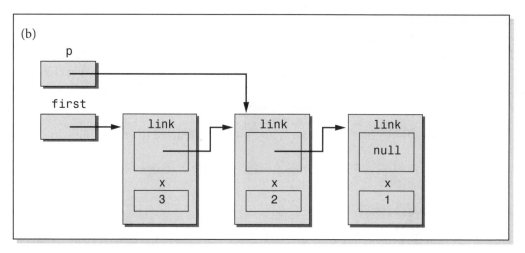

Figure 15.2 (continued)

Because p is pointing to the first node, p.link accesses the link field in the first node. This link field contains a pointer to the second node. Thus, this assignment statement assigns to p a pointer to the second node. Its effect is to advance the pointer in p to the next node (see Fig. 15.2b).

If we execute

```
p = p.link;
```

a second time (when p points as shown in Fig. 15.2b), p.link accesses the link field on the second node (which contains a pointer to the third node). Thus, this statement now advances the pointer in p to the third node. If we execute this statement one more time, p.link accesses the link field of the third node (which contains null). Thus, p is assigned null.

Each time we execute

```
p = p.link;
```

the pointer in p advances to the next node in the linked list if there is one. p eventually goes null when it advances off the end of the list.

Using the foregoing observations, it is easy to figure out how to create a loop that traverses a linked list—that is, that moves through all the nodes on the list. We simply initialize p to first and then execute a loop whose body contains

```
p = p.link;
```

Each time the loop body is executed, p points to the next node on the list. We can use p to access the data in each node. For example, the following code traverses a linked list, displaying its data as it moves across the list:

```
Node p = first;              // init p to point to first node
while (p != null)
{
   System.out.println(p.x);  // display data in current node
   p = p.link;               // advance pointer
}
```

The first time the loop body is executed, p points to the first node. Thus,

```
System.out.println(p.x);  // display data in current node
```

displays the data in the first node. But on the next iteration, p points to the second node. Thus, this same statement now displays the data in the second node. Each time this statement is executed, p is pointing to the next node on the list. Thus, as the loop traverses the list, this statement displays the data in successive nodes. After the data in the last node is displayed, the statement

```
p = p.link;
```

assigns null to p, which causes the true/false expression p != null to go false. Thus, the loop exit occurs after all the data in the linked list has been displayed.

15.3 Adding a Node to a Linked List

Let's determine the code that we need in order to add a new node to the beginning of a linked list. Suppose we want to insert a new node—the node pointed to by newNode—at the beginning of a linked list pointed to by first (see Fig. 15.3a).

To accomplish this insertion, we have to make two changes (see Fig. 15.3b):

1. The link field of the new node must be set to point to the node that is currently the first node. We accomplish this with

   ```
   newNode.link = first;
   ```

2. first must be set to point to the new node. We accomplish this with

   ```
   first = newNode;
   ```

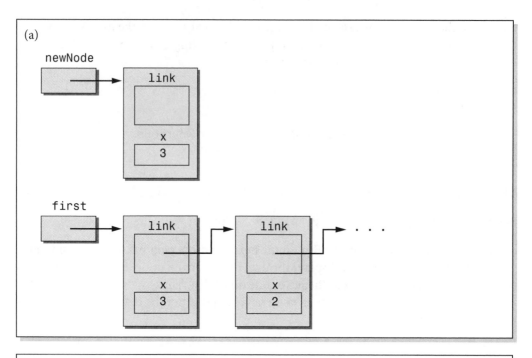

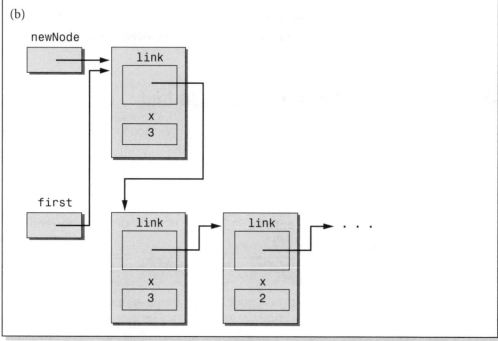

Figure 15.3

After these two changes, `first` points to the new node, and the new node points to the node that was formerly the first node. Thus, the new node is now at the head of the list.

The two changes required to insert a new node at the beginning of a list have to be done in a specific order. We must first change `newNode.link`, then `first`. If we reverse the order, we lose the pointer to the first node when we change `first`. We then do not have the pointer we need to update `newNode.link`.

To insert a new node at the beginning of a linked list, we had to update two fields: `newNode.link` and `first`. `first` contains valuable information (the pointer to the first node). `newNode.link`, on the other hand, initially contains garbage. That is, it does not contain any useful information. Thus, it makes sense to update `newNode.link` first because by doing so we do not lose any information. On the other hand, if we update `first` first, we lose the pointer it contains. This example illustrates an important rule to follow when working with linked structures: *Update the garbage fields first.*

15.4   A Linked List Class

Let's now create a `MyLinkedList` class that provides everything we need to create a linked list, add nodes to it, and traverse it (see Fig. 15.4). Notice that the `Node` class (Lines 3–7) is an **inner** class—that is, it is a class inside another class. Placing the `Node` class inside the `MyLinkedList` class provides two advantages:

1. It makes the `MyLinkedList` class complete and self-contained. We do not have to use an external `Node` class along with the `MyLinkedList` class.
2. The private members of the `Node` class become directly accessible from within the `MyLinkedList` class, and vice versa.

Because we do not need the `Node` class outside the `MyLinkedList` class, we make its access specifier `private` (see Line 3 in Fig. 15.4).

The `MyLinkedList` class in Fig. 15.4 creates nodes of type `Node` and directly accesses their `link` and `x` fields. Because the `Node` class is an inner class, its members can be `private` and at the same time be accessible from within the `MyLinkedList` class.

When we construct an object from the `MyLinkedList` class with

```
34        MyLinkedList list = new MyLinkedList();
```

we get a `MyLinkedList` object that contains an instance variable `first`. The initial value of `first` is `null`. This initial configuration of a `MyLinkedList` object represents a special list: the null list (i.e., the list that contains no nodes).

```
 1 class MyLinkedList
 2 {
 3    private class Node              // inner class
 4    {
 5       private Node link;
 6       private int x;
 7    }
 8    //-----------------------------------
 9    private Node first = null;    // initial value is null
10    //-----------------------------------
11    public void addFirst(int d)
12    {
13       Node newNode = new Node(); // create new node
14       newNode.x = d;             // init data field in new node
15       newNode.link = first;      // new node points to first node
16       first = newNode;           // first now points to new node
17    }
18    //-----------------------------------
19    public void traverse()
20    {
21       Node p = first;
22       while (p != null)          // do loop until p goes null
23       {
24          System.out.println(p.x);  // display data
25          p = p.link;               // move p to next node
26       }
27    }
28 }
29 //================================================
30 class TestMyLinkedList
31 {
32    public static void main(String[] args)
33    {
34       MyLinkedList list = new MyLinkedList();
35       list.addFirst(1);
36       list.addFirst(2);
37       list.addFirst(3);
38       System.out.println("Numbers on list");
39       list.traverse();
40    }
41 }
```

Figure 15.4

To add nodes to the list, we call the `addFirst` method, passing the data to be stored in the new node to be created. For example, the call

```
35          list.addFirst(1);
```

creates a new node that contains the data 1. In this call, the argument 1 is assigned to the parameter d in `addFirst`. `addFirst` then creates a new node that contains the value in d:

```
13       Node newNode = new Node();  // create new node
14       newNode.x = d;              // init data field in new node
```

It then inserts the new node at the beginning of the list with

```
15       newNode.link = first;  // new node now points to first node
16       first = newNode;       // first now points to new node
```

The call

```
39          list.traverse();
```

triggers the traversal of the list using a while loop:

```
22       while (p != null)       // do loop until p goes null
23       {
24          System.out.println(p.x);  // display data
25          p = p.link;               // move p to next node
26       }
```

Because `addFirst` inserts new nodes at the beginning of the list, the last node inserted is the first node on the list. Thus, the data on the list is in the reverse order. If we enter the data in 1, 2, 3 order, we get out the data in 3, 2, 1 order when we traverse the list.

15.5   Recursive Traverse

In Fig. 15.4, we traverse a linked list using an **iterative method**—that is, a method that uses a loop (the word "iterate" means "to repeat"). We can also traverse a linked list using a recursive method. Recall from Chapter 14 our approach to writing recursive methods: We use a recursive call to do most of the work. Thus, the method needs to do only a little work, in addition to the recursive call, to perform the required task. Let's use this approach to traverse a linked list. We will use a recursive call to traverse the tail of the list (the tail is the entire list except for the first node). Thus, to traverse the entire list, the method only has to visit the first node and then make the recursive call. Using this approach, we get the method on Lines 19–26 in Fig. 15.5.

```
1 class MyLinkedList2
2 {
3    private class Node
4    {
5       private Node link;
6       private int x;
7    }
8    //-----------------------------------
9    private Node first = null;     // initial value is null
10   //-----------------------------------
11   public void addFirst(int d)
12   {
13      Node newNode = new Node();  // create new node
14      newNode.x = d;              // init data field in new node
15      newNode.link = first;       // new node points to first node
16      first = newNode;            // first now points to new node
17   }
18   //-----------------------------------
19   private void traverse(Node p) // recursive version
20   {
21      if (p != null)
22      {
23         System.out.println(p.x);
24         traverse(p.link);
25      }
26   }
27   //-----------------------------------
28   public void traverse()
29   {
30      traverse(first);            // call private traverse
31   }
32 }
33 //===============================================
34 class TestMyLinkedList2
35 {
36    public static void main(String[] args)
37    {
38       MyLinkedList2 list2 = new MyLinkedList2();
39       list2.addFirst(1);
40       list2.addFirst(2);
41       list2.addFirst(3);
42       System.out.println("Numbers on list");
43       list2.traverse(first);                // illegal!!!
44       list2.traverse();                     // call adaptor method
45    }
46 }
```

Figure 15.5

Note that the `traverse` method in Fig. 15.5 is overloaded. The version on Lines 19–26 with one parameter is the private version. Because it is private, it can be called only from within `MyLinkedList2`. The version on Lines 28–31 with no parameters is the public version. Because it is public, it can be called from outside the `MyLinkedList2` class.

When the private `traverse` in Fig. 15.5 is called on Line 30, `first` is passed to the parameter `p`. `first` points to the first node and, therefore, so does `p` on this call. Because `p` points to the first node, `p.x` accesses the data in the first node. Line 23 displays this data:

```
23          System.out.println(p.x);
```

Then, the recursive call on Line 24 displays the rest of the list:

```
24          traverse(p.link);
```

In this call, we are passing `p.link`. Because `p` on the first call contains the pointer to the first node, `p.link` contains the pointer to the second node, which is the pointer to the tail of the list. `traverse` accordingly displays all the nodes in the tail. The two statements together display the entire linked list. Line 23 displays the data in the first node; Line 24 displays the data in the tail of the list.

In the call on Line 30 of the private `traverse`, we have to pass it `first`. But we cannot do that from outside the class because this version of `traverse`, as well as `first`, is private. For this reason, the call of the private `traverse` method from `main` on Line 43 is illegal. We could make the `traverse` method on Lines 19–26 public, but we would certainly not want to make the `first` variable public. `first` is a field within the class that should be kept hidden from the user of the `MyLinkedList2` class. How then do we call `traverse` from outside the class? The solution is to use a second `traverse` method that provides the proper interface between the users of the `MyLinkedList2` class and the private `traverse` method. We call a method that performs this type of function an **adaptor** method. The compiler can distinguish the calls of these two identically named methods by the arguments in the calls. If the call includes a single `Node` argument, it is a call of the private `traverse`; if the call has no arguments, it is a call of the adaptor `traverse`. Thus, on Line 44, we are calling the adaptor `traverse`:

```
44      list2.traverse();                       // call adaptor method
```

It, in turn, calls the internal `traverse` method, passing it `first`:

```
30      traverse(first);          // call of private traverse
```

By using our adaptor `traverse` method, we do not have to pass `first` when we call `traverse` from outside the class. Thus, `first` can remain private.

We have seen two linked list classes, one that uses an iterative traversal method, and one that uses a recursive traversal method. Which is better? Both approaches are quite simple. However, the recursive approach is somewhat less efficient because of the overhead of all the recursive calls that it requires. So for the simple traversal function, it is better to use the iterative approach. However, there are operations on linked lists for which the recursive approach is significantly simpler (for example, see Lab Exercise 5). For these operations, it is generally better to use the recursive approach.

Laboratory 15 Prep

1. What happens when you call `traverse` in Fig. 15.4 when the list is null?

2. What is the effect of

   ```
   p = p.link;
   ```

   where p points to a node in a linked list?

3. Change the first line of the `while` loop in `MyLinkedListP3` in `C15p3.java` to

   ```
   while (p.link != null)
   ```

   How does this change affect the behavior of the `traverse` method? Note: `MyLinkedListP3` and similarly named classes in the lab and homework exercises are all copies of `MyLinkedList` in Fig. 15.4.

4. Line 14 in Fig. 15.4 is a direct reference to a private variable x from outside its class. Why is this legal?

5. Write a `for` loop equivalent to the `while` loop on Lines 22–26 in Fig. 15.4.

Laboratory 15

1. Add a `length` method to the `MyLinkedListL1` class in `C15e1.java` that returns the length of the list (i.e., the number of nodes). Test your `length` method against both null and non-null lists.

2. Add a `getFirst` method to the `MyLinkedListL2` class in `C15e2.java` that removes the first node on the list and returns its data. If the list is empty, `getFirst` throws an exception. Test your method against both null and non-null lists.

3. Add an `average` method to the `MyLinkedListL3` class in `C15e3.java`. Your average method should return the average of all the x data on the list. If the list is null, your average method should throw a `MyLinkedListException` (a class you should create). Your average method should return a `double` value. Test your average method against both non-null and null lists.

4. Add a constructor to the `Node` class in `C15e4.java` that is passed the initial values for the `link` and x fields. Simplify the `addFirst` method (this simplification is made possible by the use of the new constructor). Test your new method.

5. Add a method `reverseTraverse` to the `MyLinkedL5` class in `C15e5.java`. Your `reverseTraverse` method should traverse and display the list in reverse order. Use recursion. Test your new method.

6. Add a copy constructor to the `MyLinkedListL6` class in `C15e6.java`. It should create a deep copy. Test your new method.

LABORATORY

Homework 15

1. Add an addLast method to the MyLinkedListH1 class in C15h1.java. This method should create a new node for the integer data it is passed and add it to the end of the linked list. On each call of addLast, get the pointer to the last node by traversing the list from the first node to the last node. Then, using this pointer, attach the new node to the end of the list. Test your new method. Be sure to consider any special cases. Calling addLast when the list is non-null is the normal case. But calling it when the list is null is a special case—you have to treat it differently than the normal case. *Always make sure you correctly handle the special cases as well as the normal cases.*

2. Same as Homework Exercise 1 but modify the MyLinkedListH2 class in C15h2.java. Include a last field in the MyLinkedListH2 class. This field points to the last node in the linked list, or is null if the linked list has no nodes. With last, it is easy to add a node to the end of the list. Without it, you have to traverse the list from the beginning to determine where the last node is, as you did in Homework Exercise 1. Test your new method.

3. Add a getLast method to the MyLinkedListH3 class in C15h3.java. Your getLast method should remove the last node on the list and return its data. If the list is null, getLast throws an exception. Test your getLast method against a null list, a list with one node, and a list with three nodes.

4. Add an equals method and a toString method to the MyLinkedListH4 class in C15h4.java. Create four lists:

  List 1: 1 2 3

  List 2: 1 2 3

  List 3: 1 2 3 4

  List 4: null list

Display List 3 and List 4 (i.e., display the string returned by your toString method). Test your equals method by comparing List 1 and List 2, List 1and List 3, and List 3 and List 4.

5. Add a get method and a set method to the MyLinkedListH5 class in C15h5.java. get(i) should return the x data in the node whose index is i (indices start at 0—thus the first node has index 0). get does not affect the list. set(i, y) should set the x field in the node whose index is i to y. Test your methods by creating a list with 10 nodes, containing 1, 2, ..., 10 (use a for loop to do this). Then use a second for loop that sets the data to 10, 20, ..., 100, using the set method. Finally, use a third for loop that gets the data with the get method and displays it. If the node index passed to get

or `set` does not correspond to a preexisting node, throw a `MyLinkedListException` (this is a class you should create).

6. Add an `append` method to the `MyLinkedListH6` class in `C15h6.java`. `append` has one parameter of type `MyLinkedListH6`. `append` attaches a *copy* of the list it is passed to the end of the list in its object. For example,

```
list1.append(list2);
```

attaches a copy of `list2` to the end of `list1`. Test your `append` method with the following pairs of lists:

List 1: 1 2 3
List 2: 4 5

List 1: 1 2 3
List 2: null list

List 1: null list
List 2: 4 5

For each pair, you should display the two lists before and after the append operation.

7. Add a `reverse` method to the `MyLinkedListH7` class in `C15h7.java` that returns a list in which the data is in reverse order. The returned list should not share any nodes with the original list. Test your method with lists that have zero nodes, one node, and three nodes.

8. Add a `remove` method to the `MyLinkedListH8` class in `C15h8.java` that removes the node at the specified index and returns its data. For example, if you pass this method the value 1, it removes and returns the second node of the list (node indices start at zero so the node with index 1 is the second node). If the node specified does not exist, `remove` should throw an exception. Test your method by creating a list that contains 1, 2, 3, and 4 in that order. Then remove the nodes that contain 1, 3, 4, and 2 in that order. Display your list after each removal.

9. Add an `addInOrder` method to the `MyLinkedListH9` class in `C15h9.java` that creates a node for the integer data it is passed and inserts that node into a list before the first node with equal or larger data. Starting with a null list, call `addInOrder` 10 times passing it random integers. Then display the resulting list.

LABORATORY

10. Draw a picture of the linked data structure that is built by the following program. What does the program display?

```
class MyTree
{
    private class Node
    {
        private int x;
        private Node left;
        private Node right;
    }
    //----------------------------------------
    private Node rootptr = null;

    public void insert(int xx)
    {
        Node n = new Node();
        n.x = xx;

        if (rootptr == null)
            rootptr = n;
        else
        {
            Node trailing = null, leading = rootptr;
            while (leading != null)
            {
                trailing = leading;
                if (xx < leading.x)
                    leading = leading.left;
                else
                    leading = leading.right;
            }
            if (xx < trailing.x)
                trailing.left = n;
            else
                trailing.right = n;
        }
    }
    //----------------------------------------
    public void inOrder()
    {
        inOrder(rootptr);
    }
    //----------------------------------------
    private void inOrder(Node p)
```

```
        {
            if (p != null)
            {
                inOrder(p.left);
                System.out.println(p.x);
                inOrder(p.right);
            }
        }
    }
//=======================================================
class C15h10
{
    public static void main(String[] args)
    {
        MyTree t = new MyTree();

        t.insert(5);
        t.insert(10);
        t.insert(2);
        t.insert(9);
        t.insert(3);
        t.insert(1);
        t.inOrder();
    }
}
```

11. Replace the insert method in C15h11.java with an equivalent recursive method.

12. Replace the recursive inOrder method C15h12.java with a nonrecursive method.

Generic Programming: Part 1

16.1 What Is Generic Programming?

Java is a strongly-typed language. That is, every variable has a type, and any value assigned to a variable must match or be converted to that variable's type. **Generic programming** is programming that creates structures that can accommodate multiple types in spite of Java's strong typing.

In this chapter, we will use the following rule, which we discussed in Chapter 10: A reference can point across or down but not up. Because the Object class is at the top of the class hierarchy, there is no reference we can assign to an Object reference variable that would cause it to point up. Thus, we can assign any reference to an Object reference variable. In other words, an Object reference variable is a **generic** (i.e., universal) **pointer**.

An Object reference can be null or can point to an object, but it cannot point to a primitive type. However, we can always use wrapper objects to hold values with a primitive type. An Object reference can, of course, point to these wrapper objects. For example, suppose we have the following code:

```
Object obj;
int x = 3;
```

Then obj cannot point to x because x has a primitive type. However, we can wrap the value of x using

```
Integer r = new Integer(x);
```

We can then assign r, the reference to the Integer object that contains the value in x, to obj (see Fig. 16.1):

```
obj = r;
```

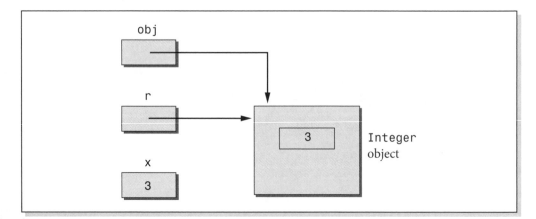

Figure 16.1

Thus, in a very real sense, obj can point to anything.

16.2   Using an Object Array

An array is a **homogeneous data structure**. That is, all the slots in an array have the same type. For example, you cannot have an array in which one slot is type int and the next is type double. An int array can hold only int values; a double array can hold only double values.

Let's now consider an Object array. For example, suppose we declare the array z with

```
Object[] z = new Object[3]
```

Then z is a reference to an array with three slots, each of which has type Object. Because an Object reference is a generic pointer, it can point to any object, regardless of its type. Thus, our z array can hold references to objects of any type. In other words, z is a generic array. In Fig. 16.2, we create such an Object array (see Line 23).

```
 1 class P
 2 {
 3    private int x = 1;
 4    public void xDisplay()
 5    {
 6       System.out.println("x = " + x);
 7    }
 8 }
 9 //=================================================
10 class Q
11 {
12    private int x = 2;
13    public void xDisplay()
14    {
15       System.out.println("x = " + x);
16    }
17 }
18 //=================================================
19 class Generic1
20 {
21    public static void main(String[] args)
22    {
23       Object[] z = new Object[3];     // create Object array
24
```

Figure 16.2   (continues)

```
25          z[0] = new P();          // initialize array with objects
26          z[1] = new Q();          // of different types
27          z[2] = new P();
28
29          for (int i = 0; i < z.length; i++)
30          {
31              if (z[i] instanceof P)      // P object?
32                  ((P)z[i]).xDisplay();    // cast to P
33              else
34              if (z[i] instanceof Q)      // Q object?
35                  ((Q)z[i]).xDisplay();    // cast to Q
36          }
37      }
38 }
```

Figure 16.2   (continued)

We then initialize the slots of the z array to point to P and Q objects:

```
25          z[0] = new P();                    // init array with objects
26          z[1] = new Q();                    // of different types
27          z[2] = new P();
```

We get the structure shown in Fig. 16.3.

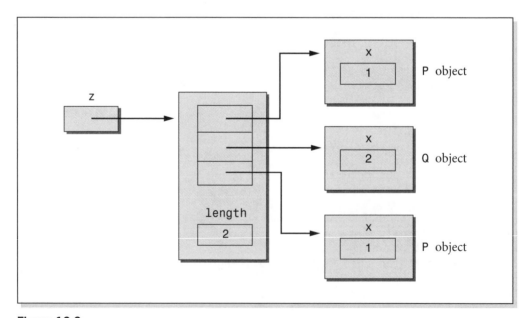

Figure 16.3

The z array is homogeneous (each slot has type `Object`), but the slots point to objects of different types. The first and third slots point to P objects. The second slot points to a Q object.

Last, we display the x values in the P and Q objects by calling the `xDisplay` method in each object:

```
29        for (int i = 0; i < z.length; i++)
30        {
31            if (z[i] instanceof P)          // P object?
32                ((P)z[i]).xDisplay();       // cast to P
33            else
34            if (z[i] instanceof Q)          // Q object?
35                ((Q)z[i]).xDisplay();       // cast to Q
36        }
```

To do this, we have to downcast each reference in the z array to the type of the object to which it points. To determine the type of the object pointed to, we use the `instanceof` operator. The `instanceof` operator returns `true` if its left operand is pointing to an object whose type is given by its right operand of the `instanceof` operator, and `false` otherwise.

But why are the downcasts on Lines 32 and 35 needed? Why can we not use the following simpler loop:

```
for (int i = 0; i < z.length; i++)
    z[i].xDisplay();
```

z[i] is a reference of type `Object`. So the compiler assumes it is pointing to an object of type `Object`. But an object of type `Object` does not have an `xDisplay` method. Thus, the compiler would flag the call of `xDisplay` in our simpler loop.

In Section 10.5, we raised the following question: Why would we ever want to upcast? We can now provide the answer: *To assign a reference to a variable that is acting as a generic pointer.* For a pointer to be generic, it has to be as high or higher in the class hierarchy than the object to which it points. Thus, assignments to a generic pointer are typically upcasts. Consider, for example, the assignment of P and Q references to z in Fig. 16.2:

```
25        z[0] = new P();              // initialize array with objects
26        z[1] = new Q();              // of different types
27        z[2] = new P();
```

Lines 25 and 27 are upcasting P references to type `Object`; Line 26 is upcasting a Q reference to type `Object`. These upcast references then have to be downcast so that the `xDisplay` method can be called (see Lines 32 and 35).

Let's modify our program in Fig. 16.2 so we can use our simpler for loop to display the values in the P and Q objects. We get the program in Fig 16.4.

```
 1 class R
 2 {
 3    public void xDisplay()
 4    {
 5       // dummy method
 6    }
 7 }
 8 //================================================
 9 class P extends R             // P subclass of R
10 {
11    private int x = 1;
12    public void xDisplay()
13    {
14       System.out.println("x = " + x);
15    }
16 }
17 //================================================
18 class Q extends R             // Q subclass of R
19 {
20    private int x = 2;
21    public void xDisplay()
22    {
23       System.out.println("x = " + x);
24    }
25 }
26 //================================================
27 class Generic2
28 {
29    public static void main(String[] args)
30    {
31       R[] z = new R[3];                // create R array
32
33       z[0] = new P();                  // init array with objects
34       z[1] = new Q();                  // of different types
35       z[2] = new P();
36
37       for (int i = 0; i < z.length; i++)
38             z[i].xDisplay();
39    }
40 }
```

Figure 16.4

Our new program has a class R (Lines 1–7), which is the superclass of P and Q. An R reference can point to either a P or a Q object because it would point down to those objects. We make z an R array rather than an Object array:

```
31        R[] z = new R[3];              // create R array
```

z[i] now has type R, and the R class has an xDisplay method. Thus, the statement within the simple for loop is legal:

```
38             z[i].xDisplay();
```

The P objects all have two xDisplay methods—the dummy xDisplay method inherited from R and the one defined in P. But the one defined in P overrides the inherited method. Thus, when z[i] is pointing to a P object, the preceding call invokes the correct xDisplay method in that object. We have the same situation for the Q object.

Because the xDisplay method inherited in R is overridden by the xDisplay methods in P and Q, the definition of xDisplay in R does not matter. Thus, we define it as simply as possible by giving it an empty body.

16.3   Abstract Methods and Classes

There is one significant danger with our use of the R class in Fig. 16.4. Suppose whoever writes the P and Q classes forgets to define the xDisplay method in those classes. Then each P and Q object will contain only one xDisplay method—the dummy one inherited from R. Our program will still compile and run. No error message will be generated. Line 38 in Fig. 16.4 will call the dummy xDisplay method inherited from R, which does nothing. Thus, although our program calls xDisplay for each P and Q object, it will not display any of the values in the P and Q objects.

We can avoid this danger if we use an abstract xDisplay method in the superclass. An abstract method has no body. It consists of the method header terminated by a semicolon. The header must contain the reserved word abstract. abstract can appear anywhere preceding the return type. For example, the abstract method for xDisplay is

```
abstract public void xDisplay();
```

A class that defines one or more abstract methods itself becomes abstract. If a class is abstract, we must use the reserved word abstract at the beginning of its definition before the reserved word class. For example, to define the class Picasso that contains the abstract method xDisplay, we use

```
abstract class Picasso
{
   abstract public void xDisplay();
}
```

The key feature of an abstract class is that it cannot be instantiated (i.e., you cannot construct an object from it). For example, if Picasso is an abstract class, we cannot execute

```
Picasso r = new Picasso();    // illegal if Picasso is abstract
```

However, a subclass of an abstract class can be instantiated, but only if it overrides all the abstract methods inherited from the abstract class. For example, if we define P with

```
public class P extends Picasso
{
   private int x = 1;
   public void xDisplay()
   {
      System.out.println("x = " + x);
   }
}
```

we can then instantiate P because the definition of xDisplay in P overrides the abstract xDisplay method inherited from Picasso. An abstract method in a class is, in effect, *an obligation on its subclasses to override that method.*

If a subclass of an abstract class does not override all the abstract methods in its superclass, it, itself, becomes an abstract class, and, therefore, cannot be instantiated.

Let's now rewrite the program in Fig. 16.4 using an abstract method xDisplay (see Fig. 16.5).

The programs in Figs. 16.4 and 16.5 have the same structure. Both use the simpler for loop (see Line 35 in Fig. 16.5). The z array in both is pointing down to P and Q objects. But the version in Fig. 16.5 has one important advantage: If the creator of the P and Q classes forgets to define xDisplay, the compiler will generate an error message. For example, suppose the creator omits the definition of xdisplay in the P class in Fig. 16.5.

```
 1 abstract class Picasso            // Picasso is abstract class
 2 {                                 // because xDisplay is abstract
 3     abstract public void xDisplay();
 4 }
 5 //====================================================
 6 class P extends Picasso
 7 {
 8     private int x = 1;
 9     public void xDisplay()
10     {
11         System.out.println("x = " + x);
12     }
13 }
14 //====================================================
15 class Q extends Picasso
16 {
17     private int x = 2;
18     public void xDisplay()
19     {
20         System.out.println("x = " + x);
21     }
22 }
23 //====================================================
24 class Generic3
25 {
26     public static void main(String[] args)
27     {
28         Picasso[] z = new Picasso[3]; // create Picasso array
29
30         z[0] = new P();               // init array with objects
31         z[1] = new Q();               // of different types
32         z[2] = new P();
33
34         for (int i = 0; i < z.length; i++)
35             z[i].xDisplay();
36     }
37 }
```

Figure 16.5

Then the P class has not met its obligation to override the abstract method xDisplay inherited from Picasso. Thus, the compiler generates the following error message:

```
P is not abstract and does not override abstract method
xDisplay() in Picasso class
```

An abstract class is a class that contains one or more abstract methods. It can also contain methods that are not abstract. For example, if we define Picasso with

```
abstract class Picasso
{
   abstract public void xDisplay();

   public void sayHello()
   {
      System.out.println("Hello");
   }
}
```

then Picasso contains the abstract method xDisplay and the concrete (i.e., nonabstract) method sayHello. Any subclass of Picasso inherits both methods. Any subclass of Picasso would have to override the inherited xDisplay method (but not sayHello) or it too would become abstract.

Abstract methods are useful for not only generic programming but also for general OO design. For example, suppose when designing a class C, we decide that all subclasses of C should have an f method. But we cannot implement f in class C because each subclass of C requires a unique version of f. However, by placing an abstract method f in class C, we ensure that every subclass of C will have an f method.

16.4 Interfaces

An abstract class can contain

- abstract methods
- nonabstract methods
- constructors
- instance variables
- static variables
- named constants, both static and nonstatic

In other words, in addition to abstract methods, an abstract class can contain everything a concrete class can contain. An **interface** is similar to an abstract class, but it is limited to what it can contain. An interface can contain only

- abstract methods
- named constants that are public, static, and final

Because all methods in an interface are abstract, you do not have to mark them with the reserved word `abstract`. Similarly, because all named constants in an interface are public, static, and final, you do not have to mark them with the reserved words `public`, `static`, and `final`. Thus, the interface

```
abstract interface Sample
{
    public static final double PI = 3.14159;
    abstract public void f();
}
```

is equivalent to the interface

```
interface Sample
{
    double PI = 3.14159;      // public static final constant
    public void f();          // abstract method
}
```

Like abstract methods in an abstract class, abstract methods in an interface represent obligations to the user of the interface. Specifically, any class that uses an interface must override all the interface's abstract methods, or else it becomes abstract.

A class uses an interface by *implementing* it. For example, suppose we have the interface I:

```
interface I
{
    public void xDisplay();
}
```

To implement the interface I, a class must override all its methods (all of which are abstract). It must also include the phrase "`implements I`" after its name in its definition. For example, the following class implements I:

```
class P implements I        // include the phrase "implements I"
{
    private int x = 1;
    public void xDisplay()  // overrides abstract method
```

```
    {
       System.out.println("x = " + x);
    }
}
```

If we create an object from this P class, it, of course, has type P. But because P implements I, it necessarily has everything required by I. Thus, the P object would also have type I. For this reason, a reference of type I can point to a P object. I is higher in the class hierarchy than P. Thus, an I reference that points to a P object is pointing down. If several classes all implement I, then an I reference variable can point to objects of any of these classes. In other words, an I *reference variable can serve as a generic pointer for all the classes that implement* I.

Let's rewrite the program in Fig. 16.5 using interface references rather than abstract class references as our generic pointers (see Fig. 16.6).

```
 1 interface I
 2 {
 3     public void xDisplay();
 4 }
 5 //================================================
 6 class P implements I        // include the phrase "implements I"
 7 {
 8     private int x = 1;
 9     public void xDisplay()  // overrides abstract method
10     {
11         System.out.println("x = " + x);
12     }
13 }
14 //================================================
15 class Q implements I
16 {
17     private int x = 2;
18     public void xDisplay()
19     {
20         System.out.println("x = " + x);
21     }
22 }
23 //================================================
```

Figure 16.6 (continues)

```
24 class Generic4
25 {
26    public static void main(String[] args)
27    {
28       I[] z = new I[3];              // create I array
29
30       z[0] = new P();               // init array with objects
31       z[1] = new Q();               // of different types
32       z[2] = new P();
33
34       for (int i = 0; i < z.length; i++)
35           z[i].xDisplay();
36    }
37 }
```

Figure 16.6   (continued)

We create an array each slot of which is type I:

```
28       I[] z = new I[3];              // create I array
```

These slots can point to P and Q objects because the P and Q classes both implement I. The compiler does not complain about the call of xDisplay

```
35           z[i].xDisplay();
```

because z[i] is type I. Any object that is pointed to by a type I reference must be from a class that implements I. Thus, that object must have an xDisplay method.

When we have a choice between an abstract class and an interface, which should we use? Here is a general rule: Use an abstract class if a strong "is a" relation exists. For instance, in our college member example at the beginning of Chapter 10, there is a strong "is a" relation between Student and CollegeMember and between Professor and CollegeMember. Thus, we should implement CollegeMember with a class—abstract or concrete—rather than with an interface.

16.5   Using an Interface to Provide Constants to a Class

Interfaces are often used to provide constants to classes. To do this, we create an interface that has the constants we wish to make available. Then any class that implements the interface automatically has access to its constants. For example, suppose we have the following interface containing the constants RATE and MINBALANCE,

```
interface MyConstants
{
    double RATE = 7.12;
    double MINBALANCE = 100.0;
}
```

and classes U and V that implement MyConstants,

```
class U implements MyConstants
{
    // can use RATE and MINBALANCE here
}
//===============================================
class V implements MyConstants
{
    // can use RATE and MINBALANCE here
}
```

Then these classes can use RATE and MINBALANCE without any qualification. For example, they could contain statements such as

```
interest = balance*RATE;
balance = balance + interest;
if (balance < MINBALANCE)
    System.out.println("Balance too low");
```

Laboratory 16 Prep

1. What is the difference between an abstract class and an interface?

2. Why can an Object reference point to any object?

3. Write the statement that calls the f method in the object to which r points. Assume f takes no arguments, r is type A, and the object to which r points is type B. Assume the B class has an f method but the class A does not. B is a subclass of A.

4. Can an abstract class be extended?

5. Define a class that implements the following interface:

```
interface Wisp
{
    public void f();
}
```

Laboratory 16

1. Comment out the xDisplay methods in the P and Q classes in Generic2.java (see Fig. 16.4). Compile and run. What happens?

2. Comment out the xDisplay methods in the P and Q classes in Generic3.java (see Fig. 16.5). Compile. What happens?

3. Comment out the xDisplay methods in the P and Q classes in Generic4.java (see Fig. 16.6). Compile. What happens?

4. Compile the following code:

```
class C16e4 implements Comparable
{}
```

Comparable is an interface in the java.lang package. Thus, you do not need to import it or use its fully qualified name. From the error message produced when you compile the C16e4 class, determine what method must be implemented to satisfy the Comparable interface.

5. Test if the Integer class implements Comparable. To do this, execute the following code:

```
Comparable c1 = new Integer(5);
```

If it works then Integer implements Comparable. Also try

```
Comparable c2 = new Double(2.0);
Comparable c3 = new String("hello");
Comparable c4 = new Scanner(System.in);
Comparable c5 = new Random();
```

You will need an `import` statement for `Scanner` and `Random` (they are in `java.util`).

Classes that implement `Comparable` have data with a linear order, and can be compared with respect to this order. For example, the integer values in `Integer` objects have a numerical order. Given two integer values, we can compare them to determine if one is less than, equal to, or greater than the other. Strings similarly have an order and can be compared. `Random` and `Scanner` objects, on the other hand, do not have an order.

6. Write a program that consists of an interface `Kons`, and two classes `C16e6` and `Cusp`, both of which implement `Kons`. The interface should contain the constants `KON1` and `KON2` equal to `1.3` and `5.5` respectively. The class `C16e6` should contain `main`. `main` should display the values of `KON1` and `KON2`. It should also create a `Cusp` object and call its `display` method. The `Cusp` class should contain a `display` method that displays the `KON1` and `KON2` constants.

7. Is the following code legal? If so, what happens when it is executed?

```
Object obj = "hello";
System.out.println(obj);
```

8. Does the following program compile and run? If not, fix it so that it does.

```
abstract class Dali
{
    private int x = 1;
    private static int y = 3;
    public abstract void f();
    public void g()
    {
        System.out.println("in g");
    }
}
//================================================
class Vincent extents Dali
{
    public void f()
    {
        Sytem.out.println("in f");
    }
    public void display()
    {
        System.out.println(x + " " + y);
    }
}
```

```
//====================================================
class C16e8
{
    public static void main(String[] args)
    {
        Vincent v = new Vincent();
        v.f();
        v.g();
        v.display();
    }
}
```

Homework 16

1. Create a class Objects that contains the following fields:

   ```
   private Object[] oa = new Object[2];
   private int nextIndex = 0;
   ```

   Objects should also contain the following methods:

   ```
   public void add(Object obj)
   ```

   Assigns obj to the next available slot in the oa array, and increments nextIndex. If there are no more available slots, add creates a new array with 10 more slots than the current oa array. It then copies the contents of the current oa array to the new array. It finally assigns to oa the reference to the new array.

   ```
   public Object get(int i)
   ```

   Returns oa[i].

   ```
   public void display()
   ```

   Displays all the objects in oa by calling println for each object stored in the oa array.

   ```
   public int size()
   ```

   Returns nextIndex, whose value equals the number of occupied slots in oa.

   Write a complete program in which main creates an Objects object to which it adds 10 strings and 10 Integer objects. main then calls the display method.

2. Create a class named Point that has an x field and a y field, both of type double. The x, y pair represent the coordinates of a point on the Cartesian plane. Point should implement the Comparable interface. Your Point class should contain a compareTo

LABORATORY

method that compares two points with respect to their distance from the origin. The Point class should also have accessor methods xGet and yGet, and a distance method that returns the distance of the point from the origin. Write a program that creates a Point array with 10 slots. Initialize each slot with a reference to a Point object that contains x and y values. Initialize each x and y field with random double values. Then call a mySort method, passing it the Point array. mySort should sort the references in the Point array so that the objects to which they point are in ascending order with respect to distance from the origin. After the sort, display the distance from the origin of each point in the order in which it appears in the array.

3. Same as Homework Exercise 2 except use an Object array to hold the Point references.

4. Create an interface named Shape that has two methods: double getArea() and void display(). Also create three classes that implement Shape: Circle, Square, and Rectangle. Each class should have a getArea method that returns the area of the object, and a display method that displays the dimensions of the object. In main, create an Object array with 12 slots to which you assign Circle, Square, and Rectangle objects whose dimensions are initialized with random numbers. Then execute a for loop that processes each reference in the Object array, displaying the dimensions and area of each object.

5. Same as Homework Exercise 4 except use a Shape array in place of the Object array.

6. Same as Homework Exercise 4 except use an abstract class in place of an interface.

7. Same as Homework Exercise 4 except make Square a subclass of Rectangle.

8. It makes sense for the String class to have a toString method. Why?

9. Implement the toString method as it would appear in the String class.

Generic Programming: Part 2

17.1 Generic Classes

The fields in all the classes we have created so far have specific types. For example, the x field in the OneInteger class in Fig. 17.1 has the type Integer (see Line 3). We say that the **base type** of OneInteger is Integer.

Every object we create from the OneInteger class necessarily has an x field whose type is Integer. We cannot use a OneInteger object to hold a string in its x field. We, of course, could create another class with an x field whose type is String instead of Integer. But there is a better way: We can create a **generic class**—a class whose base type is parameterized. When we instantiate an object from a generic class, we specify the base type we want. This type, in effect, replaces the type parameter in the generic class. Let's look at the generic class in Fig. 17.2.

The angle brackets following the class name on Line 1 indicate that the class is generic:

```
1 class OneThing<T>            // T is the type parameter
```

```
 1 class OneInteger
 2 {
 3    private Integer x;        // type of x is always Integer
 4    //---------------------------------
 5    public OneInteger(Integer xx)
 6    {
 7       x = xx;
 8    }
 9    //---------------------------------
10    public Integer get()
11    {
12       return x;
13    }
14 }
15 //===============================================
16 class TestOneInteger
17 {
18    public static void main(String[] args)
19    {
20       OneInteger p = new OneInteger(7);
21       System.out.println(p.get());
22    }
23 }
```

Figure 17.1

```
 1 class OneThing<T>              // T is the type parameter
 2 {
 3    private T x;                // Use T as if it is a type
 4    //----------------------------------
 5    public OneThing(T xx)
 6    {
 7        x = xx;
 8    }
 9    //----------------------------------
10    public T get()
11    {
12        return x;
13    }
14 }
15 //===============================================
16 class TestOneThing
17 {
18    public static void main(String[] args)
19    {
20        OneThing<Integer> p1;
21        p1 = new OneThing<Integer>(7);
22        System.out.println(p1.get());     // displays 7
23
24        OneThing<String> p2 = new OneThing<String>("hello");
25        System.out.println(p2.get());     // displays hello
26    }
27 }
```

Figure 17.2

T is the **type parameter**. We use it in the class as if it were a type. For example, on Line 3, we use T as the type of the field x:

```
3    private T x;                // Use T as if it is a type
```

On Line 5, we use T as the type of the parameter xx:

```
5    public OneThing(T xx)
```

On Line 10, we use T as the return type of the method get():

```
10    public T get()
```

To declare a OneThing reference variable p1, we specify both the class name OneThing and the desired base type. We specify the base type inside angle brackets following the class name. For example, to create a p1 reference variable for a OneThing object whose base type is Integer, we use

```
20        OneThing<Integer> p1;
```

The type within the angle brackets must be a class—*it cannot be a primitive type.* When we call the OneThing constructor on Line 21, we also specify the base type within angle brackets:

```
21        p1 = new OneThing<Integer>(7);
```

The call here of the OneThing passes the type argument Integer to the type parameter T in the generic OneThing class. Integer, in effect, replaces the parameter T in the OneThing class. Equivalently, we can both declare p1 and construct the object in one statement with

```
OneThing<Integer> p1 = new OneThing<Integer>(7);
```

Because OneThing is generic, we can construct objects from it with any base type we want. For example, to create an object with the base type String, we use

```
24        OneThing<String> p2 = new OneThing<String>("hello");
```

Because we have specified String within the angle brackets, the resulting object has the base type String.

When we invoke the constructor for a generic class, we specify the base type within angle brackets. However, the header itself of the constructor should *not* include the angle brackets and the corresponding type parameter. For example, the header for the constructor for the OneThing class is

```
5     public OneThing(T xx)
```

and not

```
public OneThing<T>(T xx)     // illegal--don't use <T> here
```

Our OneThing generic class is quite versatile. We can use it to create objects with any base type, except for the primitive types. In contrast, the base type of our OneInteger class in Fig. 17.1 is restricted to Integer.

The name of the type parameter does not have to be T. You could use any name that is not a reserved word. By convention, the first character of the type parameter name should be a capital letter.

17.2   What You Can and Cannot Do in a Generic Class

The type you pass to a generic class must be a class. It cannot be a primitive type. For example, it is illegal to replace Lines 20 and 21 in Fig. 17.2 with

```
OneThing<int> p1;            // Illegal--cannot use primitive type
p1 = new OneThing<int>();    // Illegal--cannot use primitive type
```

This restriction is not serious—we can simply use the wrapper class in place of the primitive type, as we did on Lines 20 and 21.

The BadGeneric1 class in Fig. 17.3 illustrates another restriction on generic classes.

r (see Line 11) points to an object of some type. All objects necessarily have a toString method because toString is in the Object class. Thus, it is legal to invoke the toString method via r, as we do on Line 20:

```
20        System.out.println(r.toString());  // legal
```

However, not all objects have an f method. Thus, it is illegal to invoke f via r, as we do on Line 21:

```
21        r.f();                                 // illegal
```

On Line 30 in Fig. 17.3, the class Hasf is passed to the type parameter T in the generic class BadGeneric:

```
30        BadGeneric1<Hasf> g1 = new BadGeneric1<Hasf>(h1);
```

Hasf has an f method (see Lines 3–6). Nevertheless, the call of f via r on Line 21 is illegal. Remember that BadGeneric1 is a *generic* class. It should work properly regardless of the class we pass it. If the call of f via r on Line 21 were legal, then the BadGeneric1 class would not work properly if we passed it a class without an f method, as on Line 32:

```
32        BadGeneric1<String> g2 = new BadGeneric1<String>("hello");
```

We can, however, make a change to BadGeneric1 that makes Line 21 legal. We simply change Line 9 to

```
class BadGeneric1<T extends Hasf>
```

The phrase "extends Hasf" here tells the compiler that the class passed to T will be Hasf or some subclass of Hasf. Because Hasf has an f method, the object to which r points will now necessarily have an f method. For this reason, the compiler will now allow the call

```
 1 class Hasf
 2 {
 3    public void f()
 4    {
 5        System.out.println("hello");
 6    }
 7 }
 8 //===================================================
 9 class BadGeneric1<T>
10 {
11    T r;
12    //----------------------------------
13    public BadGeneric1(T rr)
14    {
15        r = rr;
16    }
17    //----------------------------------
18    public void m()
19    {
20        System.out.println(r.toString());  // legal
21        r.f();                             // illegal
22    }
23 }
24 //===================================================
25 class TestBadGeneric1
26 {
27    public static void main(String[] args)
28    {
29        Hasf h1 = new Hasf();
30        BadGeneric1<Hasf> g1 = new BadGeneric1<Hasf>(h1);
31        g1.m();
32        BadGeneric1<String> g2 = new BadGeneric1<String>("hello");
33        g2.m();
34    }
35 }
```

Figure 17.3

on Line 21 of f via r. By adding "extends Hasf", however, we have restricted the types we can pass to BadGeneric1. We can now pass only Hasf or a subclass of Hasf. Thus, our modification causes Line 32 to become illegal because it passes String, which is not a subclass of Hasf, to BadGeneric1. In this example, we are extending the type parameter T with a class (Hasf). We can also extend a type parameter with an abstract class or an interface. In all cases, we use the reserved word extends, even if we are extending the type parameter with an interface.

```
 1   class BadGeneric2<T>
 2   {
 3      T t  = new T();                       // illegal
 4      T[] a = (T[]) new T[20];              // illegal
 5   }
 6   //=================================================
 7   class GoodGeneric1<T>
 8   {
 9      T t  = (T)new Object();              // legal
10      T[] a = (T[]) new Object[20];        // legal
11   }
12   //=================================================
13   class GoodGeneric2<T extends C>       // C is a class
14   {
15      T t  = (T)new C();                   // legal
16      T[] a = (T[]) new C[20];             // legal
17   }
```

Figure 17.4

You cannot use the type parameter in a generic class to create an object or an array. For example, the statements on Lines 3 and 4 of Fig. 17.4 are illegal.

There is a good reason why this usage is illegal: The compiler cannot translate a statement that constructs an object or array without knowing the type of the object or array. The code that the compiler generates depends on this type. For example, the code to which the compiler translates

```
Integer t = new Integer(3);
```

is different from the code to which the compiler translates

```
Double t = new Double(7.5);
```

For one thing, the objects have different sizes (it takes 8 bytes to store 7.5 within a Double object, but only 4 bytes to store 3 within an Integer object). So how could the compiler correctly translate

```
T t = new T();
```

in a generic class with type parameter T? In fact, there is no translation that would be correct. If the compiler assumes T is a specific type and generates code accordingly, then this code would be correct for that type only, and we would no longer have a generic class.

Now consider the code on Line 9 of Fig. 17.4:

```
9      T t  = (T)new Object();        // legal
```

It looks similar to the code on Line 3:

```
3      T t  = new T();                // illegal
```

However, unlike the code on Line 3, it is legal. On Line 9, we are calling the constructor for a *specific* class (Object). Thus, the compiler knows what code to generate to create the object. For the same reason, the code on Lines 10, 15, and 16 are also legal.

17.3 Extending the Type Parameter with the Comparable Interface

The Comparable interface is a predefined interface in the java.lang package. It contains only the abstract method int compareTo (Object obj). Thus, any class that implements Comparable must have a compareTo method, or else it would be an abstract class. The predefined classes whose objects have a linear order—such as Integer, Double, and String—implement Comparable. Thus, they all contain a compareTo method.

Now consider the OrderedPair class in Fig. 17.5. An object created from OrderedPair itself contains two objects: one pointed to by x, the other pointed to by y. The smaller method (Lines 11–18) returns x or y depending on which object is smaller.

To determine which object is smaller, the smaller method invokes the compareTo method via x:

```
13         if (x.compareTo(y) < 0)      // illegal
```

This invocation, however, is illegal. Because the type specified for x is the type parameter, we can invoke via x only those methods that are in the Object class (and, therefore, would necessarily be in the object to which x points). We can fix this problem simply by changing Line 1 to

```
class OrderedPair<T extends Comparable>
```

The phrase "extends Comparable" here tells the compiler that the class passed to OrderedPair implements the Comparable interface. Thus, it will necessarily have the compareTo method. This modification makes Line 13 legal. However, it also restricts the

```
1 class OrderedPair<T>
2 {
3    private T x, y;
4    //-----------------------------------
5    public OrderedPair(T xx, T yy)
6    {
7       x = xx;
8       y = yy;
9    }
10   //-----------------------------------
11   public T smaller()
12   {
13      if (x.compareTo(y) < 0)      // illegal
14         return x;
15      else
16         return y;
17   }
18 }
19 //================================================
20 class TestOrderedPair
21 {
22    public static void main(String[] args)
23    {
24       OrderedPair<Integer> p = new OrderedPair<Integer>(1, 2);
25       System.out.println(p.smaller());
26    }
27 }
```

Figure 17.5

classes that can be passed to those that implement Comparable. For example, if r1 and r2 are assigned Random objects with

```
Random r1 = new Random();
Random r2 = new Random();
```

then the following statement would be illegal because Random does not implement Comparable:

```
OrderedPair<Random> p = new OrderedPair<Random>(r1, r2);
```

17.4 Writing Our Own `ArrayList` Class

We now know everything we need to know to implement our own `ArrayList` class. We call our version of the `ArrayList` class `MyArrayList`. In our implementation in Fig. 17.6, we have included only the get, add (just the one parameter version), and size methods. The predefined `ArrayList` class has these methods and others, such as set, remove, contains, and indexOf (see Section 9.12).

```
 1 class MyArrayList<T>
 2 {
 3    private T[] current = (T[])new Object[10];
 4    private int size = 0;
 5    //---------------------------------
 6    public T get(int i)
 7    {
 8       return current[i];
 9    }
10    //---------------------------------
11    public void add(T x)
12    {
13       if (size >= current.length)
14       {
15          T[] old = current;                      // save current
16          current = (T[]) new Object[2*old.length];// get new array
17          for (int i = 0; i < old.length; i++)    // copy
18             current[i] = old[i];
19       }
20       current[size++] = x;                        // add x to array
21    }
22    //---------------------------------
23    public int size()
24    {
25       return size;
26    }
27 }
28 //=================================================
29 class TestMyArrayList
30 {
31    public static void main(String[] args)
```

Figure 17.6 (continues)

```
32      {
33          MyArrayList<Integer> oal = new MyArrayList<Integer>();
34          oal.add(5);
35          oal.add(2);
36          oal.add(3);
37          System.out.println(oal.get(0));
38          System.out.println(oal.get(1));
39          System.out.println(oal.get(2));
40      }
41  }
```

Figure 17.6   (continued)

On Line 3, we create the base data structure—an array whose size is initially 10:

```
3      private T[] current = (T[])new Object[10];
```

If on entry into the add method, this array is full, we first save current (the reference to the current array) with

```
15          T[] old = current;                       // save current
```

Next, we create a new array whose size is double the size of the old array:

```
16          current = (T[]) new Object[2*old.length];  // get new array
```

We then copy the data from the old array to the new array:

```
17          for (int i = 0; i < old.length; i++)      // copy
18              current[i] = old[i];
```

Now that our new array is larger, we can complete the add operation with

```
20          current[size++] = x;                      // add x to array
```

From Lines 16–18, we can see why MyArrayList, as well as ArrayList (which grows in the same way), can be inefficient. To grow, a new array is created and then the entire contents of the old array are copied into the new array. For large arrays, this copying process can take an excessive amount of time. We can minimize this overhead in an ArrayList object by giving it an initial capacity big enough to handle the data it has to hold. For example, if we know the ArrayList will have to hold roughly 100 elements, we can give it an initial capacity of 110. Then it is likely that it will not have to grow at all, or at most once, unless our size estimate of 100 is far too low. To create an ArrayList with a specific initial capacity, we pass the initial capacity we want to the constructor. For example, to create an ArrayList with base type Integer and an initial capacity of 100, we use

```
ArrayList<Integer> ali = new ArrayList<Integer>(100);
```

MyArrayList, however, does not have this capability, although it is easy to add.

17.5 Iterators

An **iterator** is an object that allows a user to process a collection of items in a one-by-one fashion. Iterators have two methods: next (which returns the next item in the collection) and hasNext (which returns true if there are still items to be processed, and false otherwise). Iterators are objects constructed from classes that implement the Iterator interface. Thus, a reference variable of type Iterator can point to an iterator object. Some predefined classes (ArrayList is one example) have a method named iterator that returns the iterator for that class. For example, consider the program in Fig. 17.7.

```
 1 import java.util.*;      // need to import ArrayList and Iterator
 2 class IteratorExample
 3 {
 4     public static void main(String[] args)
 5     {
 6         ArrayList<String> sal;
 7         sal = new ArrayList<String>();
 8
 9         sal.add("Bert");
10         sal.add("Ernie");
11         sal.add("Grover");
12
13         Iterator<String> itr;
14         itr = sal.iterator();      // get iterator
15
16         while (itr.hasNext())
17             System.out.println(itr.next());
18     }
19 }
```

Figure 17.7

The call of the iterator method in the ArrayList object returns an iterator for the Ar-rayList:

```
14          itr = sal.iterator();        // get iterator
```

We then use the hasNext and next methods in the itr object in a while loop to traverse the data in the ArrayList:

```
16          while (itr.hasNext())
17              System.out.println(itr.next());
```

Iterator is a generic interface. Thus, when we declare itr, we specify the base type within angle brackets:

```
13          Iterator<String> itr;
```

We specify the base type String here because the base type of the sal ArrayList is String.

Laboratory 17 Prep

1. Is the following statement legal if the OneThing class is defined as in Fig. 17.2:

```
OneThing<double> p = new OneThing<double>(3.0);
```

2. Write a generic class with two members: a private instance variable whose type is parameterized and a constructor that initializes this variable to the parameter the constructor is passed.

3. Why is the following statement illegal in a generic class, where T is the type parameter:

```
T r = new T();
```

4. Why is Line 13 in Fig. 17.5 illegal?

5. What is the purpose of Line 16 in Fig. 17.6?

Laboratory 17

All the classes in the following exercises whose names start with MyArrayList are copies of the MyArrayList class in Fig. 17.6.

1. Compile the following program. What error message does the compiler produce? What is the problem with this program?

```
class Gosh<T>
{
    T x;
}
//====================================================
class C17e1
{
    public static void main(String[] args)
    {
        Gosh<int> r = Gosh<int>();
    }
}
```

2. Can a generic class with type parameter T contain fields whose types are not T? For example, would a generic class with the following fields be legal?

```
T x;
String y;
int z;
```

Create and compile such a class to see if it is legal.

3. Compile the program in Fig. 17.3 (`TestBadGeneric1.java`). What is the error message generated by the compiler?

4. Extend the `MyArrayListL4` class in `C17e4.java` so that you can pass its initial capacity to its constructor. Also add the `set` method. Your `set` method should work like the `set` method in the `ArrayList` class (see Section 9.12). Add code to the `main` method that tests your enhancement.

5. Create a generic class `Yi` with type parameter `T` that contains

```java
T x;
public Yi(T xx)
{
    x = xx;
}
public void display()
{
    System.out.println(x);
}
```

Test your `Yi` class with

```java
class C17e5
{
    public static void main(String[] args)
    {
        Yi<Integer> y1 = new Yi<Integer>(20);
        y1.display();
        Er e = new Er();
        Yi<Er> y2 = new Yi<Er>(e);
        y2.display();
    }
}
```

`Er` is defined as follows:

```java
class Er
{
    private int n = 2;
}
```

What is displayed when `C17e5` runs? Why is the value in `y1` displayed but not the value in `y2`?

6. Can a generic class have more than one type parameter. For example is the following class legal? Use it in a program to see if it works.

```
class TwoParms<T, U>
{
   T x;
   U y;
   //-----------------------------------
   public TwoParms(T xx, U yy)
   {
      x = xx;
      y = yy;
   }
   //-----------------------------------
   public T xGet()
   {
      return x;
   }
   //-----------------------------------
   public U yGet()
   {
      return y;
   }
}
```

7. The following method is a **generic method**. Use it in a program that calls it several times, passing it arrays of different types (Integer, Double, String, and int). Does it work for all types?

```
public static <T> void display(T[] a)
{
   for (int i = 0; i < a.length; i++)
      System.out.println(a[i]);
}
```

8. Can a generic class with type parameter T contain fields whose types are also generic classes with type parameter T? For example, is the following MyStack class legal? Use it in a program that reads in the numbers in the lab13.txt file (see Exercise 2 in Lab 13) and displays them in reverse order. MyStack is in C17e8.java.

```
import java.util.ArrayList;
class MyStack<T>
{
   private ArrayList<T> s = new ArrayList<T>();
   //-----------------------------------
   public void push(T x)
   {
      s.add(x);
   }
   //-----------------------------------
```

```
    public T pop()
    {
        return s.remove(s.size() - 1);
    }
    //------------------------------------
    public boolean isEmpty()
    {
        return s.size() == 0;
    }
}
```

The class that is passed to the MyStack class is, in turn, passed to the ArrayList class within MyStack. Thus, if we execute

```
MyStack<Integer> s = new MyStack<Integer>();
```

the object constructed would contain an object of type ArrayList<Integer>. But if we execute

```
MyStack<String> s = new MyStack<String>();
```

then the object constructed would contain an object of type ArrayList<String>. The MyStack class implements a **stack**—a **last-in-first-out** (LIFO) data structure.

9. Same as Lab Exercise 8 but use the predefined generic Stack class in java.util.

Homework 17

1. Add the clear method to MyArrayListH1 in C17h1.java. Your clear method should work like the clear method in the ArrayList class (see Section 9.12). Add code to the main method that tests your clear method.

2. Add the indexOf(Object obj) method to MyArrayListH2 in C17h2.java. Your indexOf method should work like the indexOf(Object obj) method in the Array-List class (see Section 9.12). Add code to the main method that tests your indexOf method.

3. Add the remove(int index) method to MyArrayListH3 in C17h3.java. Your remove method should work like the remove(int index) method in the Array-List class (see Section 9.12). Add code to the main method that tests your remove method.

4. Add an equals method to MyArrayListH4 in C17h4.java. Add code to the main method that tests your equals method.

LABORATORY

5. Create a generic class MyQueue that creates a **First In First Out** (FIFO) data structure. Use a field qal with type ArrayList within your Queue class to hold your data. Your MyQueue class should have the following methods:

```
public boolean isEmpty()
```

Returns true if the size of the ArrayList is 0. Otherwise, it returns false.

```
public int size()
```

Returns the current size of the ArrayList.

```
void enqueue(T x)
```

Adds x to the end of the ArrayList.

```
T dequeue()
```

Removes and returns the item at index 0 in the ArrayList.

Test your class with

```
class C17h5
{
    public static void main(String[] args)
    {
        MyQueue<String> q = new MyQueue<String>();
        q.enqueue("hello");
        q.enqueue("goodbye");
        q.enqueue("last one");
        while (!q.isEmpty())
        {
            System.out.println(q.size());
            System.out.println(r.dequeue());
        }
    }
}
```

6. Add a selection sort method (see Section 9.9) to the MyArrayListH6 in C17h6.java. Test your class with

```
class C17h6
{
    public static void main(String[] args)
    {
        MyArrayList<Integer> ial = new MyArrayList<Integer>();
        ial.add(3);
        ial.add(1);
        ial.add(2);
```

```
        ial.selectionSort();
        for (int i = 0; i < ial.size(); i++)
            System.out.println(ial.get(i));
    }
}
```

7. Convert the MyLinkedListG class in C17h7.java to a generic class. Test your new class.

8. Write a program that reads integer numbers from a file, placing each on a linked list. It then traverses the linked list, displaying each number on the list. Use the predefined generic LinkedList class. Implement the traverse of the linked list using the iterator provided by LinkedList. The iterator provided by LinkedList is constructed from a class that implements the generic interface ListIterator—not Iterator. Like Iterator, ListIterator has the next and hasNext methods. It also has some methods not in Iterator. Both LinkedList and ListIterator are in java.util. Test your program on a file that contains 1 to 10 in ascending order.

9. Delete all the angle brackets and the types they enclose in the main method in C17h9.java (a copy of TestOneThing.java in Fig. 17.2). Do *not* modify the OneThing class. Does the modified program compile without any errors? Does it run correctly? If you do not pass a type to a generic class, the type Object is passed by default. Add the following line at the end of main:

```
Integer i = p1.get();
```

Does it compile without error? Now try

```
Integer j = (Integer)p1.get();
```

Why does the preceding statement with a cast work but not the statement without the cast? If the OneThing class were not generic, but its base type were Object, in what way would it be less versatile than the original OneThing class?

10. Can the type Integer[] be passed to the type parameter in a generic class?

CHAPTER 18

Graphical User Interfaces and Applets

OBJECTIVES

- Understand the advantages of a graphical user interface
- Learn how to create a graphical user interface
- Learn how to use panels
- Learn how to use action listeners to handle events
- Learn how to create and set up applets

18.1   GUI Versus Command-Line Interface

All the programs we have written so far use **terminal input/output** (also called the **command-line interface**). With this approach, input is via lines entered by the user on the keyboard, and output is via lines displayed on the display monitor. An alternative approach is a **graphical user interface** (GUI). Programs that use a GUI create one or more windows on the display screen that hold a variety of graphical components, such as menus that list choices and buttons that trigger actions on a mouse click.

The principal advantages of GUIs are

- A GUI requires less keyboard input. For example, with a GUI, a user can input a file name by selecting it from a menu with a single mouse click. In contrast, with terminal I/O, the user has to type in the file name.
- A GUI can easily inform the users of all the choices that are available using the various components on the window. For example, by displaying four buttons, a GUI communicates to the user that four choices are available.
- By giving users more choices during the execution of a program, it gives users more control over a program.
- A GUI can provide a standard user interface across a large variety of programs.

18.2   Our First GUI Program

To create a GUI program from scratch would require an enormous amount of complex programming. Fortunately, we do not have to do this. We can simply use predefined classes that support GUI. These classes are in two packages: `java.awt` (the **Abstract Windows Toolkit**) and `javax.swing`.

Before we examine our first GUI program, let's introduce some important terminology. A **frame** is a window that is displayed on the screen. A **container** is an object to which we can add components. The container associated with a frame is called the **content pane**.

To create and display a window:

1. Create a frame object from the `JFrame` class.
2. Configure the frame. Specifically, we specify its title, size, and the action that occurs when its close button is clicked.
3. Add components to the frame's content pane.
4. Make the frame visible.

Consider the window in Fig. 18.1a. It contains two components: a button and a label.

(a)

(b)

```
 1 import javax.swing.*;
 2 import java.awt.*;                // needed for Color class
 3 class GUI1 extends JFrame
 4 {
 5     private Container contentPane;
 6     private JButton button1;
 7     private JLabel label1;
 8     //----------------------------------
 9     public GUI1()
10     {
11         setTitle("GUI1");                // sets title on frame
12         setSize(400, 100);               // sets frame width, height
13         setDefaultCloseOperation(JFrame.EXIT_ON_CLOSE);
14
15         // get content pane of frame
16         contentPane = getContentPane();
17
18         // configure content pane
19         contentPane.setLayout(new FlowLayout());
20         contentPane.setBackground(Color.GREEN);
21
22         // add button and label to the content pane of the frame
23         button1 = new JButton("This is a button");
24         contentPane.add(button1);
25         label1 = new JLabel("This is a label");
26         contentPane.add(label1);
27
28         setVisible(true);                // make frame visible
29     }
30     //----------------------------------
31     public static void main(String[] args)
32     {
33         GUI1 window = new GUI1();         // create window
34     }
35 }
```

Figure 18.1

The program that creates this window is shown in Fig. 18.1b. The GUI1 class in this program extends the JFrame class (Line 3). Thus, it inherits everything in JFrame. When main creates an object from GUI1 (Line 33), it creates a frame object that represents the window that is displayed on the screen.

The GUI1 class contains a constructor (see Lines 9–29) that sets up the frame. The constructor does this by calling methods inherited from the JFrame class. These methods are setTitle (see Line 11), setSize (see Line 12), setDefaultCloseOperation (see Line 13), getContentPane (see Line 16), and setVisible (see line 28).

The title on the bar at the top of the window is set with

```
11          setTitle("GUI1");                   // sets title on frame
```

The size of the frame is specified in units of pixels. For example, on Line 12

```
12          setSize(400, 100);                  // sets frame width, height
```

we are setting the width and height of the frame to 400 and 100 pixels, respectively. A **pixel** is the smallest possible dot a display monitor can create on the screen. Pixel size depends on the size and resolution of the monitor. For example, a monitor with a resolution of 1024 by 768 pixels would have 1024 pixels in each row and 768 pixels in each column. Thus, a width specification of 1024 pixels would reach from the left side all the way to the right side of the monitor. However, on a monitor of the same size but with a 2048 by 768 resolution, a 1024 width would be only half of the horizontal screen size.

The default close operation is set with

```
13          setDefaultCloseOperation(JFrame.EXIT_ON_CLOSE);
```

The JFrame.EXIT_ON_CLOSE is a constant in the JFrame class. It indicates that the window should exit (i.e., terminate) when the close button (the button marked with x in the upper right corner of the frame) is clicked. If, instead, we specify the constant JFrame.HIDE_ON_CLOSE in place of JFrame.EXIT_ON_CLOSE, the window disappears from view but does not terminate when its close button is clicked.

The constructor calls getContentPane to get the content pane of the frame:

```
16          contentPane = getContentPane();
```

Remember that the content pane is the container associated with the frame.

On Line 19, the constructor calls the setLayout method in the content pane to specify how components should be laid out on the content pane:

```
19          contentPane.setLayout(new FlowLayout());
```

The FlowLayout object that is passed to setLayout indicates that components should be placed on the content pane in rows left to right. When one row is full, placement moves to the next row.

The constructor calls setBackground in the content pane to set the background color of the frame:

```
20          contentPane.setBackground(Color.GREEN);
```

Color.GREEN is a constant that represents the color green. The constants that are available for colors are given in Fig. 18.2.

The constructor calls the add method in the content pane to add each component to the content pane. For example, the constructor creates a button with

```
23          button1 = new JButton("This is a button");
```

It then adds the button to the content pane on Line 24 with

```
24          contentPane.add(button1);
```

For simplicity, we give each component a name consisting of its kind ("button," "label," etc.) suffixed with a sequence number. For example, we name the reference variable to the button component button1. In a GUI with multiple buttons, we would name them button1, button2, button3, and so on. If a GUI has many components of the same kind, a better naming scheme is to give each component a name that describes its function. With such names, it is easier to remember what each component does.

```
Color.BLACK
Color.DARK_GRAY
Color.GRAY
Color.LIGHT_GRAY
Color.WHITE
Color.CYAN
Color.MAGENTA
Color.PINK
Color.RED
Color.ORANGE
Color.YELLOW
Color.GREEN
Color.BLUE
```

Figure 18.2

The last step is to make the frame visible:

```
28        setVisible(true);                    // make frame visible
```

The program in Fig. 18.1b is in a file named GUI1.java. To compile it, enter

```
javac GUI1.java
```

To run it, enter

```
java GUI1
```

The window it creates will then appear on the display screen (see Fig. 18.1a). If you click on the button labeled with This is a button, nothing happens. This lack of response occurs because our program does not associate any action with this button. To terminate the window, click on the close button in the upper right corner of the frame.

18.3 Using Panels

The program in Fig. 18.1b places the button and label directly on the content pane of the frame. A more typical approach, however, is to place components on a panel and then place the panel on the content pane of the frame. The program in Fig. 18.3b is like the program in Fig. 18.1b except that it uses panels.

Figure 18.3 (continues)

(b)

```
 1 import javax.swing.*;
 2 import java.awt.*;
 3 class GUI2 extends JFrame
 4 {
 5    private Container contentPane;
 6    private JPanel panel1, panel2;
 7    private JButton button1;
 8    private JLabel label1;
 9    //----------------------------------
10    public GUI2()
11    {
12       setTitle("GUI2");
13       setDefaultCloseOperation(JFrame.EXIT_ON_CLOSE);
14
15       panel1 = new JPanel();                   // create panel 1
16       panel1.setLayout(new FlowLayout()); // configure panel 1
17       panel1.setBackground(Color.GREEN);
18       panel1.setPreferredSize(new Dimension(100, 100));
19       button1 = new JButton("This is a button");
20       panel1.add(button1);                     // add button to panel 1
21
22       panel2 = new JPanel();                   // create panel 2
23       panel1.setLayout(new FlowLayout()); // configure panel 2
24       panel2.setBackground(Color.YELLOW);
25       panel2.setPreferredSize(new Dimension(300, 100));
26       label1 = new JLabel("This is a label");
27       panel2.add(label1);                      // add label to panel 2
28
29       // get content pane of frame
30       contentPane = getContentPane();
31
32       contentPane.setLayout(new FlowLayout());
33       contentPane.add(panel1);         // add panels to content pane
34       contentPane.add(panel2);
35
36       pack();     // adjust frame size to accommodate panels
37       setVisible(true);
38    }
39    //----------------------------------
40    public static void main(String[] args)
41    {
42       GUI2 window = new GUI2();
43
44    }
45 }
```

Figure 18.3 (continued)

It creates two panels with

```
15          panel1 = new JPanel();                   // create panel 1
```

and

```
22          panel2 = new JPanel();                   // create panel 2
```

It creates and places a button on panel1:

```
19          button1 = new JButton("This is a button");
20          panel1.add(button1);                     // add button to panel 1
```

It creates and places the label on panel2:

```
26          label1 = new JLabel("This is a label");
27          panel2.add(label1);                      // add label to panel 2
```

It places both panels on the content pane of the frame:

```
33          contentPane.add(panel1);         // add panels to content pane
34          contentPane.add(panel2);
```

The preferred size of each panel is specified by a call to the setPreferredSize method in each panel object. For example, to set the width and height of panel1 to 100 and 100 pixels, respectively, we use

```
18          panel1.setPreferredSize(new Dimension(100, 100));
```

Panel1 is sized accordingly unless there is not enough room on the screen.

Unlike the program in Fig. 18.1b, the program in Fig. 18.3b does not call the setSize method to set the size of the frame. Instead, it calls pack (see Line 36), which causes the frame size to adjust so that it is just big enough to accommodate the panels it holds:

```
36          pack();      // adjust frame size to accommodate panels
```

Using panels allows for more flexibility. Each panel is a separate container. Thus, each panel can be configured differently. For example, the two panels created by the program in Fig. 18.3b have different sizes and colors (compare Lines 17 and 18 in Fig. 18.3b with Lines 24 and 25).

18.4   Events and Action Listeners

An **event** in a GUI is an action taken by the user on one of the GUI components. For example, clicking on a button is an event.

When an event occurs on a component in a GUI, the following sequence occurs (see Fig. 18.4):

1. An `ActionEvent` object is created that represents that event.
2. If the component is associated with a listener object, the `ActionEvent` object is passed to the `actionPerformed` method in the listener object. The code in the `actionPerformed` method is then executed.

To handle events, a program should import the `java.awt.event` package (see Line 3 in Fig. 18.5b).

Let's examine the program in Fig. 18.5b to see how to create a listener object and associate it with a button component. The window that this program creates contains a button and a label (see Fig. 18.5a). Each time the button is clicked, the count in the label is incremented.

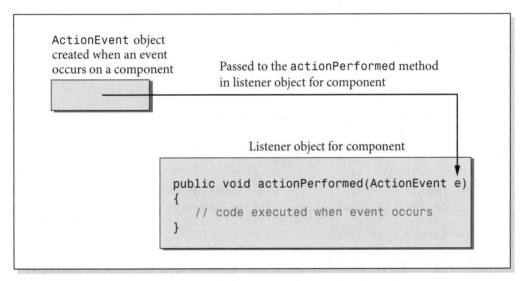

Figure 18.4

(a)

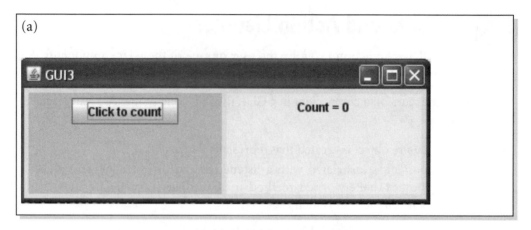

(b)

```
 1  import javax.swing.*;
 2  import java.awt.*;
 3  import java.awt.event.*;
 4  class GUI3 extends JFrame
 5  {
 6      private Container contentPane;
 7      private JPanel panel1, panel2;
 8      private JButton button1;
 9      private JLabel label1;
10      private int count;
11      //---------------------------------
12      public GUI3()
13      {
14          setTitle("GUI3");
15          setDefaultCloseOperation(JFrame.EXIT_ON_CLOSE);
16
17          panel1 = new JPanel();      // create panel
18          panel1.setLayout(new FlowLayout());
19          panel1.setBackground(Color.GREEN);
20          panel1.setPreferredSize(new Dimension(200, 100));
21          button1 = new JButton("Click to count");
22          button1.addActionListener(new Listener());  // add listener
23          panel1.add(button1);
24
25          panel2 = new JPanel();      // create panel
26          panel2.setLayout(new FlowLayout());
```

Figure 18.5 (continues)

```
27          panel2.setBackground(Color.YELLOW);
28          panel2.setPreferredSize(new Dimension(200, 100));
29          count = 0;
30          label1 = new JLabel("Count = " + count);
31          panel2.add(label1);
32
33          // get content pane of frame
34          contentPane = getContentPane();
35
36          contentPane.setLayout(new FlowLayout());
37          contentPane.add(panel1);      // add panels to content pane
38          contentPane.add(panel2);
39
40          pack();
41          setVisible(true);                       // make window visible
42      }
43      //-----------------------------------
44      public static void main(String[] args)
45      {
46          GUI3 window = new GUI3();                // create window
47
48      }
49      //-----------------------------------
50      private class Listener implements ActionListener
51      {
52          public void actionPerformed(ActionEvent e)
53          {
54              label1.setText("Count = " +  ++count);  // set label
55          }
56      }
57 }
```

Figure 18.5   (continued)

Line 22 creates a Listener object and associates it with the button1 component by calling the addActionListener method in the button1 component:

```
22          button1.addActionListener(new Listener());  // add listener
```

creates listener object

The Listener object is created from the inner class on Lines 50–56. This class must implement the ActionListener interface. This interface contains only the actionPerformed
method. Thus, only this method has to be implemented in the listener class. You can use

whatever name you like for the listener class—it does not have to be `Listener`. The code in the `actionPerformed` method is whatever you want. In the example in Fig. 18.5b, it increments `count` and then sets the text in the `label1` component to this new count:

```
54              label1.setText("Count = " +  ++count);  // set label
```

18.5 Determining Which Component Triggers an Event

If a GUI has more than one component that can trigger an event, we can either create a listener object for each component or we can create a single listener object that handles all the events. The program in Fig. 18.6b does the latter. It has two buttons: one labeled `Click to count` and one labeled `Click to count down`. Clicking the former increments the count displayed; clicking the latter decrements the count displayed.

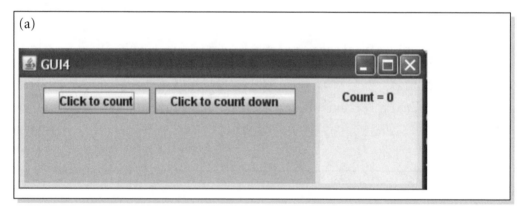

(a)

(b)

```
1 import javax.swing.*;
2 import java.awt.*;
3 import java.awt.event.*;
4 class GUI4 extends JFrame
5 {
6     private Container contentPane;
7     private JPanel panel1, panel2;
8     private JButton button1, button2;
```

Figure 18.6 (continues)

```
 9      private JLabel label1;
10      private int count;
11      private ActionListener listener;
12      //-----------------------------------
13      public GUI4()
14      {
15         setTitle("GUI4");
16         setDefaultCloseOperation(JFrame.EXIT_ON_CLOSE);
17
18         panel1 = new JPanel();     // create panel
19         panel1.setBackground(Color.GREEN);
20         panel1.setPreferredSize(new Dimension(300, 100));
21         listener = new Listener();
22         button1 = new JButton("Click to count");
23         button1.addActionListener(listener);
24         panel1.add(button1);
25         button2 = new JButton("Click to count down");
26         button2.addActionListener(listener);
27         panel1.add(button2);
28
29         panel2 = new JPanel();               // create panel
30         panel2.setBackground(Color.YELLOW);
31         panel2.setPreferredSize(new Dimension(100, 100));
32         count = 0;
33         label1 = new JLabel("Count = " + count);
34         panel2.add(label1);
35
36         // get content pane of frame
37         contentPane = getContentPane();
38
39         contentPane.setLayout(new FlowLayout());
40         contentPane.add(panel1);        // add panels to content pane
41         contentPane.add(panel2);
42
43         pack();
44         setVisible(true);
45      }
46      //-----------------------------------
47      public static void main(String[] args)
48      {
49         GUI4 window = new GUI4();               // create window
50
51      }
52      //-----------------------------------
53      private class Listener implements ActionListener
```

Figure 18.6   (continues)

```
54      {
55          public void actionPerformed(ActionEvent e)
56          {
57              // e.getSource() returns ref to triggering component
58              if (e.getSource() == button1)
59                  label1.setText("Count = " +  ++count);
60              else
61              if (e.getSource() == button2)
62                  label1.setText("Count = " +  --count);
63          }
64      }
65 }
```

Figure 18.6 (continued)

On Line 21, the constructor creates a single listener object:

```
21          listener = new Listener();
```

It adds this listener object to button1:

```
23          button1.addActionListener(listener);
```

and to button2:

```
26          button2.addActionListener(listener);
```

Because button1 and button2 share the same listener, the code in this listener must determine which button triggered the event so it can take the appropriate action. If button1 triggers the event, the listener should increment the count, but if button2 triggers the event, the listener should decrement the count.

The component that triggers an event can be determined from the ActionEvent object passed to the actionPerformed method when the event occurs. The getSource method in this object returns the reference to the component that triggers the event. Lines 58 and 61 compare this reference with the button1 and button2 references to determine which button triggered the event:

```
58          if (e.getSource() == button1)
59              label1.setText("Count = " +  ++count);
60          else
61          if (e.getSource() == button2)
62              label1.setText("Count = " +  --count);
```

Using Radio Buttons

Radio buttons are organized into groups. Within each group, only one radio button can be selected at any given time. If the user clicks on an unselected button, it becomes the selected button, and the previously selected button is automatically unselected.

Like the program in Fig. 18.6b, the program in Fig. 18.7b can count up or down. However, unlike the program in Fig. 18.6b, it uses only one count button. Clicking on this button causes the count to increase if the Up radio button is selected, and decrease if the Down radio button is selected (see Fig. 18.7a). Another difference between the program in Fig. 18.6b and the program in Fig. 18.7b is that the latter uses a text field object rather than a label object to display the count. The text field displays the current count. However, it can also be used to reset the count to any value. To do this, the user highlights the count with the mouse, enters the new count, and then hits the Enter key on the keyboard. Thus, a text field can be used to input data as well as display data. A label component, on the other hand, can be used only to display data.

(a)

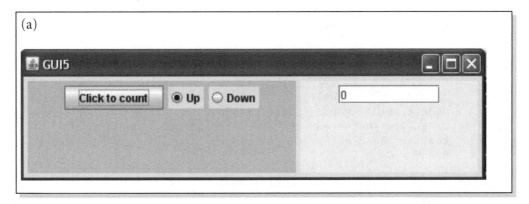

(b)

```
 1 import javax.swing.*;
 2 import java.awt.*;
 3 import java.awt.event.*;
 4 class GUI5 extends JFrame
 5 {
 6     private Container contentPane;
 7     private JPanel panel1, panel2;
 8     private JButton button1;
 9     private JTextField text1;
10     private JRadioButton radio1;
11     private JRadioButton radio2;
```

Figure 18.7   (continues)

```
12     private ButtonGroup group;
13     private ActionListener listener;
14     private int count;
15     //-----------------------------------
16     public GUI5()
17     {
18        setTitle("GUI5");
19        setDefaultCloseOperation(JFrame.EXIT_ON_CLOSE);
20
21        panel1 = new JPanel();              // create panel
22        panel1.setBackground(Color.GREEN);
23        panel1.setPreferredSize(new Dimension(300, 100));
24        listener = new Listener();
25        button1 = new JButton("Click to count");
26        button1.addActionListener(listener);
27        panel1.add(button1);
28
29        radio1 = new JRadioButton("Up", true);  // create button
30        radio2 = new JRadioButton("Down");       // create button
31        group = new ButtonGroup();          // create button group
32        group.add(radio1);                  // add radio buttons to group
33        group.add(radio2);
34        panel1.add(radio1);                      // add radio button to panel
35        panel1.add(radio2);                      // add radio button to panel
36
37        panel2 = new JPanel();              // create panel
38        panel2.setBackground(Color.YELLOW);
39        panel2.setPreferredSize(new Dimension(200, 100));
40        text1 = new JTextField(10);
41        count = 0;
42        text1.setText("" + count);
43        text1.addActionListener(listener);
44        panel2.add(text1);
45
46        // get content pane of frame
47        contentPane = getContentPane();
48        contentPane.setLayout(new FlowLayout());
49        contentPane.add(panel1);     // add panels to content pane
50        contentPane.add(panel2);
51
52        pack();
53        setVisible(true);
54     }
55     //-----------------------------------
56     public static void main(String[] args)
```

Figure 18.7 (continues)

```
57    {
58        GUI5 window = new GUI5();
59    }
60    //------------------------------------
61    private class Listener implements ActionListener
62    {
63        public void actionPerformed(ActionEvent e)
64        {
65            if (e.getSource() == text1)
66                count = Integer.parseInt(text1.getText());
67            else
68            if (e.getSource() == button1)
69                if (radio1.isSelected())  // radio button 1 selected?
70                    text1.setText("" + ++count);  // increment count
71                else
72                if (radio2.isSelected())  // radio button 2 selected?
73                    text1.setText("" + --count);  // decrement count
74        }
75    }
76 }
```

Figure 18.7   (continued)

To create the radio button group, the GUI5 constructor first creates the two radio buttons:

```
29        radio1 = new JRadioButton("Up", true);   // create button
30        radio2 = new JRadioButton("Down");       // create button
```

The true argument used on Line 29 makes radio1 the button that is initially selected. The GUI5 constructor then creates a button group:

```
31        group = new ButtonGroup();       // create button group
```

It then adds the radio buttons to this group:

```
32        group.add(radio1);               // add radio buttons to group
33        group.add(radio2);
```

Finally, it adds the radio buttons to panel1:

```
34        panel1.add(radio1);              // add radio button to panel
35        panel1.add(radio2);              // add radio button to panel
```

Note that the individual radio buttons are added to the panel—not the button group.

The constructor creates the text field with

```
40          text1 = new JTextField(10);
```

The parameter 10 specifies the width of the text field. The initial count displayed in the text field is set with

```
41          count = 0;
42          text1.setText("" + count);
```

The setText method requires a String parameter. The concatenation of "" (the null string) with count (which is type int) yields the string required by setText.

If an event is triggered by the text field, Line 66 in the actionPerformed method is executed:

```
66              count = Integer.parseInt(text1.getText());
```

The getText method returns the text in the text field as a string. The parseInt method then converts this string to type int, and assigns it to count. Thus, if the user then clicks on the count button, this new count will be incremented or decremented.

If the count button triggers the event, then the count is either incremented or decremented, depending on which radio button is selected:

```
69          if (radio1.isSelected())  // radio button 1 selected?
70              text1.setText("" + ++count);  // increment count
71          else
72          if (radio2.isSelected())  // radio button 2 selected?
73              text1.setText("" + --count);  // decrement count
```

18.7 Layout Managers

All the containers in the GUI programs we have seen use FlowLayout (FlowLayout is the default layout if a specific layout for a container is not specified). With this layout, components are added left to right in rows. If a component cannot fit on the current row, a new row is started below the current row.

A left/center/right justification of components can be specified when a FlowLayout is created. For example, in

```
c.setLayOut(new FlowLayout(FlowLayout.LEFT));
```

we are specifying FlowLayout with left justification for the container c. With left justification, any extra room in a row will appear on the right side of the row. For center and right justification, use `FlowLayout.CENTER` and `FlowLayout.RIGHT`, respectively. We can also specify the horizontal and vertical gaps between components. These gaps are passed as the second and third parameters to the `FlowLayout` constructor. For example, to specify center justification, a 20 pixel horizontal gap, and a 10 pixel vertical gap for the c container, use

```
c.setLayout(new FlowLayout(FlowLayout.CENTER, 20, 10));
```

Remember that every container is controlled by a layout. Thus, if we place two panels on a frame, the two panels and the frame can each have their own layout.

Two other layouts available are `BorderLayout` and `GridLayout`. In `BorderLayout`, the screen is divided into five regions: north (top), south (bottom), east (right), west (left), and center. Components are placed in one of these regions. For example, suppose we set `BorderLayout` for a container named c with

```
c.setLayout(new BorderLayout());
```

To place `button1`, `button2`, `button3`, `button4`, and `button5` in the north, south, east, west, and center regions, respectively, use

```
c.add(button1, BorderLayout.NORTH);
c.add(button2, BorderLayout.SOUTH);
c.add(button3, BorderLayout.EAST);
c.add(button4, BorderLayout.WEST);
c.add(button5, BorderLayout.CENTER);
```

In `GridLayout`, the screen is divided into rows and columns. For example, suppose we set `GridLayout` for the c container with

```
c.setLayout(new GridLayout(3, 2));
```

This creates a grid of three rows and two columns. Thus, each of the three rows can accommodate at most two components. To place `button1` and `button2` in row 1, `button3` and `button4` in row 2, and `button5` and `button6` in row 3, use

```
c.add(button1);
c.add(button2);
c.add(button3);
c.add(button4);
c.add(button5);
c.add(button6);
```

The components are added left to right in each row. Each row is filled before the next one is used.

18.8   Applets

All the programs we have seen so far are Java applications. A **Java application** is a stand-alone program written in Java that runs on a computer. An **applet**, on the other hand, is a Java program embedded in a web page. When a web browser views a web page that has an embedded applet, it executes that applet in addition to displaying that web page.

Because applets have the power and flexibility of programs, they can greatly enhance the capabilities of a web page. For example, you could embed a tax computation applet in a web page. Then anyone can use that program simply by visiting that page with a browser.

The power and flexibility of applets, however, present a potential danger. An applet could perhaps erase your hard disk or make confidential information on your computer available to others. To avoid these problems, the capabilities of applets are intentionally restricted. For example, an applet cannot delete, read, or create files on the system on which it is running.

A web page is a text file that typically contains **hypertext markup language** (HTML). HTML contains **tags** that tell the browser how to display or handle what follows the tag. Most tags come in opening/closing pairs. For example, in the HTML in Fig. 18.8a, `<I>` is an opening tag, and `</I>` is the corresponding closing tag. `<I>` tells the browser to display text in italic type. `</I>` tells the browser to revert back to the original type. `<BR>` is the break tag. It has no corresponding closing tag. It tells the browser to break the current line (i.e., go to the next line). The `<APPLET>` and `</APPLET>` tags embed an applet within a web page. **Attributes** within a tag provide specific information on that tag, and are specified with keywords such as `code`, `width`, and `height`. For example, the code attribute in the `<APPLET>` tag in Fig. 18.8a is

```
code="Applet1.class"
```

It specifies the name of the class file of the applet to be executed. The **width** and **height attributes** specify the size in pixels of the window in which the applet executes.

```
(a)
                        index.html

    An <I> Applet </I> Demonstration
    <BR>
    <APPLET code="Applet1.class" width=800 height=300>
    </APPLET>
```

Figure 18.8   (continues)

(b)

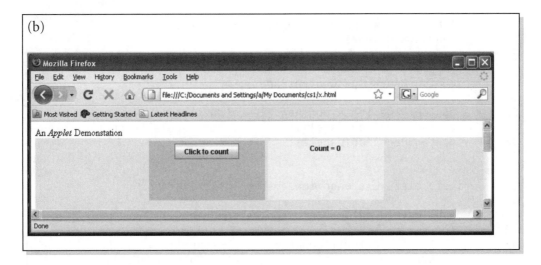

(c)

```
1  import javax.swing.*;
2  import java.awt.*;
3  import java.awt.event.*;
4  public class Applet1 extends JApplet // public, extend JApplet
5  {
6      private Container contentPane;
7      private JPanel panel1, panel2;
8      private JButton button1;
9      private JLabel label1;
10     private int count;
11     //----------------------------------
12     public void init()   // use init method in place of constructor
13     {
14         panel1 = new JPanel();                // create panel
15         panel1.setLayout(new FlowLayout());
16         panel1.setBackground(Color.GREEN);
17         panel1.setPreferredSize(new Dimension(300, 50));
18         button1 = new JButton("Click to count");
19         button1.addActionListener(new Listener());
20         panel1.add(button1);
21
22         panel2 = new JPanel();                // create panel
23         panel2.setLayout(new FlowLayout());
24         panel2.setBackground(Color.YELLOW);
25         panel2.setPreferredSize(new Dimension(300, 50));
26         count = 0;
```

Figure 18.8 (continues)

```
27          label1 = new JLabel("Count = " + count);
28          panel2.add(label1);
29
30          // get content pane of frame
31          contentPane = getContentPane();
32
33          contentPane.setLayout(new FlowLayout());
34          contentPane.add(panel1);        // add panels to content pane
35          contentPane.add(panel2);
37      }
38      //-----------------------------------
39      private class Listener implements ActionListener
40      {
41          public void actionPerformed(ActionEvent e)
42          {
43              label1.setText("Count = " +  ++count);
44              System.out.println("Orange = " + Color.ORANGE);
45          }
46      }
47 }
```

Figure 18.8 (continued)

Applets require a slightly different setup than Java applications. For example, Fig. 18.8c shows a Java applet that provides the same function as the GUI3 application in Fig. 18.5. It differs from the GUI3 application program in the following ways:

1. The class for the applet must be public (see Line 4).

2. The class for the applet must extend JApplet, not JFrame (see Line 4).

3. It does not have the calls of the setTitle, setSize, setDefaultCloseOperation, pack, and setVisible methods. These methods come from the JFrame class. But the Applet1 class in Fig. 18.8c is not a subclass of JFrame. Thus, these methods are not available to the Applet1 class. A Java application uses these methods to configure the window that it displays. However, an applet does not need these methods because it does not have its own window (an applet uses the browser's window).

4. Because the class of the applet is public, the base name of the file that contains it must match the class name. Thus, the file for the applet in Fig. 18.8c must be Applet1.java.

5. The init method that starts on Line 12 in the applet takes on the function of the constructor in a Java application. The browser initiates the execution of the applet by calling the init method—not a main method. An applet does not contain a main method.

After compiling the applet in Fig. 18.8c, we can run it and see the web page in which it is embedded (see Fig. 18.8b) by opening the file in Fig. 18.8a with a Java-enabled web browser. Alternatively, we can enter

```
appletviewer index.html
```

where `index.html` is the name of the file in Fig. 18.8a. `appletviewer` displays only the applet—not the rest of the web page in which it is embedded. `appletviewer` is a utility program that comes with the Java compiler and interpreter.

To make the web page in Fig. 18.8 available on the World Wide Web, you must place it in the appropriate directory on your web server. Check with your system administrator for specific directions on how to do this.

Laboratory 18 Prep

1. Where does the `setTitle` method called on Line 12 in Fig. 18.1 come from?
2. What is a container?
3. How does a listener object determine which component triggers an event?
4. Are radio buttons individually added to a container or are they added all together in one group?
5. Why does an applet not have a main method?

Laboratory 18

1. Run the `GUI1` program in Fig. 18.1. Resize the window by placing the cursor on the lower right corner of the window and dragging (hold the left button down). What happens to the placement of the components on the window?

2. Comment out Line 19 (the `setLayout`) in `C18e2.java` (a copy of `GUI1` in Fig. 18.1). Compile and run. What is the effect of the modification?

3. Place a `println` statement that displays `hello` in the `performedAction` method in `C18e3.java` (a copy of `GUI3` in Fig. 18.5). Compile and run. What happens every time you click the count button?

4. Add a second button to the `C18e4.java` (a copy of `GUI3`) program that terminates the window when clicked. To terminate the window, execute

   ```
   System.exit(0);
   ```

5. Compile and run `C18e5.java` (a copy of `GUI5` in Fig. 18.7). What happens if you enter a noninteger into the text field and then click on the count button? Modify the program so that it can handle invalid data in the text field. To do this, use a `try/catch` block. Test your program.

6. Add the following statements to the `performAction` method in the `C18e6.java` program. Compile and run. Click on the count button.

   ```
   System.out.println("RED:     " + Color.RED);
   System.out.println("GREEN:   " + Color.GREEN);
   System.out.println("BLUE:    " + Color.BLUE);
   System.out.println("BLACK:   " + Color.BLACK);
   System.out.println("WHITE:   " + Color.WHITE);
   System.out.println("GRAY:    " + Color.GRAY);
   System.out.println("ORANGE:  " + Color.ORANGE);
   System.out.println("MAGENTA:" + Color.MAGENTA);
   System.out.println("CYAN:    " + Color.CYAN);
   ```

The computer screen can produce red, green, and blue light. However, if these colors are mixed, our eyes will perceive other colors. For example, mixing red and green gives orange. Every color is represented with three numbers, each in the range 0–255, that specify the intensity of its red, green, and blue components. For example, pure red is [255, 0, 0] and orange is [255, 200, 0].

7. Set Line 20 in C18e7.java (a copy of GUI1 in Fig. 18.1) to

```
contentPane.setBackground(new Color(255, 200, 0));
```

Compile and run. What is the background color? Now change this statement to

```
contentPane.setBackground(new Color(255, 255, 255));
```

Compile and run. What is the background color now? What color do you get when you mix red, green, and blue?

8. Modify C18e8.java (a copy of GUI1 in Fig. 18.1) so that it adds five buttons to the frame and no labels. Compile and run. Resize the window by dragging the window's right corner. How does the size of the window affect the placement of the buttons?

9. Same as Lab Exercise 8 except modify C18e9.java (a copy of GUI1 in Fig. 18.1), and use BorderLayout.

10. Same as Lab Exercise 8 except modify C18e10.java (a copy of GUI1 in Fig. 18.1), and use GridLayout with three rows and two columns.

11. Modify the C18e11.java (a copy of GUI5 in Fig. 18.7) in the following way:

   a) Change Line 4 to

   ```
   class C18e11 extends JFrame implements ActionListener
   ```

   b) Move the performAction method to the C18e11 class.

   c) Delete the Listener inner class.

   d) Change Line 26 to

   ```
   button1.addActionListener(this);
   ```

   e) Change Line 43 to

   ```
   text1.addActionListener(this);
   ```

   Does the modified program still work? Why is this passed to the addActionListener method?

12. Open the index.html file in Fig. 18.8a with a web browser after you have compiled the Applet1.java applet in Fig. 18.8c. How are the three words "An", "applet", and "demonstration" laid out on the screen? Add extra spaces after each of these words

LABORATORY

in index.html. How does this change affect the layout? Put each item in index.html on a separate line. How does this change affect the layout?

Homework 18

1. Write a GUI application program with two text fields, one button, and one label. Use the text fields for input. When the button is clicked, the sum of the numbers in the two text fields should be added and displayed in the label. (*Hint:* To set the text in a label, use the setText method [setText is in label objects as well as text objects].)

2. Modify C18h2.java (a copy of GUI5 in Fig. 18.7) so that it does not use a count variable. Instead, it should use the text in the text field to keep track of the current count. Each time the count button is clicked, access the text in the text field, convert it to type int (with Integer.parseInt), add or subtract 1 depending on which radio button is selected, and store the result back in the text field as a string. Using this approach you do not need a listener for the text field component.

3. Add to C18h3.java (a copy of GUI5 in Fig. 18.7) a second group of five radio buttons that specify the size of the increment/decrement. The five radio buttons should correspond to the increment/decrement sizes 1, 2, 3, 4, and 5. For example, if the radio button 4 is selected, then the count should be incremented or decremented by 4 each time the count button is clicked.

4. Write a GUI program that has two panels. One panel should have three text fields and a button labeled Show Color. Label the text fields Red, Green, and Blue. When the Show Color button is clicked, the color specified by the three text fields should be displayed in the other panel. If any of the text fields do not hold an integer in the range 0–255 when the Show Color button is clicked, set the offending field or fields to 0. Then proceed to display the color.

5. Radio buttons are used to specify mutually exclusive options. Check boxes are similar to radio buttons, but are used to specify options that not mutually exclusive. Any combination of check boxes can be checked at one time. A check box is created from the JCheckBox class. Add two check boxes to the C18h5.java (a copy of GUI5 in Fig. 18.7) program, one on each panel, that control the background color of its panel. When a checkbox on a panel is checked, the background color on that panel should go white. When unchecked, the background color should revert to its original color (yellow for panel1 or green for panel2).

6. Convert the GUI5 application in C18h6.java to an applet. Embed in HTML and view with a web browser.

7. JOptionPane is a "quick and easy" GUI. Run the following program. What does it do?

```java
import javax.swing.JOptionPane;
class C18h7
{
    public static void main(String[] args)
    {
        String s = JOptionPane.showInputDialog("Enter number");
        double d = Double.parseDouble(s);
        JOptionPane.showMessageDialog(null, "Root = " + Math.sqrt(d));
        System.exit(0);
    }
}
```

8. What does the following applet do? Experiment with different arguments to see how they affect the display.

```java
import javax.swing.*;
import java.awt.Graphics;
public class C18h8 extends JApplet
{
    public void paint(Graphics p)
    {
        p.drawOval(0, 0, 50, 50);
        p.fillOval(100, 0, 50, 50);
        p.drawArc(0, 200, 50, 50, 0, 90);
    }
}
```

9. Write an applet that displays a happy face with eyes, eyebrows, nose, ears, and mouth on the screen. See Homework Exercise 8.

Sample Exam 3 (Chapters 12–18)

Each question is worth 20%

Name _____

1. Write a recursive method (just a method—not a complete program) that returns true if the string it is passed is null or is made up exclusively of one or more occurrences of the letter 'A,' and false otherwise.

2. Write a method rotate (just a method—not a complete program) that removes the first node on a linked list and places it at the end of the list. If the list is empty or has only one node, rotate has no effect on the list. Assume each node has a link field

LABORATORY

that points to the next node. The link field of the last node on the list contains `null`. Assume your method is in the linked list class. Thus, it has direct access to the `first` field that points to the first node on the list.

3. Write a program that reads in a text file whose name is specified on the command line. Your program should determine and display the sum of all the integers in the file that are bounded by whitespace, the beginning of a line, or the end of a line. For example, if the file contains the following text

```
6x 7y 2 &8 *9
3 4
```

your program should sum 2, 3, and 4 only. Do *not* use the `hasNextInt` method in your program. (*Hint:* `nextInt` in the `Scanner` class throws an `InputMismatch-Exception` [in the `java.util` package] if it attempts to read a noninteger. It throws a `NoSuchElementException` [in the `java.util` package] if the input data is exhausted [i.e., no more data to be read].)

4. Create a generic class `Deque` (just the class—not a complete program) with type parameter T. A `Deque` ("double-ended queue") object should use an `ArrayList` to hold the objects that are added to it. Your `Deque` class should include the following methods:

`public void addFirst(T x)`

Adds x to the beginning of the `ArrayList`. Implement with add method in `ArrayList`.

`public void addLast(T x)`

Adds x to the end of the `ArrayList`. Implement with the add method in `Array-List`.

`public T removeFirst()`

Removes and returns the first element in the `ArrayList`. Implement with the remove method in `ArrayList`.

`public T removeLast()`

Removes and returns the last element in the `ArrayList`. Implement with the remove method in `ArrayList`.

`public int size()`

Returns the size of the `ArrayList`. Implement with the size method in `Array-List`.

5. Write a listener class for a button that displays one of five randomly selected greetings. Also give the Java code that creates the button, the label (for the greeting), and the listener object, and associates the button with the listener.

Installing the Java Development Kit (JDK)

 Macintosh Installation

You're in luck. The Macintosh comes with the JDK preinstalled.

 Windows Installation

Download and install the Standard Edition (SE) of the JDK:

1. Using a web browser, go to `java.sun.com/javase/downloads`.
2. Click on `Download JDK`.
3. Follow the directions to download the JDK installation file for Windows.
4. When the download completes, run the installation file.

You now have to set the Path variable so that the Windows operating system can find the JDK programs:

5. Click on the start icon in the lower left corner ⟶ Computer (or My Computer).

6. Double click on the icon that represents the drive on which you installed the JDK (it's probably the C: drive).

7. Double click on Program Files ⟶ Java.

8. Double click on the folder whose name starts with jdk.

9. Double click on bin. This folder contains the JDK programs.

10. Right click on the address window at the top of your screen that contains the full name of the bin folder.

11. Click on copy (Windows XP) or copy address (Windows 7). Close the window by clicking on the x in the upper right corner.

12. Windows XP: Click on Start ⟶ Control Panel. If the control panel is in Category View, click on Performance and Maintenance ⟶ System ⟶ Advanced. If the control panel is in Classic View, double click on System. Then click on Advanced.

    Windows 7: Click on the start icon in lower left corner ⟶ Control Panel ⟶ System and Security ⟶ System ⟶ Advanced System Settings.

13. Click on Environmental Variables.

14. Under System variables, click on Path _ Edit. You may have to scroll to find the Path variable.

15. This is a critical step. Be careful! Hit the Home key. Position the cursor at the beginning of the entry in the Variable value window. Right click at this position. Select Paste to insert the full name of the Java bin folder. Then enter a semicolon to separate the entry for the Java bin folder from the rest of the value. Click on OK to exit from each of the active windows. If you accidentally corrupt the Path variable, click on Cancel and then go to Step 14.

 ## Linux Installation

In the Synaptic Package Manager, search for jdk. Select the latest version of the Sun jdk and mark for installation. Then click on Apply.

Index